NOW *THE* WOLF HAS COME

NOW *THE* WOLF HAS COME

❖

THE CREEK NATION IN THE CIVIL WAR

By Christine Schultz White
&
Benton R. White

TEXAS A&M UNIVERSITY PRESS
COLLEGE STATION

Library of Congress Cataloging-in-Publication Data

White, Christine Schultz, 1956–
    Now the wolf has come / by Christine Schultz
    White and Benton R. White — 1st ed.
        p. cm.
    Includes bibliographical references and index.
    ISBN 0-89096-689-3 (cloth : alk. paper)
    1. Creek Indians—History—19th century.
    2. Creek Indians—Relocation—Indian Territory.
    3. Creek Indians—Government relations. 4. Indians
    of North America—History—Civil War, 1861–1865.
    5. Confederate States of America—History. 6. United
    States—History—Civil War, 1861–1865. I. White,
    Benton R. (Benton Ray), 1949– . II. Title.
    E99.C9W55   1996
    973.7'1503973—dc20   95-40697
                                                CIP

❖ To the heritage and glory of the ones who called themselves the PEOPLE.

❖ And to the sunshine in our lives, *Amy*.

You said . . . no white people in the world should ever molest us . . . and should we be injured by any body you would come with your soldiers & punish them. but now the wolf has come. men who are strangers tread our soil. our children are frightened & the mothers cannot sleep for fear . . . we want you to send us word what to do. . . . My ears are open & my memory is good.

—Opothleyahola to Abraham Lincoln
Summer, 1861

CONTENTS

PREFACE

This book was written for several reasons, but chiefly because it recounts a story that deserves to be told. In the fall of 1861 nearly nine thousand Native Americans, mostly of the Muskogee Confederation, found themselves surrounded and about to be consumed by a war not of their making. Their three hundred-mile trek to escape in the face of overwhelming odds and countless hardships ranks as one of the great feats of frontier American history. It rivals, and in ways surpasses, the experience of Chief Joseph and the Nez Percé. We believe those who suffered and died from the experience are entitled to a better fate than to be relegated to a footnote in history or wholly forgotten.

Over the past two decades a number of books have been written on the subject of Native American history. The majority of these works have been sympathetic to the Native American experience and in particular the encounter with western civilization. Yet we believe precious few have been written from an Indian perspective. It is the purpose of this book in part to offer such a perspective.

We have no illusions about the limitations placed on our labors. In certain ways our work has been an exercise in frustration and even futility. The differences in culture and language between our world and theirs have inevitably imposed restrictions on what could be accomplished. There are innumerable words, phrases, and thought patterns from the Muskhogean language group for which there are no adequate English equivalents. The subtleties and nuances in speech—and behavior—that separate a preindustrial tribal society from our own are countless. Even the spelling of place names and personal names is a problem for, ultimately, there is no exact or proper English spelling for anything Muskhogean. Also, by the 1860s, the period we cover, Native American cultures and traditions had long since been fundamentally altered and hopelessly intertwined with those of white society. Thus, a study and interpretation of events from a purely Indian perspective, void of any other influence, has been impossible.

Likewise, we have been just as handicapped by the culture of our own reading audience. In our view, latter-twentieth-century Anglo America is largely unequipped to deal with certain aspects of Native American life, for example, torture. As a result, we have largely omitted materials on the subject. We did so not to hide the fact that Muskogee warriors practiced torture, but because Anglo Americans are so divorced from the more brutal realities and will invariably stymie on the topic in emotional disgust. So in one sense our ambitions were doomed before we began.

Still, we think our work and approach have not been totally in vain. We believe human nature has remained essentially unchanged for thousands of years and that an understanding of the past, even the ancient past, is everywhere around us if only we will open our eyes. Events in eastern Europe, following the collapse of the Soviet empire, for example, have proved again that bloody retribution and tribal vendetta are more than dark memories. We maintain, further, that people everywhere have always behaved in amazingly similar ways. In our view, if circumstances had been reversed, with Native Americans in possession of modern technology first and Europeans void of immunities to smallpox and measles, the last five hundred years would have included the story of whites being largely swept from the earth. Also, and most important perhaps, we chose this approach after having lived a large portion of our lives with peoples and in cultures that closely resemble the ones of which we write. This work is no mere compilation of research from archives and academic papers. It is based in part on real life and very personal experience.

Our primary academic research derives from records at the Oklahoma State Historical Association Archives in Oklahoma City, the District Federal Archives in Fort Worth, Texas, and government documents sections from several university libraries, as well as personal interviews with members of the Muskogee Nation.

We should add that our research includes seeing and walking much of the land. To the extent possible, we have retraced the route followed by the nine thousand as they sought to escape their enemies. When we depict a hill, a forest, a tree-lined creek, or a meadow, it is as we found it, and largely as they found it, too. We visited these sites at the same time of year they saw them to add to our understanding. From windswept ridges we have looked out on winter sunsets and rising moons, and we have seen the land as they viewed much of it, covered in ice and snow.

We realize there will be detractors to our approach, if for no other reason than our narrative style. At times we draw near to writing in the first person. Yet we concluded that the common vernacular and an intimate, almost personal, depiction offered the best hope of capturing the thoughts, feelings, and passions of our subjects; certainly an academic style would have been inadequate. We suspect we may risk confusing others. The reader will notice the lack of dates, figures, familiar time lines, and, in some places, even linear logic when depicting events from an Indian perspective. Only when we shift focus to the whites or their allies do we apply such conventions. For the Muskogee Nation, there is no month of November, for instance, only the month of Frost. There are no minutes or hours, only moments, instances, or eternities. Some, no doubt, will also squirm at our analysis of the dynamics among politics, money, and war. We will lead our readers, but require that you accept nothing. It is left to you to determine what is real and what is illusion—in politics and in life.

We have written this book as well to shed light on a major part of Native American history and culture that is usually ignored or at best passed over quickly. To a considerable extent, Native American history can be interpreted as endless bouts of infighting, factionalism, and blood feuds: between nations, tribes, sets of towns, and clans. It has always been so. Long before the arrival of the European, tribal and intertribal rivalry and war were a way of life. To be sure, whites exploited and exacerbated these rivalries in pursuit of their own purposes, as you will discover from reading this book. But to depict Native American history of the last few centuries as a struggle only between red and white is grossly simplistic. Certainly, there were Indians who tried to transcend tribal rivalries and build large and more powerful Native American political movements. This book is the story in part, of one such person, the Speaker of the Muskogee Nation, Opothleyahola. Yet his primary focus was always inescapably the local community. His life, like that of his kin, was built around ancient feuds, vicious petty rivalries, and a worldview that was forever provincial.

There will be some who feel we have erred in emphasizing Indian factionalism, who will argue that we are overstating our case. Others may contend that our emphasis on rivalries between Indian factions has come at the cost of depicting our subjects as too one-dimensional, as single-minded beings consumed with hatred. We disagree on both counts. We stand in awe of the complexity of Native American culture and thought patterns; our respect for Native American ways of life continues to grow. But we find ourselves unable to ignore an essential part of so many Native American civilizations—factionalism and infighting.

Our only genuine concern in taking this approach is that we might be misunderstood as depicting one faction as essentially right or good and the other as wrong or evil. We do not believe that the central character of this work, Opothleyahola, was any better or worse than his great protagonists—the McIntosh family. We believe that they were all faced with difficult, if not impossible, choices for survival as the world they had known disintegrated around them. We are convinced that Daniel McIntosh was as great a man as Opothleyahola. We refuse to judge the actions or motives of either.

Finally, we have penned this work as something of a rebuttal. We are often disappointed with the way Indian history is taught and written today. Part of the problem, we suspect, is that the subject is largely in the hands of individuals who have had very little personal experience with Indians, to say nothing of experience living on the land, or struggling to survive by one's wits and skills. Mostly, the story of Native American history has been told by a sheltered upper middle class that has done little but go to school and teach school. Not surprisingly, its views of Indians are largely a syrupy brew of racial romanticism and well-intentioned but condescending "noble savage" muck, usually mixed with a judicious portion of contemporary political dogma centered around an ecological theme.

And that brings us back to a theme of our own. The ones we call Indians or Native Americans were like peoples everywhere then and now. Some were brilliant and even great; others were incredibly loathsome and deceitful, or even stupid. Most were a mixture of these traits and many more. If, through the distance of language, time, and culture, we can view them only as images through a dark and very smoky glass, still we think we can see them. And if the reader finds an occasional sentence or passage that gives even a glimpse into a way of life that is in some ways as ancient as the ice ages, then we shall have succeeded.

Several thank yous are in order for helping make this work possible: our friend Tom Wilkinson, who would not rest, or let us rest, until we had seen the job through; our major professors R. David Edmunds and Don Worcester, who trained us. We cannot forget our parents. Neither can we overlook our friends and colleagues at the Alabama School of Mathematics and Science— Howard Nicholson, Sandy Hicks, and Jeff Goodman—who read the manuscript and offered many excellent suggestions. And we offer thanks also to Jim Kettle, our friend and editor extraordinaire. We acknowledge as well those talented and lovable students at the Alabama School—Shane Estes, Jeff Lawley, Amy Bischoff, Rhonda Perdue, Sarah Walker, Karen Faison, Gina Carman, Margaret Janer, and many others—who also read our work and inspired us. Finally, we salute the life and works of Louis L'Amour and their impact on our approach to writing.

A final word of caution. If yours is a world of linear logic, scientific empiricism, and sensory perception only; if your understanding of reality is limited to mass, energy, and contemporary concepts of time and space; if you cannot concede that there are at least other possibilities, you need read no farther. You will find our approach hopelessly superstitious and even laughable. But those still of the old ways will believe. And we think, too, that the old gods will hear us and smile.

PROLOGUE

When the daylight ends its cycle and darkness settles on the land, a wild, mournful cry sometimes rises into the night. It is an unforgettable sound, causing even the largest creatures to cock their ears or glance about with anxious eyes, for the animals grasp instinctively that the time of the hunter has come, and that the predator beast is somewhere near. Nothing can escape the sound; the air seems to fill with a lingering, dreadful wail that rises above the trees, touching the stars. It is the howl of the wolf pack, the sound of wild fury and pitiless doom.

Wolves are impatient killers. They stalk an animal in a deliberate way, trailing along hollows and hillsides, pausing only to catch the scent. With their translucent eyes focused always straight ahead, they are utterly remorseless and driven by the most primal needs. When the wolves finally flush their prey, they give chase. Dashing through moonlit woods and stygian shadows, they can run an animal for what seems an eternity. If the prey is quick and cunning, like a deer, it might rush ahead of the pack and seem to escape. Darting and leaping over logs and ravines, a deer will quickly outdistance a loping pack. But escape is only an illusion. All the while other wolves quietly circle to the left or right, then ahead of their quarry. In the end, the wolves close in from all sides.

The kill is merciless and savage. Circling their exhausted captive, the wolves tear at hamstring and loins until the animal, in agony, can no longer hold up its head and is finally dragged down by the throat. It ends with the wolves feasting on a lifeless, shredded form. And later perhaps, just before dawn, the eerie faraway howl comes again, before fading into the darkness. It is the pack staking its claim to the land and all its creatures.

It is instinctive, this killing, a way of life for the wolves. They feed off the weak and lame of the forest and keep the living animals strong, swift, and free-running. The hunt is part of a natural pattern as old as the cycle of life and death. But the wolves kill only to survive, never out of greed or blood lust, never just because the game is there.

That alone distinguishes the wolf from another predator beast that stalks this world.

THE MONTH OF FROST

(November)

Opothleyahola of Tuckabatchee.
Courtesy Universities Libraries, Western History Collections, University of Oklahoma.

CHAPTER ❖ ONE

Grandfather

He sat on the floor, staring into the embers of a dying fire. All around lurked the evil and dread that always seemed to come with the dark. Glowing coals struggled to outline cabin walls and overhead beams. Somehow the very air carried a presence that was sinister and threatening and just out of sight. Occasionally, the coals popped and hissed, spitting flame and sparks. Images of light and shadow would appear—dancing, magical forms that filled the room with their power. Light and motion would drive away the dark, and the spirit world would come to life. But the flame would die down and the images vanish. Back would come the night.

He was utterly alone. In all of his long life he had never felt so alone. Yet he knew the decisions he made would affect thousands and could mean life or death. Every decision or act, no matter how small, was woven into the lives of others, just as individual threads created a piece of cloth. There was no separating of one man from another. There was no deed or thought that existed apart. The fate of every man was bound to the rest, with inescapable results. When a rock is thrown into a pond, ripples move away from the splash in ever-widening circles until finally the whole pond has been touched. It was the same with life.

At still another level—a deeper inner realm—he also realized their fates were inescapable no matter what he chose, and that all of life was a cycle. Birth begot still more birth; spring begot a summer that turned into winter then spring again. And every tragedy resulted in another tragedy. All existence was linked to a recurring, rhythmic pattern from which there was no escape. The most ancient teachings and his very soul told him it was so.

From outside came the sound of wind and the scratching of a tree limb against wooden roof boards. Sometimes a heavy gust caused the cabin to creak and groan, as if the winds were about to speak. But they would quickly pass away, leaving only the slow hissing of the coals. There was nothing more, nothing but a chilling wind, a world of darkness, and a man peering into a dying fire—and clutching something in his hand.

It was a letter, wrinkled and ink-smeared from the touch of so many. The letter was a promise of help from the government, or so he was told. Growing up in the old country, he had never learned to read. If only he and his following would remain true, all would be safe, the letter promised. Peace, security, and, above all, the protecting arms of the military, all of this and more the government could provide if only he would cast aside his fears and remain loyal. If only he would trust.[1]

The old man looked down at the yellow parchment, his dark eyes scanning the strange marks, wishing he could look as easily into the heart of the one who had written. Gently he rubbed his callused fingers over the paper as if hoping to feel the truth. In the past, policymakers and letter writers would not have cared if he or his kind had lived or died. They had never so much as called them by their proper names. Now the same men were promising safekeeping for everyone. He could think of no reason why the politicians should be trusted or why they should even want to help, except perhaps for one—it was in their interests. Maybe that was enough.

Help he needed desperately. His people were deep in enemy territory, nearly surrounded. Every day their lives grew more uncertain. Already there had been fighting near the town of Thlophlocco; and to the east and south, only a short distance away, enemy forces had gathered in overwhelming numbers. At other places houses had been burned and families driven out. At any moment the enemy might raid the valleys and plunder and kill. They would come for him, too. They would seek him out and take his life, no matter the cost. The old man could accept his own fate, for he had lived long and well. All creatures, man or beast, must finally die. But he would never accept the death of the others and of their way of life. Better to suffer endless cycles of agony and death than to

4

see the end of a civilization that was ancient before his enemies had ever come into the world.

It was impossible to know exactly what was happening, for contact with the outside had been cut since summer. Troops and government agents had abandoned the forts, and there was no one to turn to for support or advice. A delegation had left to contact authorities farther north, but no one expected to hear from them anytime soon. Rumor had it that great battles had been fought and Washington City overrun. Everywhere were powerful and influential men telling any who would listen that the government was bankrupt, that the new president, Abraham Lincoln, was dead. Perhaps it was all true. The omens had warned of disaster. Last year a serpent's tail had appeared in the sky, a sure sign of war. And there had been dreams: twisted dreams of mankillers swooping from the sky, dreams of lands turned lifeless as stone, and of shiny metal ribbons wrapped around the bodies of the dead; nightmares of a power more vast and wicked than had ever been imagined. All that could be known for certain was that many would suffer and even perish if they remained where they were.[2]

The old man knew about suffering. It had been nearly a lifetime, but the images haunted him still. Even in the darkest nights he could see the men fighting, then running for their lives. He could still hear the screams of the women and the little ones, still see their faces twisted in agony and terror. He would never forget the sight of a river turned red with the blood of the slain. And he would always see the enemy: their long matted hair, their sallow skin, and, most of all, their eyes—piercing, clear, and horribly evil.[3]

He kept staring at the letter and the strange marks on the paper, wondering what to do, but he could think of no easy answers. The lines of experience and worry seemed to etch even deeper into his face. Last night he thought he had heard an owl hoot, an omen of death, but death for whom? Old Megillis Hadjo would have known what to do, for he could foretell the future and even change the weather. But Megillis Hadjo was long dead.

Every instinct told him to throw the letter into the fire. In the old country another government and invading army had destroyed nearly everything he had known. Then, too, there had been omens: plagues, droughts, storms. But the People ignored the signs until it was too late. Into the towns and villages came the invaders—like swarms of locusts. They came with their long rifles, their false promises, and their hate.

At first the People showed them kindness and generosity, offering the strangers food, shelter, whatever they desired. It was the custom of the People and the civilized everywhere to be generous and hospitable, for a man was measured by his courage and the size of his heart, not by his possessions. But the invaders had no heart. It was said they were from an island beyond the sea, but as far as anyone could tell, they might have come from the land of shadows and death. They were strange, frightening, and terrible, their kind; perhaps they were not even human.

Slowly at first, the outsiders took what they wanted from the People through trade, treaties, and promises of friendship. But their gains only whetted their appetite for more. Some of them carried bogus land titles and forged treaties that claimed the country was theirs. First the land, then the stock, then even personal belongings and sacred relics—nothing escaped their grasp. Next came the bloodletting. If it suited them, they seized homes and beat families bloody and senseless as they drove them from their own doorways. Other times they took the families as well, reducing boys and men to slaves, converting wives and daughters into prostitutes or members of their personal harems. Even the bones of the dead were unsafe as they dug up the graves of ancestors for silver and gold.

Some tried to resist, at first believing they could drive their enemies away, but resistance was in vain. The invaders hunted them like animals—shooting on sight, siccing dogs on them—young or old, it made no difference. Babies they bashed against trees; mothers they raped, then slit open with knives as their children stood by helpless. Bounties went out on scalps, sets of ears, then skulls, until at last the survivors could only scatter to the woods and hide in terror, or submit.

When there was nothing left to steal and they had grown weary of slaughter, the invaders turned their fury on what was left of the People's spirit, killing the soul as well as the flesh. In came their priests to poison minds with wicked tales of incest, burning lakes, three-headed gods, and sorcerers. Close behind were the peddlers and hucksters enticing the hapless and confused with useless trinkets, mechanical wonders, and the trappings of their own perverse way of life. To keep the People forever weak and powerless, the outsiders turned them against one another: town against town, clan against clan. To the greedy they offered land and gold taken from the rest. To the foolish they held out the illusion—but never the reality—of power. To the vain and stupid went meaningless

❖ NOW THE WOLF HAS COME

titles and hollow honors, and always to the dispirited went alcohol. It was all part of a grand design: to break down, kill, and utterly destroy; to instill a hatred and shame for all that was sacred and dear; to cause a people to question or despise their own existence and convert them into disheartened beggars who pleaded for bread and acceptance from the very ones who had tried to murder their way of life. Some of the invaders promised that all would be right again, that the People would someday regain their lands and live in peace. But their words were as empty as their souls, and in the end an entire civilization was nearly swept away. The few survivors, broken and impoverished, were strangers and outcasts in their own land: mocked, ridiculed, beaten, laughed at, spat upon, raped, murdered, and, finally, driven away. All of this and more the People suffered, and all because they dared to exist and to stand in the path of a dreadful, remorseless enemy.[4]

But in their blackest moments, when the People seemed stripped of even hope, those who had clung to the old ways rallied around a leader. Against all odds their leader held them together until at last, as if by a miracle, he led them to a new home in another land, the American frontier. He was a man who stood against corruption and fear and the many dreadful changes, the same man who now stared at a letter before a dying cabin fire.

Out of the forests and swamps of the old country and across the Muddy River the People traveled to the new land. They left in the winter, force marched and under guard, some in chains. The invaders drove them out like cattle, then torched what was left of the old villages, for they wanted nothing to remind them of who had once owned the land. Lean men and haggard women, crying children, hollow-eyed and with bloated bellies, an entire race was sent away, starved and half naked. The old, the stooped, even the lame stumbled along, grasping for another chance at life, with rain and sleet cutting into their faces as they plodded west. The strongest led the way, carrying the heavenly plates and the sacred fire. Then came families of the many towns, in overloaded wagons or on broken-down ponies. Alongside were countless others on foot.

Many perished, for there was never enough food or blankets to keep warm. Sometimes there was not even wood to build fires, for other nations and peoples driven ahead of them had already stripped the land. Other times the People were forced to bed down in swamps and knee-deep water. As they were forced along at gunpoint, even as women gave birth and the aged collapsed, their trail became a bitter memory of graves and tears. If possible they buried their dead, but too often the armed guards rushed them on with the last glimpse of a child or a grandmother nothing more than a cold, lifeless form lying on the open ground. Yet whenever the People despaired, certain they could go no farther, their leader was there to help them to their feet. Always he was there to help the mothers and the little ones. A better world awaits us somewhere, he would tell them. We can begin again, he would assure them; once more we can be strong and well, if only we are true to the old ways and to one another.[5]

Life in the new land was hard at first, a struggle just to survive. They found themselves in the open, without food or tools. The invaders had planned it that way, hoping they would all die. The People put up lean-tos and hovels of sticks, mud, deerskin, and bark. But raw winds swept down from the plains that first brutal winter, winds like they had never known, filling their homes and lives with a numbing cold. Water froze in bowls away from the fire. It seemed that no amount of blankets or clothes could protect against the merciless winds that rushed through every crack. Sometimes they rose in the mornings to a blanket of snow inside their homes.

With the cold came the starving time as well. Men and women suffered in silence, but the children cried piteously. They lived on wild nuts and berries, then roots and grass—anything they could find, for there was no ammunition to hunt game. Some of the old ones took their lives rather than burden the rest. Others, too weak to kill themselves, simply lay down and refused to eat.

Then came spring. Cool rains and balmy winds replaced the cold. Gaunt men and lean ponies struggled with crude hand-fashioned plows. Others, using only sticks, dug holes and planted the last of their seed. Soon corn shot up from the rust-colored soil, and the survivors took heart. But the rains went away and the soft winds grew hot. The cornstalks that had stood upright and fresh began to droop, then turn yellow. Every morning fleecy clouds hinted at rain only to vanish in a pallid sky. In the end there was nothing left of the corn but brown stalks jutting from cracked ground. Instead of joy and the sounds of laughter, there was only the grating buzz of locusts and the rustling of dead stalks in a fiery air. There was no one to turn to for help; a forgotten race in a forsaken land, they endured and starved.

But the People survived, and somehow they began to piece their lives back together. Slowly they replaced thickets and prairie

8

with fenced pasture and fields. Once again there was food, and broken dreams and bitter memories faded. Children began to smile and play once more, the women grew beautiful, and the men strong and vigorous. There was laughter and love and thanksgiving. In time, the mud huts gave way to homes of siding and lattice, and along the rivers some of the families grew wealthy planting corn and cotton, or raising horses. The People learned again to believe in themselves and in one another.[6]

Most of all they learned to trust their leader. He was the one who had led them from sure death to a fighting chance on the American frontier. When there was cold that first terrible winter any were welcome to sit by his fire. When hunger had driven them all nearly mad he shared the last of his corn. It was he who had helped wring promises of land and protection from the U.S. government. He was their spokesman and their shield against the outside world.

He was known as Opothleyahola[7] of Tuckabatchee, though he went by many names: Old One, Speaker, Ambassador, the Wise One. To others he was Father or Grandfather—even to those who were not blood kin. To many he was as much a spirit as a man. Some of the young ones had never seen him, but he was as real and as much a part of their lives as their own fathers and grandfathers. More than anyone else he had restored their souls, replacing misery with hope and purpose. He had taught them all how to live again, how to be great and good. But it could not last.

A war had spread across the land, a brothers' war some called it. At first many of the People tried to avoid choosing sides; they had known enough killing for a lifetime in the old land and wanted only to be left alone. But they soon discovered that no one would be allowed to live in peace. One of the warring factions nearly surrounded them and was demanding submission. If the People refused they would be killed. Their journey to the West had ended as it began, a cyclic nightmare that again promised devastation and ruin.

When the crisis came there were many who tried to lead and advise. But as danger drew closer, the People instinctively turned to one leader above any others—Opothleyahola. He was a man of great wealth in the Territory, with fields, pastures, and fine horses, and with political influence even in Washington City, it was said. Never mind that he was old. Never mind that he wished only to spend his last days in solitude. Never mind that for months he had struggled with a cough that was so bad he sometimes had spat blood. They were certain he could save them as he had in the past. Opothleyahola would find a way out, they told themselves. He was their best hope; he was all they had.[8]

The fire was dead but the room had filled with light. Morning sun angled through windows, striking the barren floor. All of the furniture had been shipped away days before. Nothing remained but the solitary figure still squatting before the hearth. Finally, the old man raised his head and looked about. The time was right; it was time to leave, for the enemy would soon come. Carefully he folded the letter and tucked it inside his shirt, then stiffly rose to his feet, trying to ignore the pain in his knees. He would have to be strong in the days ahead. Somehow, he told himself, he would find the strength, for he had always been there when the People needed him. Was it not the way of those from Tuckabatchee to lead and protect? Had it not been so for lifetimes? Since the beginning, when the wind first blew away the fog and all could see, there had always been leaders to guide and protect.

Perhaps he was old but his dark eyes still burned with life. Silver hair neatly combed back from a face with chiseled, angular features; in another reality he might have been called Senator or Tribune. His was a face marked by a lifetime of struggle. Yet age and hardship had made him tough and durable like the flint hills that surrounded his home. He wore a tailored coat and hand-crafted footwear, a ruffled shirt, and a sash tied at the waist. A medicine bag hanging from his neck held the root of wild king, a charm to bring good fortune. Over his shoulder was an embroidered pouch colored green, gold, and black.[9]

There was only one chance for the People. They would have to flee, and he would lead them. Somehow they would have to cut their way through enemy territory, moving north to the Arkansas River, and link up with Union forces coming from Kansas. It would take many risings. Before they were safe it would be the month of Big Winter, perhaps even later. But there was no other way. Everyone must leave: the young and the old, the sick, the lame. To remain would mean being left to those without pity or mercy. Stock, wagons, personal belongings—everything would have to go or be left to plunder and ruin.

Somehow, too, he would have to find a way to pull from them their last bits of strength and devotion. It would take everything the People could scrape together in courage and wits even to have a chance of getting through. An entire population trapped in a battle zone, they would have to fight their way free.[10]

The old man wondered how many truly realized what lay ahead. The young talked eagerly of war. They spoke of guns burning in their hands and of knives and hatchets thirsty to drink the blood of enemies. They had no idea what they were facing. They could not imagine the rage and fury of the ones who were coming. Some of them had never seen a white man, except at the missions.

He was frightened, Opothleyahola, as frightened as he had ever been in his life, but he could not afford to show fear. He was puzzled, isolated, and confused, yet he could not afford to show hesitation or bewilderment. Somehow, some way, he had to get them through. It would be worse than when the People had come west, more deadly perhaps than when they were hunted down in the old country. They would be stalked day and night. The men might hold their own in an open fight, but with the women and the little ones to care for they would all be vulnerable. If caught in the open they might all be slaughtered.

He walked across the room to the door and carefully took down the rifle that rested over the frame. The old gun was a muzzle loader with a long single barrel, scratched and worn at the stock. Under the barrel was a whittled hickory stick for a ramrod. They had been through much together, man and rifle.[11]

Opothleyahola opened the door and stepped out on the porch, not looking back, not bothering to shut the door. The wind still blew in uneven gusts from the north—not a cold wind, but chilling and unsettling; in it was the promise of change. The sun burst through a turquoise sky, lighting up fields and pastures and the woods that sloped down to the river. The distant hills were ablaze in color as bleeding leaves poured out their last days of life.

Suddenly, forty or fifty mounted men appeared from a nearby thicket of blackjacks—his men. They rode up at a gallop, their rifles glinting in the sun. Some wore buffalo robes, and a few had on suit coats. Most were in buckskins or wrapped in blankets to keep out the morning chill. They wore every kind of headgear: straight-brimmed hats, straw hats, even top hats—some with feathers drooping from the crowns. One had on the hide of a deer head. Others wore turbans in the style of the old country, colored green, blue, or red. They were the rear guard, these men, the last to go. They had camped all night in the thicket waiting for their leader.

11

They pulled up in front of the house. But one of the riders, a young lieutenant, leading another horse, came closer; he rode up to the porch before stopping.

Carefully the old man eased onto his mount and took the reins. He looked up and nodded, and the riders began to form into a single column. Not a word was spoken, yet everyone seemed to understand. He nodded again and the column passed him in single file, moving toward the trees and the river. As they rode by he studied every face, wondering what would become of them. It would take a miracle—divine providence—to get everyone out.

The last rider passed, but before joining them Opothleyahola paused and turned his horse to face the sun. He dropped his reins and slowly raised his arms with hands outstretched, palms turned upward. Then, as was his custom, he offered thanks to the One who gave meaning to the world and breathed life into every creature. This morning he asked for special guidance as well. At last the old man lowered his arms. With head bowed he sat motionless. Once again he was leader of his nation. To outsiders and the thoughtless they were called Indians, or the Creeks, but among their own kind they were forever the Muskogee, or the People.

The wind whispered something. He looked up, then turned his horse and galloped off to join the others and meet his destiny. But in the distant hills other men on horseback, scouts for the enemy, were also riding. They had news to report—Opothleyahola was moving.[12]

❖ NOW THE WOLF HAS COME

CHAPTER

TWO

The Outsider

The men followed the river all of the morning, splashing through a murky bottom of rust-colored water, trees, thickets, and vines—a wooded red swamp. The wind peppered them with leaves colored gold and crimson, raining down from giant sycamores and elms. To others the tangled canopy of limbs and vines might have seemed a dreary place of half-light and shadows, but the riders knew where they were safest. There were no tracks for an enemy to follow in a swamp. For as long as anyone could recall, the People had lived near the creeks and amid the forests. The huge trees were like grandfathers, ancient and reassuring.

Occasionally, an animal darted ahead of them, skipping across the water or scrambling up a tree. Sometimes the faint sound of geese could be heard overhead. The geese had come early that year, earlier than anyone could remember. There had been much rain, too, after a dry and very hot summer. Something seemed strangely out of balance, more than the usual change of seasons, as if the cycles and patterns of life were no longer in place. Perhaps it was witchcraft or perhaps the white man now had the power to cause the rivers to flood or run dry. Yet there was nothing for the men to do but move on in nervous silence, glancing left and right as they rode.

As the sun rose high, the river narrowed, cutting through long rolling hills. The bottomland and swamps gave way to steep rocky banks that forced the riders up the slopes. As they moved along, the men could not help but wonder at the hills, for it was said they were the graves of giants. In olden times giants had walked the earth and the animals could speak. Along with man, the giants and animals had lived together. But man was tempted away from happiness by his own nature as he learned to cheat, lust, and steal. When the animals realized what had happened, they went away, and the giants grieved themselves to death. Only the silent hills remained as testament to past glories.[1]

The white man scoffed at such notions, that animals could speak or that giants had lived. But the white man's world was empty and confused. His eyes saw only the surface; his ears heard only what was near. He could not feel the soul that was a part of all life. He could not see or hear what was never meant for nonbelievers.

Along the crest of one of the hills the men happened upon a ragged little clearing of weeds and cornstalks. Behind the clearing, and nearly hidden in the trees, stood a cabin, chinked with red clay and blending with the autumn colors. As the men rode up to the cabin no one greeted them. In the yard were wagon ruts and hoofprints leading in the direction they were headed. Nothing more. Two of the riders carefully slid off their mounts, walked onto the porch, and stepped over the open door frame. Inside there was no one. The only hints of life were a few bits of broken pottery.

They traveled on through the woods and hills, seldom out of sight of the river. At one point the men thought they saw a flash of light behind them in the distance, but no one could be sure. Keeping watch for the enemy in the rear, their thoughts were also for their families ahead. Had everyone made it to their campsites? Were the wives and little ones all waiting safely for their men? Were the members of the towns also packing and moving to join them as planned?

Every rider had loved ones ahead he had entrusted to another. Though he barely had time to think of family matters, Opothleyahola could not forget that somewhere ahead were his daughters, Kisila and Asihi. He had not seen them since the troubles had begun; there had been no time. But they were never far from his mind. They were the ones who would forever hold his name in sacred honor and carry on the memory of all he had been. He could only hope that the gods would watch over them.[2]

Still deeper in the day the men came upon another cabin, this one burned to the ground and smoldering. A single rider slowly rode up to the homesite while the others waited. On a fence post away from the charred ruins was a rooster, and in the distance a

❖ NOW THE WOLF HAS COME

barking dog. No one was in sight, but that was no guarantee they were alone. Did the owners burn the cabin before leaving, or was it the enemy? Somewhere near was the answer. The men rode on, but not before checking their weapons. When danger was close there was something reassuring about the feel of a rifle or a bow and a full quiver of arrows.

Before night the riders worked their way down to the river, searching for a campsite. It was always wise to choose a camp before dark, especially if there was danger. They camped that night half-hidden amid plum thickets and huge, moss-covered boulders that had rolled down from the hill. Some of the men watered and hobbled the horses while others spread out blankets. Soon there were small campfires of twigs and dry wood flickering in the twilight. The dry wood gave off little smoke, cutting down on the chance of being noticed. Squatting around their fires, some began puffing pipes shaped as turtle shells and with stems like alligators. Always the men stared just above the flames, but never into the light. The spirit of fire was too bright to behold. To stare into the fire meant blindness. Before long there was a meal of jerky and roasted sweet potatoes, and a chance to share thoughts from the day.

There was much to think about. Over the range of hills to the west were other campfires, some as far away as the plains. Every night the number of campfires grew throughout Indian Territory. It had been going on since the end of summer. Neighbors converged and camped around farms or along creek bottoms or meadows. Families linked up then joined with other families, towns merged with neighboring towns.

Every household had been given a bundle of sticks to take with them when they left. With each rising, a stick would be thrown away as they traveled. When none remained they would be at a meeting point with others. Always moving in the same general direction—like human streams merging to form a river—it was all part of a larger plan. The People would have to gather before the enemy understood what was happening, then somehow escape.[3]

Opothleyahola had planned it all. Keeping the details only in his head, he had outlined the routes, meetings points, and schedules of every town and family that was forming to join him. And while his followers slipped away he had bought time, holding back those who would do them harm with nothing but words and cunning. For days, by hinting at submission and alliance, then war, then peace again, he had kept them at bay. It was an old trick and one Opothleyahola knew well, for when someone is outnumbered there is often little left for him but wits, cunning, and a will to survive.

Opothleyahola understood something very basic about the white man. For the white man tomorrow was all-important; not the past, not the present, but tomorrow. Greatness or failure, happiness or despair, in the white man's world it was all based on tomorrow. Strategies, goals, outcomes, power, worth, status; all of it was forever organized around tomorrow and what was yet to be. Tomorrow was more important to the white man than the air he breathed moment to moment. And so the white man could be delayed, tricked, and fooled: tomorrow Opothleyahola would consider a meeting; tomorrow he would begin preparations for a conference; tomorrow he would send an emissary to make arrangements for peace. In the old land Opothleyahola had served as ambassador for the nation many times. He knew how to sway others with promises and eloquence, even an audience of enemies. He had endless ways as well to hint at peace or war, to raise hopes or fears, to mislead and misdirect. He was not a warrior or a general; he was not a chief; he was a speaker, an orator—a man of words. There was no higher honor. When the white man spoke he was blunt and colorless, for his words, like his soul, were empty, but with the People it was different. There were subtleties and nuances in their every phrase. They had countless ways to describe fire, wind, water, birth, or death. They were a nation of poets, the Muskogees. Words to them were an art form and there was no greater artist than Opothleyahola.[4]

But there were no words left that could keep away the ones who wished them harm. When they discovered that Opothleyahola had slipped away to join the People they would come searching, and they would come for blood. And what troubled Opothleyahola most was not the white men who would follow, but another enemy riding with them.

Above all, the enemy was not the white man, but the McIntosh of Coweta. In the old country there had long been bitterness between Opothleyahola of Tuckabatchee and the McIntosh of Coweta. Before Opothleyahola was born, even before the time of change, there had sometimes been bad blood between households and towns. A new life together on the frontier could not put an end to the old feuds—nothing could.

McIntosh—the very name stuck in the throat like bitter bile. The white men who had seized the old country were hated and feared for the grasping nothings they were. But for the McIntosh there was a special kind of loathing only people of the blood could understand. It was the McIntosh who had been quick to embrace the invaders, sensing there was something to gain. They traded with them, learned their savage tongue, mated with them, and finally took a name from the outsiders in place of their own, the name McIntosh. The McIntosh had been some of the first to reject the old ways and walk the white man's path; but it didn't stop there. They saw to it that others at Coweta and surrounding villages were corrupted as well. Once the Cowetas were mighty warriors, protecting all of the Lower towns from harm, but they became as vile and corrupt as the ones who had led them astray. Everywhere they went, the McIntosh spread their poison, until half of the old nation—the Lower towns—were forever lost to a world of change.

They were a curse, the McIntosh, and like the white men they served, they reduced all of life to lies, murder, and money. Always they managed to reap fortunes from the misery of others, even their own kind. The McIntosh and their henchmen made sure they got more than their share of the white man's bribes and government annuities. Turning away from their heritage while selling their sacred motherlands, they had sold their birthright as well. Among the white men there was a holy book and in it a man named Judas. Many times Opothleyahola had heard the story from insipid missionaries. He wondered what the McIntosh thought of Judas?[5]

All of his life Opothleyahola had fought and feared the McIntosh, for whenever they appeared the white man was usually near. He would never forget them at Tohopeka. He still recalled how William McIntosh had come with men from Coweta and the other Lower towns, as well as with anyone else who would follow, to slay people of their own blood. No one who survived that day would ever forget.

At Tohopeka, like a demon relishing slaughter, was the one called Jackson. Even at a distance the warriors spotted him: that tall, rigid form standing on a bluff, leering at them. The battle began when Jackson unleashed his artillery against the warriors and the breastworks. Then came the infantry, endless lines of bearded, howling white men. The warriors fought back in desperate fury. They fought until their ammunition was exhausted; then it was hand-to-hand. And just at that critical moment that always comes with mortal combat—when everything hangs in the balance—billowing smoke clouds appeared to the rear. It was William McIntosh. Along with his following, William McIntosh had slipped behind the others and struck the campsite, killing those he had known all his life, even the women and children. Exhausted and surrounded, the warriors finally broke and ran for the river along with what was left of the families. The enemy cut them off. A few of the families tried to surrender but were butchered. White men and Cowetas alike scoured the woods and fields for victims— scalping and mutilating, gutting the wounded as well as the dead. Entire clans were swept away. By the end of the day, bodies littered the riverbank and the waters of the Tallapoosa were red with the blood of a dying nation.[6]

Now the McIntosh were coming again to unleash the killing and the terror, this time on the American frontier. In the name of states' rights, or southern independence, or some other myth that existed only in the minds of white men, the McIntosh were riding. And this time, coming with them was a special kind of evil, the ones called Texans.

Opothleyahola already knew something of the Texans. Long ago he had visited Texas hoping to find a refuge for the Muskogees. Texas was empty territory in those days, with creeks and forests that reminded him of home. He met with the Texas leader Sam Houston to see about land and a new beginning. Houston promised land and Opothleyahola paid him $20,000, the treasury of his nation. All of his life, Houston assured him, he had been a friend of the Indians. Houston lied. He pocketed the money and the People never saw the new land that was to be theirs.[7]

There were other stories, too, from those who had once called Texas their home—half understood, frightening tales from the Tonkawas. The Texans, it was said, thought nothing of slaughtering humans or animals until there was nothing left to kill. They were enemies of everything that breathed. With axes the Texans had swept away entire forests. Their steel plows had turned up soils that washed into the rivers, making the very water they drank foul and muddy. Always they carried filth, disease, and strange, revolting habits. Their lives seemed mindless and utterly savage. And now they were one with the McIntosh.

Such thoughts haunted Opothleyahola and those with him as they sat around their campfires that first evening. What would become of them all, they wondered: the families, the villages—the whole of the Muskogee Nation? What would happen if Union troops did not arrive in time? How could they even be sure of linking up with the other campsites ahead?

18

It had been a long day, filled with uncertainty. Every man had been careful to cover his tracks. As far as anyone knew, they had kept from sight, but none could be sure. That night the ground seemed cold and hard to the old man. The only sounds were a cracking fire and the last few insects from summer. As he lay against the earth, staring at the heavens, he wondered again about his daughters and what was ahead. All that could be known for certain was that he would do his best. Perhaps that would be enough. It was said that if the days were lived properly and fully, the seasons and the years took care of themselves.

They rose early the following morning, for the men were anxious to join their families. But before leaving they waded into the river to bathe. Every day the People bathed if they could, even in the winter, even if it only meant rolling in the snow. Bathing was a symbol of purity, and nothing was more important. When a man made himself pure in body and spirit, his life was in balance, and so, too, was the world around him. But if he became unclean or corrupt, if he chose to steal or lie, if he took another man's wife, committed murder, dishonored his town, or turned his back on a neighbor or the gods, he brought down disaster. The forces of nature would rip apart, leaving only chaos and death. All of life was a struggle to walk the path of righteous purity in order to maintain harmony and balance.[8]

Such was why the People had suffered so terribly and nearly been destroyed. The white men who had invaded their lives were merely symptoms of a deeper evil. The true cause of despair was the People's own impurity. Too many had turned from the old ways, hunting and trading deerskins for the white man's trinkets and listening to false promises of those like the McIntosh. Too many had become unclean, and so they had disrupted the balance between man and the rest of the world. If it seemed that the old gods had deserted them, it was only because the People had first deserted the gods. If it appeared the People were powerless before their enemies, it was only because, lusting for the trappings of the invaders, they had lost their magic and power.

In the past, there were those who had tried to warn against impurity and corruption. Two of them were Tecumseh and his brother Tenskwatawa. Opothleyahola was little more than a boy when Tecumseh had come to his village, but he would never forget. Tecumseh and his men were covered in blue powder and wore the sacred feathers and the tails of the buffalo. He was a mighty man that day, Tecumseh. He spoke against impurity and change and implored the People to return to the ways of their grandfathers. And there was magic and power in his words, for when he stamped the ground the earth shook and the stars fell. But too few listened. Too many were already hopelessly lost to those like the McIntosh, and so the old nation was doomed.[9]

Now there were none left who followed the old ways but the ones searching desperately for a chance to escape their enemies. They were the last of their kind, the keepers of the true faith. And leading them was the last of the ancients, the one called Opothleyahola.

After breaking camp, the men rode all morning, still following the river, careful always to remain hidden amid the trees. On the slopes above they spotted another homesite and, later still, another cabin, burned to the ground. Finally, the men left the river and the trees and rode west into the prairie country. Then came more woods and meadows, pastures with fences, and a road. They stayed on the road for the rest of the day and camped that night in a grove of post oaks. One more rising and the men would be with their loved ones. But that night in camp, someone else entered their lives.

It was a man on horseback, riding in from the darkness and carrying a white flag. He rode to the edge of the firelight then pulled up his horse. Peering from the dark, he was a stranger to all but one. Opothleyahola recognized him instantly; the man was John Taylor—a merchant and a cheat—one of those penniless hucksters who forever lurked about Indian Territory. Taylor wore a coat covered in dust and a dingy shirt. The shadow from a slouch hat hid his face from the firelight, except for one feature—his eyes. Somehow they caught the glint of the light and flashed back at the men on the ground. They were the kind of eyes that chilled the soul, the empty eyes of a white man.

Taylor looked about, then turned to Opothleyahola. He had come to offer peace, he said, and a last chance for the Indians. The Texans had not been fooled. They knew the Indians were organizing and would try to join with Yankees farther north. They had trailed Opothleyahola since he had first tried to slip away. For weeks the McIntosh and their scouts had shadowed all that was happening: the planning and the moving. Little more than a day's ride away was a column of Texans and McIntosh warriors. But there could still be peace, Taylor added. If Opothleyahola and his followers would surrender and swear allegiance to the Confederate States and to the McIntosh, there would be no bloodshed. If they refused, sure death awaited.

Opothleyahola listened carefully to every word, searching, perhaps, for the trace of a lie or a hint of uncertainty or hesitation in the white man's words. Taylor went on about war and killing and the women and little children who would suffer. Then at last there was silence. . . . The white man leaned forward in the saddle and the firelight caught the trace of a bitter smile. In his eyes was the look of a hungry animal. He was waiting for an answer.[10]

CHAPTER
THREE

The Tuckabatchees

Opothleyahola rose slowly to his feet. The only sound was the hiss and pop of a burning log. He seemed older than ever in the half light and shadows, silver hair in long, ragged strands hanging to his shoulders. But as he straightened himself and looked squarely at the white man, he seemed to grow in power and might, and his eyes flashed like burning coals.

For a few more moments there was only the crackling fire and the two men locked in a frozen stare. Suddenly from the dark came faint rustling and a wisp of movement. Behind John Taylor shadowy forms on horseback eased into the light, holding rifles. It was Opothleyahola's men. They had allowed the white man to slip into camp and now he was surrounded.

Opothleyahola peered up at Taylor, glaring hatred and contempt, but never uttering a sound. Finally, he glanced left and right, then snapped out commands. Some of the men on horseback moved in closer with rifles leveled at the intruder. Others on the ground began rolling up blankets and bridling horses. They would ride all night to join their families. The white man would come as a prisoner. For the moment, there was little left but to ride through the dark with the prisoner and hope that endless amounts planning had not been undone.[1]

If the enemy were waiting for news from John Taylor, perhaps there would be confusion or uncertainty if he did not return. Maybe they would quarrel over what to do next. In time the white men and the McIntosh would come, for the doling out of misery and death was how they fed their souls. But the longer the Confederates waited, the better the chance for escape.

Opothleyahola wondered about his enemies as he left camp. Why had they sent John Taylor? Who was behind it all? Did someone really believe that threats from a single white man could frighten him into surrender? Could anyone be so truly ignorant? The McIntosh would know better; someone else must have sent Taylor. But who? What sort of commander imagined the Muskogee people would put aside their fears and memories? Who was foolish enough to think he could sweep away the years with a single messenger riding in from the dark? Did the enemy not grasp that present troubles were merely part of an ancient pattern? If there had never been a white man's war, if there had never been a United States, rivalry and hatred would still have been a way of life between Opothleyahola and the McIntosh, for one was Tuckabatchee, the other, Coweta. It had been so for lifetimes, even before the Cowetas grew corrupt. Since a dimly remembered past when warriors had battled by a river, often there had been bad blood between different towns.[2]

As Opothleyahola and his men rode into the night, their fears closed in around them, thick as the dark. If the Texans and the McIntosh were aware of their plans and as close as John Taylor said, it was disaster. There could be a massacre. What would happen to the families, what would become of the little ones if all of the mothers and fathers lay dead? The world would end in chaos and everlasting darkness.

Plans to protect against chaos and war had begun that summer, even before the McIntosh had joined the Texans. Opothleyahola had ridden into the open country to meet with the western tribes. Riding with him were other leaders as well: White King and Sands, and headmen from the Cherokee and Chickasaw nations. Everywhere they went Opothleyahola spoke to the many nations, urging them to stand with him through the coming war. It was not their fight, he told them. Let the white men slay one another until the earth was soaked with their venomous blood. All of the tribes should unite as one, just as Tecumseh and Tenskwatawa had urged long before. Let the many peoples join as brothers of the same fire; let them all shun the white man's war, and the gods would protect them.

They met first with the Seminoles, then the Delawares, and the Kickapoo. Wherever they went it was the same, Opothleyahola urging and pleading with any who would listen to keep out of war. Everywhere, too, the results were similar: some listened, others walked away. Many promised to stand with Opothleyahola, but just as many refused.

As he rode west from one nation to the next, Opothleyahola soon learned as well that a number of leaders had committed already to the white man's war and the southern army. The United States was no more they told him, and Confederate troops were everywhere promising protection and support. Any who tried to resist would surely die; joining the South was the only way to save their nations. For others, the reasons for joining with the Confederates were merely self-serving; it was an old story and one Opothleyahola had seen many times. For gold, horses, a rifle, or a title, many tribal leaders had allied with the South, and to a war—Opothleyahola believed—that promised only ruin. But always behind the many voices and factions were endless rivalries and petty feuds that were forever a part of life. Always there was a score to settle, or some injustice to avenge; the war would furnish an excuse for blood.[3]

As Opothleyahola and the others rode farther west, the land grew wild, windswept, and open. Antelope replaced the deer; dry gullies and draws took the place of free-flowing streams. It was an endless, drought-stricken country, the Far West, a land where even the grass and insects struggled to live. But it was also a place for Opothleyahola to try to forge an alliance with still another nation—a fierce and mighty people—the ones called Komantsi.

In the shadow of the ragged Antelope Hills, Opothleyahola met with the many bands of the Komantsi. Of all of the nations, none was more fearsome. Entire countries trembled at the mention of their name; savages like the Texans feared them instinctively. Even those in a faraway world called Mexico lived in terror of their raiding parties. If Opothleyahola could persuade the Komantsi to stand with the Muskogees, if they became brothers of the same fire, no one amount of evil could destroy the People—not even a white man's war.

There must be a way for the many nations to survive the white man's war, Opothleyahola told them. There could be no honor in fighting alongside such beings. The Muskogees and every eastern nation could move west and live with the Komantsi until the white men had finished their war. Perhaps when the war was done, the white men would all be dead. Then all of the nations could again live their lives free from change.

24

❖ NOW THE WOLF HAS COME

A few of the Komantsi listened and believed, but the rest were unmoved. The Komantsi feared no one and saw no reason to join others for protection. They had not yet experienced endless numbers of white men trampling across the land, killing everything with their touch. When Opothleyahola had finished speaking, the Komantsi simply rode away, vanishing into the flat, bluish horizon of the plains. Before leaving, they warned Opothleyahola never to return, alone or with others.[4]

When Opothleyahola returned from the plains, there was more news and it was mostly bad. As in the past, the McIntosh had betrayed the People, this time joining with the new Confederate States, and half of the Muskogee towns had followed. The Confederate States were not only Texas but even those farther east that had seized the old country long ago and driven out the People.

Already Confederate authorities were swarming over the Territory. Soon their troops would follow. While Opothleyahola was in the West, the McIntosh had made alliances with Confederate authorities, bribed a number of tribal leaders into submission or silence, and forged the names of others to their bogus agreement with the white man. As in the old days, they had dared to speak for all of the nation. The McIntosh had even forged the names of those who had ridden west with Opothleyahola.

Quickly, Opothleyahola and the other leaders called a meeting at the Council Grounds to denounce what had happened. The McIntosh and the rest who had signed a Confederate treaty spoke for no one but themselves, they declared; the McIntosh would never lead the People. Their skin was brown, but their souls were white, their hearts black.

It was after the meeting at the Council Grounds that a letter came from Washington City promising help, and plans began for leaving the country. If the People could not move west and wait out the war, they would flee north and join the Union forces. Anything was better than submission to the McIntosh. All of the true believers from the Muskogee Nation, or any nation, were to follow Opothleyahola north to the Arkansas River, where they would join John Ross and the Cherokees, then link up with northern troops.[5]

Then came still more news. While all were making ready to move to the Arkansas River, a rider from the Cherokee Nation arrived: John Ross and the Cherokees, he reported, had allied with the Confederates. It was said that John Ross had no choice, that many of the Cherokees wanted a Confederate alliance, and that his bitter rival, Stand Watie, would have killed him had he not joined. The reasons were not important. What mattered was that the Muskogee people were betrayed. It was John Ross who had first urged Opothleyahola to remain neutral in the coming war. It was John Ross who had offered the Cherokee country as a place where they could stand as one against the Texans and the McIntosh after the Komantsi refused a refuge in the west. Instead of a refuge the People were now in a trap.[6]

The Texans and the McIntosh were closing in from the south while other Confederates and the Cherokees were poised to strike from the north and east, moving between the People and Union troops from Kansas. There was no chance of escaping to the west and joining the Komantsi. There was no longer any hope of uniting the nation and standing as a single people, or even of remaining in their homes. The only option was to ally with the federal government and somehow reach northern troops coming from Kansas before the enemy could cut them off. All of the demons from the past were again at work: greed, treachery, confusion, ancient rivalries, and, above all, the McIntosh and their masters, the white men.

There was no moon that night, and the sky was very black as Opothleyahola rode with his men and their prisoner. The riders had to pick their way through brush and woods, yet before first light they hit more prairie country, and with sunrise spotted wagons in the distance. It was the campsite of their neighbors and families, the people of Tuckabatchee. The ones in camp came from a number of clans—the Snake, the Bear, the Wind, and many more—but they were bound together by town and by the knowledge that they were to guide the others to safety. Soon other towns would join them: Greenleaf, Arbeka, Topolothoco. But those from Tuckabatchee would lead them all.[7]

Campfires and wagons scattered in every direction across the open land and into a line of trees. Horses and mules stood hitched to some of the wagons. A few were already moving out, heading north for the Arkansas River. As the men rode up they noticed the sounds of cattle—hundreds of them lowing and bawling somewhere nearby. Then came barking dogs, the rattle of trace chains, and voices, for when they saw them riding up, the People ran to greet the men on horseback. Some of the fathers and mothers held up the little ones so they might see Opothleyahola.

There was joy and celebration at the sight of loved ones riding into camp. In normal times there might have been a feast and a festival as well. But the times were anything but normal. Everyone had to pack and get out. Carry what you can, burn or bury the rest, or leave it, but get out for the enemy was near. Opothleyahola sent riders to the south and west, dashing across the countryside to alert every homestead and wagon party. Others rode north to warn of the danger.

For the rest of the day the wagons moved out, creaking and groaning under their loads. Over an open rise to the west herds of cattle and horses were moving out as well. A few of the households owned some of the largest herds in America. Some of the stock would have to go, too, for the People would need cattle and horses to rebuild their lives when the war was over, after the McIntosh and the Texans were driven away. The cattle and horses would be needed as well to survive the hard days ahead. Raising and selling stock to Union authorities would be a way to live until the People were again on their land. And only the ponies and oxen could pull the wagons.

Even with danger so near, there was a strange calm about the camp. Men and women paused to visit as they packed, children played, and the old ones sat in the wagons or by the campfires quietly watching and waiting, keeping company with their memories. They seemed possessed, all of them, of a strange inner sense that told them when to rush and when to take their time, as if they could feel the danger and would know instinctively when it was right to hurry.[8]

But as the sun moved across the sky the People left, each in their own time, not in a single orderly column but in scattered bands, and moving out in several directions. Wagons dotted the landscape to the horizon: some heading north, others veering to the west and northwest, and a few traveling east. For a day or more they would fan out, leaving a spider web of horse tracks and wagon ruts to confuse the enemy. But in time every wagon would turn north to meet near a collection of springs and sloughs called Big Pond. At Big Pond all of the Nation would assemble to form a mighty river of humanity flowing northward. And the Tuckabatchees with Opothleyahola would be there to lead them.

Riding among the scattered wagons were men on horseback. Beside the wagons and riders were other men on foot as well as women, boys, and girls. Some of those on foot led ox teams, others drove milk cows with whips or prods. Many trudged along with bundles thrown over their shoulders. There were covered wagons, buggies, buckboards, and carts—all of them bulging with belong-

27

THE TUCKABATCHEES ❖

ings from a lifetime of labor and sacrifice. On top of a loaded buck-board might be a boy with a puppy, waving to other children on the ground, on another might be a grandmother or a woman heavy with child.

As the last wagons pulled out, another party of men rode with them—the warriors. Most sat clutching shotguns or bows astride their ponies. All of them had knives or hatchets at the waist. A few of the warriors galloped back and forth across the prairie or circled the others as they all rode away. Their ponies had caught the mood and the chill in the air; prancing and snorting, the animals could hardly be held to a trot. Somewhere in the distant hills to the south-east were still other men, the scouts. They would ride slowly and carefully, the scouts, alert to any sign or movement: startled birds, fleeing animals, a dust cloud—anything that might hint at approach-ing danger. The scouts were the eyes and ears of the People. They would be the first to signal an alert when the enemy appeared.

Even as the last few wagons creaked away from camp, a rider came galloping in with news. Many of the People were still far behind, he reported. Some were on their way, but a number were still packing or rounding up cattle and horses at their homes. Oth-ers had decided not to come at all—the omens and signs had warned against leaving, they said. Still others believed it was not the time to go. And a few had decided Opothleyahola could not be trusted—that he was too old, or had lost his wisdom or his magic. Then, too, there were the towns that would never follow and would side with the enemy.

It was no surprise to Opothleyahola. He knew the People well and realized not everyone would come. A Muskogee leader drew power by virtue of heredity or from proven and demonstrated quali-ties such as wisdom and honesty. But his power was usually lim-ited to his town. Only a few had the strength and influence to touch the lives of the whole Muskogee Nation, only those like Opothleyahola or the McIntosh. And even they could not speak for all. There were no presidents or governors who ruled for a set period, no matter how much they might grow to be despised. Nei-ther were there third parties hiding in the shadows, discreetly man-aging the affairs of the one who pretended to govern. There was only a loose confederation of towns: some that would follow Opothleyahola; others that were forever lost to the McIntosh.

Those who planned to come later would have to get out as best they could. If they were cunning and brave and the gods looked after them, they would be safe. If not, they were doomed. The ones who chose to remain at their farms or follow another path would soon discover if their way was best.[9]

At last the wagons were out of sight. There was no one left in camp but a small band of riders. No signal had appeared from the scouts, so apparently the enemy was still some distance away. Someone shouted a command and the last few riders moved out as well: fanning across the open country, following the web of tracks and wagon ruts. But two men on horseback still remained, holding torches. Finally they galloped through the camp, setting the grass ablaze. Perhaps there were too many wagons to slip away or hide, but it would be difficult to sort through the maze of tracks and blackened earth left behind. The enemy was clever and would find the right path, but it would take time.

The fire spread quickly through the yellowish grass, and the smoke billowed high in great rolling clouds. Even if the enemy spotted the smoke, it was a welcome and reassuring sight to the People—like a grandfather shielding them from harm. It had always been so. Was not fire a gift from the gods to their children? Was it not a living spirit; was it not an earthly symbol of the Master of Breath?

The riders galloped off, disappearing into the smoke. Nothing remained in camp but the litter of broken wagons, and something else. Jutting from the ground and pointing in the direction of the enemy were four sticks—a magic number four. The sticks were painted black and red, the colors of death and war.[10]

29

CHAPTER
FOUR

The Boy

He went by the name of James Scott—a white man's name—though in body and spirit he was Muskogee. He was only a boy, not more than eight or ten years old. But his was a world where manhood came early, and now more than ever he needed to be a man. His raven hair glistened in the sun, and his dark eyes peered straight ahead as he worked his pony in and out of the blackjack and post oak thickets. The pony seemed huge for one so small, but he managed. Just ahead, on the trail, cattle trotted along the winding path. At a bend in the path, a deer darted ahead of the cattle, then into the brush. In another direction a pair of wild hogs scampered away. The little boy ignored them; his only thoughts were for the stock.[1]

With every rising James Scott went alone into the brush and surrounding hills to gather cattle. There was no one else who could help. His father and mother were busy at the farm and his sister, Lizzie was little more than a baby. At night James watched his father and mother cooking, salting, and packing slaughtered beef. It had gone on this way for days.

In time others arrived, neighbors and family from surrounding farms. They came on horseback, on foot, or in wagons filled with furniture and bedding. Some drove small herds of cattle, horses, and sheep. A few even herded flocks of guineas and geese. At the farm the men butchered still more stock, then sliced and cooked the meat. The women ground corn or dried and packed sweet potatoes, onions, peppers, and beets. Everything they would need went into the wagons: cooking pots, clothes, tools. Anything of value that could not be brought along, they buried. It almost seemed like a festival at first: everyone busy, children playing, dogs barking, men and women talking far into the night.

But it was not a festival. There was no music and little laughter. Something was terribly wrong and even a boy could sense it. There was tension in the voices of his father and mother, and a certain strained look in their faces. Somehow the air itself seemed charged with fear. And there were whispers, too, about someone coming to take away the women and the children.

At last the work ended. On a gray, chilly dawn the wagons pulled away from the farm. Shouts and whistles, the crack of whips, the rattle of trace chains: all mixed together with the groans of overburdened wagons as they began to move. One of the children in a wagon was crying while others on the ground laughed and played. Some of the women were in wagons but others walked alongside. James rode with the men on horseback to help drive the cattle.[2]

Slowly they made their way north, keeping to the brush wherever possible, until they joined with another wagon party at a muddy stream called Hillaby Creek. For several risings the families camped amid the trees at Hillaby Creek. As they waited, others joined them, adding to the number of wagons and campfires. And every night, as their numbers grew, the People shared their hopes and fears. All would be right again, they assured one another; their grandfather would protect them as he had so many times before. The Old One had powers that the McIntosh and the Texans did not even suspect.

For as long as he could remember, James had heard of the Old One. Once he had seen him; Opothleyahola had come to speak to his father and mother. To James, Opothleyahola resembled a god as much as a man: the wrinkled features, the long white hair, the warm and reassuring voice. He was dressed in green, black, and gold, with a copper gorget and red turban. Like the hills and mountains, Opothleyahola seemed ancient and all-powerful. Yet, at the same time there was a certain indescribable sadness that never left him.

At the farm Opothleyahola had warned of the dangers that lay ahead, but he spoke as well of courage, loyalty, and how the Muskogee people must survive. He showed them a letter from someone who had promised help. If the People would only stand together, the letter read, there would be troops to protect them. The

Great Father Abraham Lincoln with his mighty army would sweep away the enemy and restore the lands. After Opothleyahola left, the family started packing and James began rounding up cattle.[3]

From Hillaby Creek the wagons and families moved north again to join with others. They were far behind the rest, and the McIntosh were somewhere near. If they could reach Big Pond they would be safe, at least for a while; all of the towns and clans would be there. But they would have to move carefully if they were to go unnoticed, for Big Pond was still far away. As the wagons crept north, men on horseback fanned out to surround them and form a shield. Most of them carried guns: old flintlocks and muzzle loaders, and other rusty castoffs from the past. Still, their firearms were probably as good as those of the enemy. Others rode with a bow and a quiver of arrows slung across their backs. A few carried war clubs tucked in their belts. The old ways of war—the club and the bow—were vanishing. The white man's weapons had seen to that, but not for everyone. The memories and the old style of combat still lived for some.

Next came the cattle, driven along by other riders. After Hillaby Creek, James was no longer with the cattle but in a wagon with his sister; the country was too dangerous for any but warriors to ride in the open. No one lit fires to scorch the earth as they moved. The smoke would have been spotted by the enemy, and the People were too few to stand against an army.

For several days they rode, glancing over their shoulders at the distant hills as they moved, looking always for signs of danger. No more wagons would be joining them until Big Pond. If they faced trouble, they were on their own. Sometimes they would cross an ancient hunting trail. Other times they might happen upon a small pile of stones. As they passed the stones, some of the men would get off their ponies to pick up other rocks or bits of flint to pitch on the pile. The stones marked the spot where someone had met death, perhaps from an animal or in combat with an enemy. Adding stones was a token of respect and a way to feed the spirit of the dead. Half of the land they crossed was rolling prairie; the rest was a brush country of stunted oak and hickory—the sort of ground where the wagons could remain half hidden. At night the People camped amid the oak and hickory thickets, the only sign of life their small smokeless fires and the nearby cattle. Every night the People studied the heavens, searching for a sign of what lay ahead: smoke stars, serpents' tails, anything that might foretell what was to come. The heavens and the earth were filled with prophecies and omens for any with the gift to understand. In the northern sky was the star that never moved. There was also the image of the canoe, the spirits' road to the other world, and countless other stars and constellations. All of them could foreshadow what was to be. And later in the night, perhaps in dreams, the spirits would come as well to speak and offer counsel.[4]

Every morning the People rose before light. If they had camped by a creek or stream, they bathed and purified themselves for the day. With first light the wagon caravan would be pushing north again. But one morning as they were moving out, a wagon lost a wheel and they had to call a halt for repairs. The following day, one of the women gave birth and they waited longer still. The newborn was healthy and without markings; that was a good sign. But they were falling behind. The pattern continued, the People moving when they could, stopping when they must. There were signs that others had been their way: hoofprints, wagon ruts, old campfires. But whose campfires, and whose horses? Were they friends or the enemy? Then came more ominous signs: charred fields and burned-out cabins. And sometimes in the night they could make out an eerie red orange glow to the south and the east. Still they saw no one. As they traveled farther, even the birds seemed to vanish. It was as if all life had fled from the evil that was nearing. They found more wagon ruts, camp litter, and hoofprints leading in every direction, though never the ones who had made them. But just when some began to wonder if they had been left behind and it seemed they were the only ones on earth, their fate changed. They came to the crest of a gentle rise and caught sight of something none had ever seen in Indian Territory. In the distance rose smoke from countless campfires: it was Big Pond.

Not since the old country had there been such a gathering of the towns. With every day cycle, more wagon parties arrived, adding strength and numbers, camping wherever there was room. On the campfires were great pots of sofki to share, and venison and beef aplenty. Spreading in every direction were buggies, wagons, carriages, buckboards, and carts; and farther away grazed herds of cattle, horses, and sheep.[5]

And as the People grew in numbers, far from the white man's world, they embraced once again the old ways and the true faith. Men put on leggings and breechcloths, wrapped themselves in blankets, and braided their hair. The air filled with the sounds of drums and rattles, and of old songs and ancient chants. The wail of flute mated with the smoke of campfires. And in the dark, Opothleyahola prayed to the spirits to give him strength and wisdom. Once more there was hope. Some dared believe that a new age had come: that the white men would be swept away by their own war, that the People would again inherit the earth as the prophets had foretold. There were mighty speeches, promises sworn in blood. And there was magic. The hills moved, the animals spoke, and the gods, too long forgotten, came again to their children, the Muskogees.

Still more wagon parties arrived at Big Pond, swelling the numbers. Then came a single large party from the south. As they rode in, a late sun caught the glint of their rifle barrels and the metal gorgets they wore across their chests. In front were some of the warriors, striking figures on horseback. Every man held a weapon: a gun or a bow. They wore breechcloths and leggings and shirts colored red, green, black, and gold. Fringe and ribbons streamed from their sleeves and feathers drooped from their long raven hair. Behind the warriors followed the women and children in wagons or on horses. It was the wild ones—the ones called Seminoles.

Leading them were the war captains: Alligator, Holata Micco, Halleck Tustenuggee. Many times before the war captains had led their men into battle against their enemies, no matter the odds. When Halleck Tustenuggee surrendered to the white man's army in the old world, he was down to eighty warriors. Had it not been for the women and the little ones, he might have fought until they all lay dead. Some of the Seminoles were still fighting and hiding in the swamps and glades of the old land. When the bloodletting came, as it must, the Seminoles would stand against anyone.

But despite the power or courage of the Seminoles, and no matter how many warriors had gathered from the towns, no one could remain for long at Big Pond. Even if the warriors were great in number, those of the enemy were greater. Already scouts reported a large, hostile party to the southeast. It was only a question of when they would come. Soon the People would have to leave for the Arkansas River.[6]

There were far too many wagons to travel together, and the stock would starve for lack of grass if not broken into smaller herds. They would all have to move, instead, in parallel columns and several days apart. Any of the wagon parties could be overwhelmed if caught alone, but it was the only way. With the wagons would be the women and the little ones, the sick and the aged. Then would come the stock. Once the wagons and the stock were away from Big Pond, a large body of warriors would follow, riding between the families and the enemy. At the same time a second and smaller party of warriors would race ahead to secure the fords at the Arkansas River. If they were lucky, Union troops might be there waiting.[7]

With the wagon parties and the warriors were slaves as well, for slavery had always been a part of Muskogee life. In the past, slaves had come as prisoners in war. If a captive was spared from death, he became a slave. A slave might become a servant or a laborer when taken prisoner. Often though, he won his freedom through service or deeds of courage. Sometimes he was adopted by the family that had enslaved him. A few rose to become great warriors or the leaders of towns. Some became slaveholders themselves. Black slavery came with the white man, and there were many black slaves in the Muskogee Nation. But there were black warriors, elders, and slaveholders, too. As in the past, a slave could rise to freedom if he was great and good and the gods were with him. It was all part of an endless cycle that ebbed and flowed with the fortunes of war and fate.

There had been a change, though, brought on by the current troubles. Opothleyahola had made a promise: if the slaves remained true to their masters and the Union in Washington City, when the war was over they would all be freed. Soon other blacks, runaway slaves from plantations of the enemy, joined the People as the word of freedom spread. They came by the hundreds. Some were from plantations of the McIntosh. All were welcome; all were freed.[8]

The McIntosh and the southern white men talked of preserving slavery. Growing numbers in Kansas and Washington City declared it evil and spoke of sweeping slavery from all of America. It was of no concern to the People, for they cared nothing about the white man's values. Their troubles were never over slavery or even a choice between North or South. For them the struggle was between the old ways and impurity, tradition and change. Theirs would be a war between Upper towns and Lower towns, Tuckabatchee and Coweta, Opothleyahola and McIntosh.

A few wagons and families were still arriving at Big Pond when the first parties began to leave for the Arkansas River. It would be several days before everyone was away. The clouds were low and heavy the morning the first wagons broke camp. A mist sifted down—the kind of dreary mist that often comes with autumn— slowly soaking everyone to the skin. As the wagons moved out, wheels soon caked with a heavy red clay that had to be knocked off by men and boys following on foot.

The column of wagons stretched across the prairie like a snake, fading into the mist and fog. Next went the cattle and horses, then the sheep. The mist kept away the dust clouds, but nothing could stop the bawling and bleating of the herds. Then another column moved out, heading north but veering away slightly from the first wagon party. Still later went another party of wagons.

In the days that followed, the pattern continued: wagon columns leaving camp and heading north for the Arkansas River, followed by still more columns. Finally there were only a few wagons left, and the main body of warriors, who would ride always between the wagons and the enemy.

Opothleyahola was with the last of the wagons at Big Pond. The day they left he was on horseback, near the head of the column, but not for long. The many days in the open, the nights sleeping on the ground, it was too much for one so old. He began to ride in a buggy, and at night the young ones made him a bed from blankets and a feather mattress in one of the wagons. It didn't help. He grew wearier still. But he would not stop to rest, for too much time had been lost already. There were others just as old, and they were all in deadly peril. He would find the strength to go on.

Not everyone could keep up the pace. Some had traveled their last, in this world at least, the very old and the sick. Sometimes a small crowd and several wagons pulled away from the others to bury a loved one. The dead were buried facing east with a few personal belongings: a blanket, a pipe, perhaps a looking glass or some tobacco, and maybe a bow and arrows—the kinds of valuables one might want or need in the spirit world. Maybe buried alongside was a favorite dog or even a horse. After the body was placed in the ground, everyone present pitched a handful of earth into the grave. And then, perhaps, a small fire was kindled by a son or wife before departing. It was all part of a last token of respect to a life lived well.

As the wagon parties passed towns and farms, still more joined Opothleyahola. At Tiger Town it was the Yuchis—the Children of the Sun. The Yuchis, it was said, were formed from the dripping blood of eagles that flew too close to the sun; through their veins flowed fire. When the Yuchis first came to live with the People, they had settled near the Cowetas and counted themselves as a Lower town. Now they followed the path of Opothleyahola. It was the same for several of the Lower towns. They would pin their fate to the old ways and the old gods, not the traitors and the corrupt.

Then the Alabamas joined them. So far as anyone knew, the Alabamas were as ancient as the land and the rivers. They revered still the memory of animals from the time of the deep cold—the ones with the great trunks and long tusks, and the mankiller cats with knives for teeth. From the west in small bands came foreigners and distant kin: the Delawares and the Shawnees. The Shawnees, it was said, could make themselves invisible. Then came others, even more foreign and remote: the Quapaws, the Kickapoo, and the Piankashaws. Next the Wichitas arrived, and even a few of the remaining Kadohadachos. And there were other peoples on the way, coming along the Delaware-Shawnee Trail.[9]

They came in wagons, on foot, and on horses stolen from the enemy. Every day there were more who joined, pouring in from all directions and nearly every nation in the Territory: some running or hiding, hoping to escape; others hoping only for a chance at vengeance, or to prove themselves in battle when the fighting began. All of them, though, were willing to cast their fate with a single, determined leader. Finally, riding in from the east to join were some of the Cherokees, in spite of John Ross and Stand Watie.

There had been a time when the Muskogees and the Cherokees were enemies. There had been a time long before when the Muskogees were enemies of any they met. They were a mighty nation then, rich and powerful, and they feared no one. It was the time of princes when the cities and temples of the People spanned nearly half a continent. Their influence stretched even farther: to the deserts and jungles of the South, to the snowy mountains in the West, and perhaps as far as the western sea. But no more. Now the Muskogees were but a remnant of past glories, joining with the Cherokee Nation or any other that might protect against the savages who were closing in.[10]

Before long there was trouble between the Muskogees and some of the foreigners. Insults were traded and horses turned up missing. Warriors from the different nations challenged one another, threatening to convert campgrounds into battlefields. Many of the foreigners had strange and revolting ways, it was said; some did not bathe and others ate their meat before pitching an offering to the fire. One of the Delawares had killed a fox, sacred symbol of the Potato clan, and he refused to make reparations. The Quapaws would not show the Hitichis proper respect. Some were refusing orders from the Tuckabatchees, and the Kickapoo would listen to no one.

But whenever blood ran hot, Opothleyahola would make peace

and push them on. He was one of them, but at the same time different. Most of his life Opothleyahola had dealt with the white man and was forever changed by the experience. For as long as he could remember, he had stood against the McIntosh as well. More than any other, perhaps, he understood the enemy who was coming for them. He knew that if they were to survive, the nations would have to work as one. Over and over he reminded them they were brothers of the same fire, that they were the True People, all of them, that their enemies were demons or traitors. If the nations failed to stand as one, all would perish.

Moving north, camping, then moving again, their numbers continued to swell. Finally, the wagon party with Opothleyahola passed a four-sided post shaped from the stump of a tree. On each side was a carved symbol: the sun, the buffalo, the snake, and the wild goose. A few rotted strands of fringe and beads, swaying in the breeze, hung from the post; on top was the skull of a buffalo. The marker was the site of the Osage War Trail. In the old days, the Osage traveled south along the trail every spring and fall, raiding as far as Texas. But the Osage, like so many others had been forever broken as a power by the white man. What was left of them were in Kansas. Only the Komantsi still had the power to defy the white man or any others who crossed their land.

When they camped that night, the People knew they were nearing the Arkansas River. Another rising, maybe two, and they would be at the fords. But before they could move again, something happened; it came with a dark bluish cloud rolling in from the west. The wind rose in gusts—a sharp chilling wind. Snakes danced across the sky, and in the clouds was the roar and thunder of giants at war. Hawks and crows swirled overhead, just in front of the storm. Then came the rain, a cold gray wall, swallowing everything as it moved across the prairie and the distant ridges, heading straight for the wagons. It hit with a single volley of water and wind. The People huddled under wagons and carts hoping to stay dry, but it was no use, for the wind and rain lashed them. Others simply turned their backs to the storm and endured. The entire camp was but a speck on the rain-washed land, at the mercy of the storm. Puddles quickly formed, growing and merging with others to become small ponds. Every ditch and draw was soon gushing water. And then, just as suddenly as it had hit, the storm was over. The rain ended, the sun appeared, and the black warring clouds moved away toward the enemy and the Kiamichi Mountains beyond. Only the sharp chilly wind remained. There was no traveling that day, for loaded wagons could not cross flooded draws and soaked ground. But by dark only a few puddles remained as reminders of the storm. That night the winds died, but the air turned colder still. The following morning a ghostly frost coated the ground and there was ice in the puddles. Yet with first light the People and wagons were moving again.

Somehow in the storm the white man, John Taylor, had escaped, or perhaps he was allowed to get away; no one was troubled. If the enemy already knew their plans, as Taylor said, then he could tell them nothing new. Before long, however, there was another matter to consider.[11]

It was a man on horseback riding in from the south, a slave of the McIntosh with a warning from his masters. He rode in holding up an arm, waving to the wagons and buggies. The Confederate army was nearby and closing fast, he shouted. Everyone must turn around; otherwise, they would all die; no one would escape. He rode the length of the column shouting, waving, then warning and ordering: "Turn back, go back. They're coming for you if you don't surrender." Some of the People mocked and jeered. Most simply rode in silence, staring ahead, as if the rider did not exist. At last the slave drew reins, wheeled about, and galloped off in the direction he had come.

For the rest of the day the People wondered about the slave. How close were the Texans and the McIntosh? What was the enemy planning? Was it possible that Opothleyahola had been fooled and led into a trap? Was it possible that Union troops were not coming? That night in camp no one could forget what had happened. Then came more news when one of Opothleyahola's scouts rode in from the dark. Most of the wagon parties were across the Arkansas, safely on the other side, he reported. But not everyone. There had been too many delays: storms, broken wagons, childbirth, sickness, and death. It might take days to get everyone across. Opothleyahola listened as he sat beside the fire, then rose stiffly and walked out to the edge of camp, into the darkness. In the distance, in the direction of the enemy, he could see the faint orange glow of Confederate campfires.[12]

CHAPTER

FIVE

The Chase

There would be no stopping to rest that night. Children hurried into the wagons while women gathered pots and blankets and men hitched up the teams. They were still a night's ride from the Arkansas River. But if everyone moved swiftly and the gods watched over them, the women and children at least might slip away to the river before the enemy tracked them down. At the Arkansas the one called Little Captain, along with his warriors, would be waiting to protect them. Little Captain and his men had been at the river for days, helping everyone to the other side; they were the ones who had gone ahead to secure the fords. Soon the moon rose in the east to light the way. As they moved out, there was nothing to do but follow the soft shadowy outline of the wagon in front—and pray there was time enough to escape.[1]

Opothleyahola and most of the men remained behind. Once the last wagons faded into the night, they took another path. Keeping some of the wagons and buggies, the warriors veered away to the northwest. They would leave a deliberate trail as they moved: abandoned buggies and wagons, camp litter, lame ponies. It was an old trick but one that had worked before. While the women and children slipped away to the river, the men hoped to lure the enemy into battle. The men with Opothleyahola were now a small army of warriors from nearly twenty nations. Like the women and little ones they, too, would ride through the night, but never swiftly, never working to hide their trail. Just as the women and children, the warriors also prayed, but not for escape. They prayed for battle. Too soon the warriors' prayer would be answered.[2]

By sunrise Opothleyahola was nearing a low range of hills rolling off to the east. Away from the hills, and higher than the rest, was a single rounded mountain shaped like a haystack. The country was mostly prairie except for the dark clusters of cedar and scrub oak clinging to life in the draws and ravines of the hills. It was a land of coarse grass, flint ridges, and brush, all colored gold by the morning sun.

The men were painted for war. Some had colored their faces: half red, half black. Others had lines streaking away from their eyes, to strengthen sight. A few had even stripped away their shirts, in spite of the chill, and colored their chests and arms with the marks of blood and death. All of them had cornhusks and feathers in their hair. The cornhusk was a symbol of loyalty to Opothleyahola. They rode with guns and bows ready, hoping desperately the enemy would follow their trail instead of that of the women and children.[3]

So far they had all been lucky. Some of the People had been on the trail or in campsites for many risings, all the while avoiding the enemy. Yet it was more than luck. Opothleyahola, mostly by feigning an interest in Confederate promises, had drawn on every instinct to keep the enemy from their throats. Not until the last moment had he slipped away to join the People. At one point he had met with Confederate authorities at his home. Another time, even after condemning the McIntosh and their forged treaties, he had parleyed with the enemy at the Council Grounds. A peace agreement needed time for thought, he had told them: there were terms and guarantees that needed clarification; there was also a matter of where the parties should meet, and who should represent the many towns. He yearned for peace and a treaty with Confederates, he assured them. But it would take time. Perhaps the white men could return and resume their talks. Perhaps the white men could come again—tomorrow.[4]

The McIntosh had never been misled. From the beginning they knew Opothleyahola was stalling. The McIntosh understood there could be nothing between themselves and Opothleyahola but an endless cycle of hatred and bloodletting. But their leader was a Confederate commander who fancied that he knew the Indians and believed his personal bearing would convert Opothleyahola if only they could meet. The Confederate was a fool.

For half a lifetime Opothleyahola had dealt with senators, kings,

41

princes, and presidents. Such had always been his lot at Tucka-batchee. Yet throughout his long life no one had impressed him so little as some of the white men he had known. It was true that the whites had power, and their numbers were greater than the leaves of the forest. But they were a grasping, treacherous people. And they were without magic. It was true even of the Great Father in Washington City whom Opothleyahola had met long ago. The Great Father could not vanish through a ring of smoke; he could not see or hear the spirits. The Great Father was in charge of a nation of nothings from a heritage of nothing. And now a lowly Confederate commander imagined he could somehow overawe the Speaker of the Muskogee Nation? The insects had more bearing.

In the past it had been right to stall and mislead the enemy with words. But as he led his warriors that morning near the rounded mountain, Opothleyahola prayed like the rest that the enemy would come quickly for war. Let the Texans and their wolves called McIntosh seek him out; he was weary of talk. Let them come and die, for the women and children must not perish. Somehow the women and little ones had to get across the Arkansas River.

The People and the wagons were clustered along the bank of the river, into the trees and up the bluff. One thin line of families and wagons stretched across the river at a ford. Around the bend a collection of log rafts and flatboats connected with ropes ferried back and forth, carrying still more wagons and families to the other side.

Everyone patiently waited their turn, then one by one crossed the river at the ford or on the rafts. Earlier, several wagons and families had tried to cross by simply plunging into the water, but they were lost in the currents. The wagons drifted into a series of whirlpools, tipping and bobbing, then finally turning on their sides and vanishing beneath the waters. Most of those who went down with the wagons were never seen again.

As the People waited to cross the river, more rode in from the south to join them. An entire party of wagons, those that had been with Opothleyahola, arrived during the morning. A few more families on horseback and foot straggled in still later. It was said many more were farther south, trying to slip through enemy lines.

Beneath the water at the ford were the tie snakes, watching the People cross to the other bank. The tie snakes were powerful and dangerous beings who lived beneath the streams and rivers. Theirs was the kingdom of the underworld where shadows and spirits forever reigned. None, except the corrupt like the McIntosh, and also the white man, questioned their existence. Sometimes the tie snakes came out of the waters to wrap themselves around their enemies on land, leaving them helpless. Other times they would hang from trees and fall without warning on their foe.

Since time began and the wind blew away the fog, the People had lived near the snakes at the rivers and creeks. They felt none of the white man's hatred for snakes; instead, they revered them. As the People waded the Arkansas River, some could see the snakes beneath the water even through the red muddy currents. Some spoke to them and chanted prayers of thanksgiving as they struggled through the chilly waters, for the tie snakes often answered the prayers of the faithful.

All morning it went on: the log rafts and flatboats ferrying back and forth; others carefully picking their way across the river at the ford. Watching on a bluff above the river was Little Captain. Young, lean, and painted for war, he stood with his rifle and looked anxiously at the line of wagons and families struggling through the water. Once across the Arkansas they would be safe, at least for a while. The Confederates could not mount a charge through a river. But it would take time to get everyone across. If the People were caught in the open crossing the river, they would be butchered. Scattered along the bluff on either side of Little Captain were his warriors—half hidden behind rocks and trees—with their backs to the river and facing the direction of the enemy. They would stand and fight until every woman and child was out of danger, or every warrior lay dead.

Deeper in the day Little Captain ordered the remaining wagons away from the river. Scouts reported the enemy was near; there was no time left to get every wagon across. Slaves began cutting branches and small trees to cover the wagons that remained. Others on the bluff started brushing the ground with branches, away from the river and toward the enemy, trying to cover any hint of a trail. All the while families continued wading across the river at the ford in a slow steady line, depending on the gods and Little Captain to protect them. And the warriors on the bluff kept facing south, waiting and straining for the first distant glimpse of the enemy.[5]

A line of buggies and empty wagons bounced along, surrounded by painted warriors on horseback. In the lead buggy was Opothleyahola. They had been on the trail for a night and nearly a day.

THE CHASE ❖

Once again shadows were lengthening, signaling the close of another day cycle. Opothleyahola was nearly sick from exhaustion and his cough had returned, a deep rattling cough. But there was no time to rest.

Sometimes a rider would race in with news. Then another would gallop away just as quickly. But the wagons and party of warriors kept moving, purposely leaving a trail. Then news came they had all been waiting for: the enemy was following—and moving away from the women and children. Still later another rider arrived to report that the enemy was following, and closing fast. But Opothleyahola was in no hurry. The land had grown rugged and broken, with gullies and draws filled with brush and timber. It was a country the gods might have carved out for ambush and war.

A day or two before the warriors might have been trapped on the same ground, for every gully and stream had been a torrent after the storm. But this was a land where streams and creeks could rise and fall in less than a day. At a half-flowing stream called the Red Fork of the Arkansas, they left some of the wagons and buggies. But the warriors and the rest of the wagons pushed on, and the enemy kept closing from behind. For the rest of the day they rode, moving slowly, crossing prairie, thickets, and draws, and still more gullies and muddy, half-alive streams. Soon the day would end as it had begun, the sun washing the land in rays of golden light. Soon, too, the ground would be colored red with blood.[6]

The warriors were eager for battle. Through combat a warrior gained status and worth with the People. There would be bloodletting, death, and stories of men in battle that would live forever, for man is a hunter and warrior by nature. Animals that are hunted—like the deer—have round, stubby teeth and eyes on the side of the head. But the animals that kill—bears, panthers, wolves—always have sharp, pointed teeth and piercing eyes that look to the point of attack. So does man.

Suddenly, the war party reined in on the prairie. Far to their right, some thought they had heard the faint popping sound of gunfire. Yet when they stopped there was only silence. Just to be sure, Opothleyahola ordered several riders to the right as a scout; in an instant they were off. The rest of the warriors and the wagons moved again, down an open slope toward a tree-lined ravine.

Once in the trees Opothleyahola called a halt. He ordered campfires built, large billowing fires that would attract an enemy. Then he placed his men along the ravine. The ravine curved in from the direction they had come, in the shape of a gigantic bow.

Soon every tree and bush hid a warrior. Other warriors piled up rocks, then sank down behind them. There was magic in the rocks, and their grandfathers—the trees—had always protected them. Facing the prairie, the way they had come, they waited.

At dusk one of the scouts came racing back, reining in his sweat-soaked horse as he entered the ravine. The sound of guns was Little Captain, the scout reported. A few of the enemy had found his hiding place at the river. But Little Captain and his warriors had stood their ground until the last of the women and children had crossed the Arkansas. Then he, too, had slipped away with his men to the other side. The main party of Confederates was still closing on Opothleyahola. Part of their column was just beyond the rise to the south, the rider went on, pointing behind him. They were nearly in sight.

Opothleyahola knew the enemy was near, even before the rider began to speak; he could feel their presence. In the distance an owl hooted four times. Overhead a single star glistened in a red orange western sky, the star of death. And all around the spirits stirred to life as in olden times.[7]

CHAPTER

SIX

The McIntosh

They rode in a column of twos—a long, uneven, loping column that stretched for a mile or more over the open country. Hoofbeats mixed with the clank of tin cups against canteens and the occasional chatter of the men. Their clothing was a wild array of tattered homespun, cheap jackets, tailored suits, and even buckskin. A few wore hunting shirts of red or white; but most were in colors of brownish butternut and gray—sweat-stained and specked with mud. Everyone had something covering his head: slouch felt hats, broad-brimmed straw hats, caps; a few even had on Mexican sombreros. And every man wore a red or white string dangling from an arm, a makeshift badge to symbolize Confederate forces.

Most were in their teens, little more than boys. They were lean, wiry, and tanned, though some were sickly as well, with blotches and sores on yellowish skin. Their hair was matted and greasy. It had been days since any had bathed; for some it was weeks. A few of the older officers wore frazzled, unkempt beards flowing wildly down to their chests. But despite their raggedness and squalor, they all had a certain look that made the whole command seem remorseless and unstoppable. Perhaps it was the smooth, easy way they carried themselves in the saddle. All of them had learned to ride soon after they could walk. They were probably the only white men in America who could match the Indians on horseback. Then again, it might have been their weapons. Nearly every man carried a shotgun or a rifle. Some had Colt revolvers as well, tucked in pants or in pistol belts strung across their shoulders. A few had extra pistols hanging from their saddle horns. And every rider had a huge knife carried in a leather scabbard and hung from the saddle. That they were all very dangerous, no one could doubt.

They came from the pine barrens and river bottoms of Texas: lonely, half-hidden places with names like White Oak, Lone Star, the Big Woods, Daingerfield, and Sulphur Bottom. A few of them were learned and versed in the ways of politics and the world; one or two perhaps had even read Aristotle and Cicero, but such were the exception. Mostly they were men who had never before traveled thirty miles from home. Some could not read, though they carried Bibles; others had never seen a newspaper. They still believed in witches, devils, trolls, and luck—a remnant perhaps of their ancient tribal past. And when they spoke through jagged, tobacco-stained teeth, what they said was often garbled and disjointed, for most of them had a vocabulary of only a few hundred words.

They fancied themselves as paladins and cavaliers, these men, defenders of a way of life that had begun with the earliest settlements in Virginia. They had it on what they believed was good authority that the Indians and a Yankee host were massing to invade their homeland, that every family and farm in Texas might be put to the sword or the scalping knife. They were certain, too, that they would deal with the enemy, just as surely as they knew they would win their war for southern rights, no matter the odds. They were a wild, tattered, and deadly pack, these white men. Already they had lynched two of their own, one for rape, another on the rumor that he was an abolitionist. Yet for all that was deadly and even savage in their nature, they were devoted to their beliefs and their cause and would face almost any hardship or danger for the sake of those beliefs. To an outsider, most of them would have seemed coarse, frightening, and even brutal. Yet in their own world they were good and brave and were dearly loved. Like mankind everywhere, they feared and hated what they did not understand. The white men on horseback were prisoners of their times and their way of life as surely as were the ones they trailed.[1]

Behind the Texans, at a distance, came another column, the First Confederate Creek Mounted Regiment. Leading it was Daniel McIntosh: strong, proud, and vigorous, wearing a broad-brimmed hat and a cotton duster that came down to his boots. His hair was long, black, and flowing, and he was sporting a neatly trimmed beard. He was a wealthy and powerful man, Daniel McIntosh, with slaves, good bottomland, blooded horses, and a fine, spacious home. He was leader of the Lower Creeks and of a family that had led half of the Muskogee Nation for a hundred years. And he was a Baptist preacher, too. In all of Indian Territory there was only one with more influence—the one he stalked and planned to kill—the man called Opothleyahola.

Daniel knew all about the bad blood between his following and the ones who rode with the other side, how it had gone on for years. There had been rivalry between Lower and Upper Creeks for lifetimes. But for Daniel McIntosh there was a special and very personal hatred that drove him as well. All of his life Daniel had heard the stories of what had happened when he was a baby: the storming of the family farm in Georgia, the slaughtering of stock, the torching of the home, and finally, the driving out of the owner, killing him in the yard. In the old land years before, Opothleyahola's savages had murdered William McIntosh, Daniel's father. In his worst nightmares, Daniel could still hear the soul of his father crying out for vengeance, unable to rest until Opothleyahola lay dead.

To a man like Daniel McIntosh, Opothleyahola was the embodiment of all that was evil and depraved. He was everything that Daniel, his father, and his father before him had opposed. To Daniel, Opothleyahola was nothing but a political schemer who refused to accept reality, who thrived on his own ignorance and superstition and led his wretched followers to certain destruction. Opothleyahola of Tuckabatchee, and those from the Upper towns, prayed to the sun, still held the Green Corn Dance, and passed on inheritance through the mother's family. And they made no attempt to learn English. They imagined somehow they were still living apart from the white man—in purity and isolation, as if the last three hundred years had never happened. They were deluding themselves.

Did they not realize that everything they stood for had forever passed? The Indian could no longer live in isolation and independence. Long before Opothleyahola was born, the Indian had lost his ability to stand alone. His whole way of life was hopelessly intertwined with that of the white man: raising cattle and horses, using metal tools, black slaves, and a thousand other luxuries and necessities from the white man's world. Opothleyahola and those with him were no longer even Indian, Daniel believed, whether they chose to admit it or not. If somehow Opothleyahola and his people could drive the white man into the sea, they would have no choice but to follow. How many of them were willing to throw away their guns, drive off their stock, or farm again with only a stick? How many were willing to forsake their cabins and return again to drafty huts of bark and mud? How many, including Opothleyahola, were willing to walk away from their government annuities?

And what of Opothleyahola's personal possessions: his pastures and fields, his slaves and blooded animals? What of his mercantile interests? For years Opothleyahola had owned the largest store within miles of his home. He was the richest man in Indian Territory, with even more than the McIntosh family. Was he willing to give it all up and return to communal farming?

What Opothleyahola feared and hated most, Daniel was certain, was the loss of power that would come with change and a new and better way of life, for Opothleyahola was a demagogue. He was a man who had built power and wealth by shrouding his following in isolation, ritual, and ignorance—skinning them all the while of their annuities and lands, Daniel believed, in fraudulent or unfair trade. Stripped of his power and his tricks, he would be forced to compete for status and wealth like anyone else. What Opothleyahola and his following called the old ways, Daniel argued, were nothing but fading remnants of savagery and darkness laced with hypocrisy, and the sooner it all vanished the better.

That Opothleyahola was also an ignorant and stubborn man could be seen in the way he clung to the fiction of a United States still honoring a treaty of allegiance with a nation that had ceased to exist. He was a dangerous man, too. Wherever he went, Daniel believed, Opothleyahola brought out the worst in everyone by encouraging others to throw off civility and revert to a raw, primitive past that some imagined was a golden era. He was like a disease, eating away at all that was good, decent, and civilized. His followers had seized slaves and enticed others to run away. On some of the farms, it was said, wives and daughters had been seized as well and made into concubines. Every husband and father dreaded that their family might be next and had sworn to destroy the ones responsible. Lifetimes of hard work and progress were being swept away. If he were not stopped, there would be utter chaos and desolation. More slaves would be freed, more women seized, more pasture and field would be laid to waste, more homes would be put to the torch, and all for naught. For no matter what, Opothleyahola was doomed.

The United States was a thing of the past, Daniel was convinced, as surely as were the old ways of the Muskogee Nation. Nothing could stand before the southern white men and their guns.

Every experience of the Muskogee people for the past hundred years had taught that lesson, first in Georgia and Alabama, then in Indian Territory. The North would be swept away, for the southern white men were like the wind, everywhere and unstoppable. The Muskogee peoples—weak and scattered—could bend with the breeze, or like Opothleyahola they could stand rigid and finally snap like a twig in a gale. There were no other choices. Even the animals understood something so basic. Did not the buffalo herds move with the summer and winter breezes from one range to another? Did not the birds come and go with the seasons? Any but a savage could see that the future lay with cotton and slavery, with a free confederation of southern states and a system of inheritance that passed through the father so that each generation could live better than the last—just as the McIntosh family had done. Above all, the future was with those who were bold enough to forsake a dark past and assimilate into the white man's world.

Following close behind Daniel McIntosh was his Creek Confederate cavalry. Nearly a dozen of them were family. Some of the riders wore long drooping feathers from their hats and a few had colored blankets wrapped about their shoulders. Others were in breechcloth and leggings and had their faces painted. Only a few resembled the Texans, with uniforms of tattered and ragged butternut, though they all wore red or white strings from their arms.

Behind Daniel and his regiment came still more Creeks, a mounted battalion under Daniel's eldest brother, Chilly McIntosh. In the old days in Georgia, Chilly had nearly lost his life the morning Opothleyahola's warriors struck the family farm. He had seen his father shot down and stabbed. Had Chilly not put on a dress and slipped out with the women, he, too, would have died. Old, gray, and toothless and riding in a carriage, Chilly was obsessed by a single purpose—to kill the one who had murdered his father. He wanted desperately as well to erase the memory and, some said, the shame that came with saving himself by dressing as a woman.[2]

Farther behind the Creeks came other Indian units: portions of the First Choctaw and Chickasaw Mounted Rifles, then a small band of painted and feathered Seminoles led by a hulk of a man, John Jumper. Captain Jumper carried a sword he had received along with his Confederate commission. He had joined the Confederate army because, like so many other leaders, he believed it the most logical course. His decision had little or nothing to do with affinity for the South. Also, the Confederates had given him that sword and a promise of more treasure in the future.

50

The Seminoles in the ranks, like other Indians, had rallied to the Confederate cause mostly out of loyalty to particular war chiefs or out of hatred for those who had joined the other side. Only a handful of men on either side had studied the causes of the white man's war; fewer still cared. There was an occasional Daniel McIntosh, who imagined himself a southern planter, but he was largely an aberration. For every Daniel McIntosh there were two like John Jumper. Despite what Daniel wanted to imagine, there were hundreds more who would follow and fight because they were still Muskogee warriors at heart. Most of his own people spoke no English and still half believed in the old gods. War meant a chance for deeds of valor, and always it furnished an excuse to strike old enemies and even old scores.[3]

For more than a week the Confederates, staring into the distance as they rode, had trailed Opothleyahola in the hopes of a chance to strike. But there had been delays and mishaps from the beginning. A lack of forage had caused them to waste time; then it was necessary to wait on reinforcements to guard the commissary trains. Even when the men finally moved out, they were living on little more than parched corn and hoecakes, sometimes sharing the corn with their mounts. Always, it seemed, when they were closing in on the savages, another mishap slowed them and Opothleyahola slipped away: storms, illness, pasturelands that had been scorched by the enemy to keep the horses weak and famished. Sometimes springs they were depending on had been trampled down or filled in. The whole affair seemed plagued with problems and rotten luck. And though they would never admit it—even to themselves—there was a gnawing suspicion among the Texans that the Indians had outsmarted them. Several times Opothleyahola had hinted at peace and a chance to meet and talk, even as recently as a month ago. But whenever Confederate authorities had tried to oblige, they discovered later that the Indians had continued with their packing and moving northward, and that still more time had been wasted.

Even as the Confederates had begun to regain lost ground and time, they were still haunted by the knowledge that not everything had gone as hoped. Within a few days of trailing Opothleyahola, they were so low on food that some were supplementing provisions with wild acorns and roots. As they rode north they were usually shadowed as well by several enemy scouts on distant ridges, and always by one, a single Indian on a white horse. Often in front of them, at other times on their flank: the single warrior was never out of sight. The men had tried to capture or kill him. But no one could run down the warrior on the white horse. Some of the men had ridden close enough to fire at the Indian with rifles. A few swore they had him in their sights when they fired, but none had brought him down. Some of the Confederates had come to believe the warrior was a ghost, not a man. Perhaps it was so.[4]

But at last it seemed their luck had changed. The trail of wagon ruts they followed was growing deeper and more distinct; even footprints of children were visible. And the droppings from Indian ponies were fresh. Then on a clear chilly morning the Confederates encountered a few Indians who had fallen behind the main party fleeing north. The Indians swore that Opothleyahola was not far ahead and promised they would return home if left alone. The Confederates, with no time to waste, released the fugitives then pushed ahead. Later in the morning, the column of Texans rode into an abandoned campsite with smoldering fires. At the camp the trail seemed to fork in two directions: one path leading north toward the Arkansas River; the other trail—more clearly marked—veering to the northwest.

The Confederates drew reins. A few got down from their mounts and walked over the campsite and the trails. One or two stopped to touch the ground and the hoofprints. Finally, they made a decision. They would divide their column. A small company of Texans would follow the lesser trail to the Arkansas River. The main body of troops would move on the larger trail to the northwest. Some of the Confederate Indians were not so certain about the meaning of the forked trail. Daniel McIntosh in particular was worried. But he understood who was in command and kept his thoughts to himself, as he had learned to do so many times before.[5]

After they left the campsite, the main body of Confederates rode hard, every man sensing they were nearing the Indians. Soon they would end this foolish, time-consuming chase, they told themselves, and get on with the real war against Yankee oppression and Abraham Lincoln. Then in the afternoon the men heard rifle fire in the distance. Later came news that the Texans moving on the Arkansas River had ridden into an ambush. Reports were fragmented and confused, but it seemed that some of Opothleyahola's band had again escaped, this time across the Arkansas River. The white men raged at what they heard. It would have been different, they assured one another, if they had all been there: "Injuns" could not whip white men in an honest fight.[6]

The Confederates followed the trail of wagon ruts and hoofprints with new determination. Across the prairie they galloped, toward a low range of hills and a single haystack mountain. The country grew rough and rocky, laced with gullies and half covered with blackjack and cedars. The column began to break and scatter from the hard riding and rough terrain, but the Confederates would not be slowed. The supply wagons fell far behind, and the main body of troops scattered a mile or more behind a lead unit of perhaps a hundred Texans. Yet the entire anxious, overextended column kept moving. For too long the Texans had been tricked, fooled, and delayed; finally, some of their number had been shot down in battle. There was simply no place in their world for a white man's army that could be defeated or outmaneuvered by a savage like Opothleyahola. They would strike him down before another day had passed.

The lead unit of Confederates continued to trail the Indians to the banks of a half-flowing river, the Red Fork of the Arkansas. Hardly pausing to glance at two abandoned wagons, they splashed across to the other side. Across more gullies and prairies they raced, until at last the Texans saw the smoke of Indian campfires. The last fleeting rays of sunlight were striking the top of the haystack mountain to the east, but there was still time enough to finish off the Indians before dark. Spurs dug into horseflesh, and with a yell the men raced ahead.

The Texans burst into the campsite, guns raised. But they found only a few broken ponies, camp litter—and blazing, freshly built campfires. Once more there was the sense of having been fooled.

The Confederates pushed on. Soon it would be dark, but there was still a chance to strike the Indians before another day, for the campfires they had found were less than an hour old. They raced across more prairie, and then a rock-strewn gully, galloped up the other bank, hardly breaking stride. That was when they noticed something ahead. It was the warrior on the white horse; this time he was squarely in front of the column. He sat his horse at the crest of an open gentle rise, a dark mounted form outlined against a bluish twilight, not two hundred yards away. Slowly the Indian turned his mount, then almost casually, he rode over the rise, just out of sight.

The Texans rushed for the top of the rise, after the Indian. But when they reached the crest, they paused. In front lay a dark prairie set against a distant faint outline of trees, and among the trees glimmered a hundred campfires—it was Opothleyahola.

The Confederate officer at the head of the column waved an arm, ordering his troops and their sweating mounts into a single

53

line for a charge. The main body of Confederates was far behind, out of sight, but there was no time to waste. And there was no doubt of what lay ahead. The Indians had been chased down and would now surrender or die. The officer in front raised his pistol and motioned forward. A howl went up, and the entire line of mounted white men lurched ahead. In an instant their horses were at top speed.[7]

Just as quickly, the Indian on the white horse began to race away, straight for the distant timber and the twinkling campfires. But as the warrior rode he began to lean to the side of his pony nearly touching the ground with his body, first to one side, then the other. Like magic, fire sprang from the ground as he leaned left, then right, lighting the prairies.

In the timber the warriors waited, rifles leveled, bowstrings pulled taut with arrows. Every rock and tree hid a man. The enemy, in the open and unprotected, was charging straight for the warriors. And somehow fires were sprouting from the prairie, making the white men an easy target. Surely it was the work of the gods.

As the Texans drew closer, the warriors could hear them shouting and howling like beasts, then came the hoofbeats of their horses. Closer still they came, their dark forms outlined against prairie fires and the last trace of light in the western sky.

Every warrior readied himself and took aim. One of them, standing at a tree nearest the prairie, slowly raised his hand. The enemy was in range, but not a warrior moved. Still closer the enemy came, screeching and howling, their horses pounding the earth. A hundred steps away. Seventy steps. The warriors could almost see their faces; they could feel their evil. Suddenly, the warrior standing by the tree turned and dropped his arm—"Now"![8]

❖ NOW THE WOLF HAS COME

CHAPTER
❖
SEVEN

Fire and Blood

Guns, spitting fire and death, roared into the night. Horses and riders tumbled to the ground. Some of the men stumbled to their feet. Others lay where they fell. Arrows filled the air with a quick swishing pop, and some found their mark. There were screams and shouts and the sounds of horses wild with fright or pain. A man on the ground staggered aimlessly with arms outstretched and groping as if he were blind. A horse trampled one of the wounded.

Those still on mounts tried to steady their bucking, rearing animals, and somehow a few men got off shots from revolvers. The unit commander, still on horseback, tried to rally the men. Waving and firing a pistol, he turned to lead another charge at the warriors and the timber. It was his last act. A second volley roared from the woods; the captain tumbled from his mount with a bullet through the brain.

The Texans on horseback tried to rescue those on the ground, letting them ride double. Some Confederates tried to make a stand, firing at the woods, shouting to one another to hold their ground. But already it was too late.[1]

Warriors on foot burst from the woods, on the left, then the right. Quickly, they were on the flanks of the Texans and threatening the rear. Another blast of gunfire exploded from the timber and more Texans fell. Others felt the sharp, stunning blow of arrows. A man by the flag bearer slumped in his saddle; another fell to the ground. A few more deadly moments and the Indians would close the only chance of escape to the rear.

For the Texans, the choice was run or die. The white men fell back on foot and horseback, everyone racing for their lives. As they ran, prairie fires swirled about, making them easy targets. As in the past, the Master of Breath was with the People, whipping up the flames. Warriors would appear in the firelight, quickly firing guns and arrows, then darting back into the night. Sometimes a warrior, too close and in the light, would be shot down by the fleeing Texans. The whole affair was random, savage, and chaotic.[2]

There is little about combat that is planned. It is wild, maddening, bloody panic. No matter the race or the nation, it brings out the beast that is always just beneath the surface. When men close in face to face and hand to hand, they fight terrified or in blind rage—almost never in a deliberate way. Most of what they imagined war to be vanishes in an instant with the first blast of gunfire, with the first shrieks of agony. Men had been known to load their guns over and over, forgetting to fire, jamming ten or more minié balls down the rifle barrel, never realizing what they were doing until they finally fired and the weapon exploded in their faces. Others had fought on in mad fury after they were run through with a sword or even disemboweled, tripping over their own entrails, but still struggling and slashing back. It isn't planning, or ideals, or discipline that causes men to fight this way; it is instinct, and it comes with a rush. Strategists will plan and commanders may lead, but once in combat there is only a single basic truth that overrides all others—one must kill, die, or flee. There are no other choices.

At last, other Confederates began to arrive: the Choctaws and Chickasaws, some of the other Texans, and part of the Creek units. Close behind, hundreds more would soon be on the field. As they came over the rise, the reinforcements looked down on swirling prairie fires and figures moving in and out of the light. Away from the flames, in the dark, rifle fire lit up the night like fireflies. Some of the retreating Texans, wild-eyed and panting, faces covered in soot, stumbled up to meet them. A few had arrows sticking from legs and arms.

The reinforcements quickly formed into a battle line. The Confederates dismounted and knelt on the ground with their rifles while every third man held the mounts. Retreating Texans and runaway horses passed through the ranks, but the fresh troops could not begin pouring volleys into the open country in front. There were still too many fleeing Confederates in the line of fire.[3]

The reinforcements sent out mounted patrols to scout their front. They rode slowly into the flickering firelight and shadows, sometimes shouting to any ahead, asking if there were any Texans. One rider spotted something in front. He paused and called out, but received no answer. Nosing his mount ahead for a few more cautious steps, he shouted again, "Are there any Texans in front?" He got his answer: a blast of gunfire, and bullets whizzing about his face.[4]

No one could be sure any more of what was around him, or what he saw. One of the white men thought he could make out a large moving column of Indians in the distance, where the battle had begun. Moments later he had second thoughts, maybe it was only the grass, swirling and whipping about from the prairie fires. Perhaps it was neither; perhaps it was the spirits.

A blast of gunfire from the dark ripped the main Confederate line: horses fell and a man pitched to the ground. The Choctaw and Chickasaw units moved forward a few steps; they managed to get off several volleys and the enemy seemed to melt away, at least for the moment. But the pattern of fighting had already been set. Men blazed away at the slightest motion in the dark, their officers unable to control them. In every direction officers barked out orders or demanded identification. Before it was over Confederates were firing at any sound, probably at one another as well.[5]

While Confederates squinted into the night, firing at Indians and their own fears, other warriors had slipped around and behind the white men. A handpicked body, they moved swiftly on foot to the south—toward the Confederate commissary wagons.

Miles from the fighting, the Confederate supply train had formed into a circle, camped for the night. The mules were staked; teamsters were either asleep or sitting around fires. A few sentries stood watch, leaning against their rifles or sitting on wagon tongues, but they were more concerned with keeping out the evening chill than with watching for Indians. No one felt himself in danger, so far behind the lines. Probably no one even knew about the fighting that had already taken place. It had been a long, exhausting day chasing Opothleyahola across the prairies and by midnight they were all asleep, perhaps even the guards.

Suddenly there was a stir, then a shout; the sleepy Confederates leaped to their feet. All around the prairie was ablaze with spreading fires. Cinders from the burning grass drifted into camp

57

and across the prairie, starting still more fires. Within minutes the entire campsite was alight from the flames. The mules began to kick and bray. Men rushed up to steady them, but it was no use. Arrows rained into camp, causing teamsters to duck and dodge. Then came gunfire from the dark and more white men hit the ground or scrambled under wagons. The mules broke from their ropes then scattered from camp, racing between the wagons and into the night. There was no time to organize and fight back. A few Confederates got off several rounds, firing wildly into the brush and burning prairie, but they saw nothing. Then it ended, as quickly as it had begun. The gunfire and arrows stopped, and those who had fired them simply vanished. A party of guards swept the area around the camp while others went after the mules. But there was no trace of Indians, except for the scattered fires still burning on the prairie.

The main body of Confederates remained all night on the battleground, at the crest of the rise: still in formation, still squinting into the dark and trying to make out any movement around them. Before light the last of the Confederates rode in and took their positions along the line. By dawn nearly fifteen hundred men were in battle formation. But before they were ready to make their move, Opothleyahola had made one of his own.[6]

CHAPTER

EIGHT

Cooper

At dawn the Confederates peered across a blackened, smoldering prairie littered with weapons, lifeless men, and dead or dying horses. A few of the animals still struggled for breath. Lying flat on the ground, they whinnied piteously from pain. One or two had the strength to raise their heads, but their ears remained lowered, their eyes half shut. The whole field seemed awash in agony and drifting smoke. And mixing with the smoke was the faint, sweetly pungent smell of charred human flesh. Some of the white men, at least the younger ones, grew sick to their stomachs. They had all seen death many times where they lived: animals slaughtered, family funerals, public hangings. But few had witnessed wanton killing, much less been a part of it. They had never seen a man stiff or mangled, his eyes open and still wild with the shock that comes from sudden death. In a single night the Texans had learned more of war than all of the armchair strategists and political demagogues could have furnished through a lifetime of speeches. And for all of the Confederates, there was also the numbing realization that they had been routed.

On the rise overlooking the field, the entire Confederate command was in the saddle: Creeks, Seminoles, Choctaws, Chickasaws, and Texans. Squinting into the smoke, they could see the blaze of campfires and what seemed to be some of Opothleyahola's wagons in the distant timber.[1]

In front of the Confederates a man with raised field glasses sat on his horse and stared at the distant campfires. It was Colonel

Douglas Cooper, the commanding Confederate officer. Other men rode up to the commander: two adjutants and several other officers, including Daniel McIntosh. Cooper was practically surrounded. But always the commander stood out from the rest. His men recognized him even at the farthest point of the line. He was splendid in appearance, Douglas Cooper, dressed in an officer's uniform, proud and erect, with gray hair and a graying beard. To the men in the ranks he seemed a natural leader. If anyone could restore confidence after the night before it was Cooper, or so it seemed.

A closer look told another story. When he finally lowered his field glasses, the officers and aides saw the same bloodshot eyes and red bulbous nose, the same glazed stupor that had come to mark nearly every morning with their commander. Cooper was so drunk he could barely sit his horse.

All of his life Cooper had moved among the powerful and successful, though he had never been a success. Always he had aspired to wealth, though he had long since squandered his own inheritance. But despite the personal disappointments, he had a talent that so far had served him well: worming his way into the confidence of the rich and influential. In the old days, before the war, his friend Jefferson Davis had managed to get him appointed as Indian agent to the Choctaw and Chickasaw nations. When the war began it was Davis who again found a place for Cooper, this time as commander of Confederate forces in Indian Territory. But no amount of influence could erase what had been a jaded life, laced with incompetence and gross corruption. Courtly manners and resplendent uniforms would not long hide the truth. If Opothleyahola had a secret weapon in his flight for survival, it was Douglas Cooper.[2]

Cooper had plans to make money off the Indians, just as he had done when he was agent to the Choctaws and Chickasaws. But this time he had far more in mind than selling off Union Indian rations or rustling cattle from the ones he had sworn to protect. For some time, there had been rumors of Indian cattle and horses sold to Union agents in the western country, even as far west as Santa Fe. There were rumors, too, of a fortune in gold from the sales. The war would furnish Cooper an excuse to steal it. True, there would be Confederate Indian authorities who might pry into such matters, but Cooper had taken care of that. The Confederate superintendent for Indian affairs was his old friend Elias Rector, a man who detested Indians. Perhaps for a cut of the treasure Rector would keep Confederate authorities out of the way. Only a few months earlier Cooper had shown his true mettle, writing his friend

60

on the matter of Indians, the war, and how they might benefit: "if we work the thing shrewdly we can make a fortune each, satisfy the Indians, stand fair with the North, and revel in the unwavering confidence of our Southern Confederacy."[3]

Rumor had it that Opothleyahola had hidden the gold on his land. Slaves had buried the treasure, it was said, and then had been killed so that only Opothleyahola would know the location. Other rumors spoke of gold buried along the trail as the Indians had fled, or of a vast treasure still with Opothleyahola and his wagon parties. Whatever the truth, even in an alcoholic fog Cooper understood that the key was Opothleyahola. If he could meet with Opothleyahola, perhaps they could negotiate a deal. That was why Cooper had been so reluctant to fight and why he had held back again and again—even when his troops were in striking distance of Indian campsites and wagon parties.[4]

The young men he commanded, at least the Texans, never imagined what was happening. Like most men, they believed war was over righting an injustice, or protecting home and hearth. They could not grasp how a few with influence and power might cynically use everyone else for personal gain. In their limited experience, there was no place for a ravenous ambition so dark and sinister that it would relish carnage in exchange for wealth. It never occurred to them that there are those who long for war and even create war to serve their vanity and greed. And so the white men, like men everywhere, were easily exploited.

Always, the Confederate commander had believed if he could but meet with Opothleyahola he could bribe the Indian, just as he had bribed a set of henchmen on the Choctaw and Chickasaw lands to help him cheat his wards when he was their Indian agent. Maybe Opothleyahola would settle for a personal cut of the gold, or perhaps some of his neighbors' horses and cattle. Maybe Opothleyahola would even be happy with a military title. It had worked with others.

But now Cooper's plans were in jeopardy, for bloodshed the night before had probably ended chances of an understanding with Opothleyahola or any of the other Indians. As Cooper scanned the charred prairie, he knew the best and only alternative was war. If he could capture Opothleyahola or some of the women and children to hold as ransom, he might still cut a deal. There was probably no other way.

Sitting on a horse nearest Cooper was Daniel McIntosh. He was still dressed in his duster and wide-brimmed hat. It had been a hard night for Daniel and his Creek Confederates. They had missed their chance to come face to face with the enemy. It had been the Choctaws and Chickasaws—if anyone—who had finally stopped Opothleyahola's warriors by pouring volleys into the flames and darkness. When Daniel and most of the Creeks arrived it was largely over. Throughout the night they had remained in line, anxious and ready, staring into darkness and dying fires. But nothing more had happened. By dawn, the Creeks were tired and hungry; some had not eaten for two days. Yet none of them, least of all Daniel, would have left the field the following morning.[5]

Daniel was staring across the same blackened field as Douglas Cooper, but his thoughts were not of gold. His mind was on vengeance. Soon his father's spirit would rest, for on this day Daniel McIntosh would destroy Opothleyahola. Underneath his duster was a long-barreled Colt .44 revolver. A thousand times Daniel had gripped its wooden handle as he rode after Opothleyahola. Soon he would fire it at his enemy—point-blank—execution style.

As the smoke began to clear, something irresistible stirred in Daniel. Despite his Christian education and his tailored ways, despite a lifetime of denying his heritage and blood, there was a part of Daniel that was still Muskogee. The old urge for retribution, the need to redress an imbalance, consumed his very soul. Every unavenged injustice lay before him. The ghosts of his father and of the kinsmen and tribesmen who had followed the McIntosh for a hundred years screamed out for blood. It was only a matter of charging across the blackened ground and into the distant line of trees.

Two long lines of mounted men stretched across the open rise, one reinforcing the other. In the center of the first line were the Creek Confederates, some of them in war paint. They would spearhead the attack, and Daniel McIntosh would lead the charge. For several minutes more the entire command sat in silence, poised and eager, waiting for a party of scouts who had been sent ahead to reconnoiter the front. There was camp smoke in the distant woods and something that looked like wagons, but no one could be sure. Even with field glasses, the Indian lines were too far away to view clearly. Finally, the scouts came racing back across the prairie. They rode straight for the officers in front and drew in their horses. Not bothering to salute, they gave their report. The Indians were gone: not one of them remained.

Daniel glanced left, then right, at his line of men. Then he faced straight ahead, staring at the distant trees. Slowly he loosened the grip on his revolver and lowered his eyes. For a few moments there was only silence. Finally Cooper, struggling to fight through his drunken haze, uttered something and the other officers rode away to order the lines out of battle formation.[6]

Except for a few who would bury the dead, the entire command moved toward the Indian campsite at a trot. They rode over the charred prairies and past the bodies of men and animals from the night before. A few more minutes, the line never breaking stride, and they were at the trees. Once in the woods, the Confederates headed straight for the camps, past breastworks of luggage, past horses and cattle, scattering them in every direction. The men began to fan out in every direction as well. Some began rounding up cattle; others galloped up to abandoned wagons.

In camp, Daniel pulled up his horse and looked about. He rode a few steps more, then stopped again as his men rushed by. Rising in the saddle, he turned to scan in every direction, peering into the smoky woods around him. Rage filled his soul. It was a trick—the wagons, the campfires. It was all a ruse. Opothleyahola and his warriors had been gone for most of the night, probably since the fighting had ended.

Behind Daniel and his men came more cavalry, the Texans. They burst into camp and went straight for the wagons. Only one contained food, and it was found to be laced with poison. Other white men began gathering up hides of buffalo and bear left in the campsite and mumbling, no doubt, about spoils and victors.[7]

A few scouts tried to pick up the trail of Opothleyahola, but it was no use. The tracks led away in four directions, then simply vanished, as if the ones who made them had stepped into another world. In a few minutes the Texans found something else, dead white men—casualties from the night before. The bodies had been stripped of clothing. One had a row of acorns across the chest. Another had a crushed skull. Still another body bore the marks of burns; and they had all been scalped. Among the dead was the merchant John Taylor; he would not escape again.

Daniel sat on his horse watching. By then Chilly McIntosh, furious that Opothleyahola had escaped, caring nothing for what was going on around him, was in the campsite as well. Finally, Daniel turned and slowly rode away, pretending not to hear the Texans and their remarks about Indian savages and "red niggers" committing torture. A few white men still skulked about looking for something to steal, but it was over. Soon the entire campsite filled with an eerie quiet. There was only the faint faraway sound of mocking crows.[8]

CHAPTER NINE

The End of the Earth

A north wind whipped through the grove of blackjack and hickory. Only days before their leaves had been golden and yellow; now they were brown and lifeless. Rattling in the wind, the leaves, still clung to the trees unwilling to fall, as if they could not accept a death that had already come. But with every gust a few more drifted to the ground, vanishing forever. In a nearby ravine, a squirrel rustled through the dry, dead leaves in search of acorns. Small birds flitted about, picking at seeds. And overhead, a final wayward flock of geese flew southward with the chilling winds. Everything living seemed to sense in its own way the change that was coming.

Near the grove of blackjack sat several men on spotted ponies and thoroughbreds. Slightly in front of the rest was their leader, Opothleyahola. A red turban covered his head, while a long blue coat protected him down to his buckskin leggings. His silver hair, sometimes moving with the gusts of wind, fanned out on his shoulders. Resting across the pommel of his saddle was his rifle.

All of the riders, transfixed by what they saw, stared motionless into the wind. It was the plains country: open, rolling, and endless. Some of the younger men had never seen the plains and wondered what would happen to any who set foot on such a land. Without trees and mountains, what would keep up the sky? Where would the owls roost, and what would shield the mother earth from cold and heat? Surely a man would fall off the earth if he ventured far onto the plains. There were those who had traveled the plains and returned. Opothleyahola was one of them. But many had ventured into the treeless country only to vanish.[1]

Across the plains to the north was Kansas and the safety of the U.S. government. Beyond the horizon, only a few days' ride away, was the Kansas border. Some of the war captains advised making a break to the north, straight across the open country. As the wind rolled across the grass in waves, the land beckoned, inviting the men to cross. But just as many feared it was an invitation to death.

On the plains were the Komantsi. Once the open country to the north and west had belonged to the Osage, but no more; now only the Komantsi reigned. They would be waiting, the Komantsi, in the tall grass. Their war parties might strike without warning. Even worse, what if the McIntosh and the white men were to catch the People in the open? They could all be ridden down. It could end in a slaughter. Yet the People could not remain forever where they were. Standing against them to the east and northeast was John Ross, Stand Watie, and all of the Confederate Cherokees. And soon the white man and the McIntosh would return. No one, not even Opothleyahola, had bothered planning what to do if Union troops had not arrived when they reached the Arkansas River. It was not their way. Yet plan they must, for the enemy would come again.

For a moment someone believed he saw movement in the distant grass, maybe the Komantsi. Opothleyahola hoped it was Union troops. He was betting everything on their support. Perhaps the objects in the distance were runners with news. Perhaps they were Union cavalry. Or maybe it was the miccos and headmen from the many nations that had ridden north seeking help. It had been many risings since they had left, and no one had heard from them; maybe some were returning. The men on horseback kept staring into the distance, straining to make out the movement in front. Suddenly it disappeared, and there was nothing but the endless waves of grass.[2]

The gods had been with them so far. At the battle of the rounded mountain the People had lost only a handful of warriors. And in the confusion of darkness and prairie fires every man had slipped away to join the women and little ones north of the Arkansas River. The enemy had not followed. Instead, they had ridden east to regroup.

Countless numbers of the People had camped in the timber by the Arkansas River, or along the nearby streams: Horse Creek, Walnut Creek, and many others. And still more families continued to join them, late arrivals who had slipped north after the enemy had ridden away. Every night their campfires flickered through the woods and surrounding bluffs. But they were at the edge of their world. Since the beginning of time, the People had never known a life away from the creeks and the forests. In the old country they had lived under an endless canopy of trees. Even in Indian Territory—even if on the prairies—they were always in sight of the woods. Had John Ross and the Cherokees not joined the Confederates, the People could have stood against the enemy along the forested banks of the Arkansas River until help arrived from the north. That option was gone.[3]

In the camps, the People put up wooden lean-tos or tied awnings between wagons to form open-air tents to keep out the rain. Others took refuge amid the ruins of an abandoned fort where root cellars and basements from crumbling buildings offered shelter. The men spent their time hunting and trading, or pitting wits and skills against one another in gambling and horse racing, or marking themselves with tattoos of serpents, turtles, and birds. As always, the wives and daughters gathered firewood, cooked, and sewed.

Among the People a wife was loved and cherished; her husband addressed her always with courtesy and respect. She was the one who owned the house and carried the blood from one generation to the next, for the family always passed through the line of the woman. But she was never an equal. A woman made her man's camp, kept his bed warm, bore him children, walked in his shadow, and honored his name. She was more like a first among little ones. Always, a woman belonged to someone. She was someone's wife or a daughter or part of a clan. She gave a man status by her very existence and by serving. She was valued and prized but she was not a partner. Sometimes she was one of several wives.

She was also a reason the People were running to escape. The McIntosh and the white men, it was said, were coming to take away the wives and the little ones, to make them slaves and prostitutes, as they had done in the past. Already women had been seized to serve the enemy's lust in drunken revels. Better a warrior and his woman should die first.[4]

Many of the aged passed time in camp with the children, for with age came love and respect, especially from the little ones. The old with their memories were the keepers of knowledge and wisdom for the young. They were the ones who would pass along the ancient truths: teaching the children of a fog that had shrouded the earth until the wind came to begin the world; telling them of ani-

❖ NOW THE WOLF HAS COME

mals and spirits that stalked the woods and spoke to any who listened and believed. Always, they taught, the spirits were near if only one would notice. If a man or even a child looked quickly to the left or right, from the corner of his eye there was movement—the spirits.

The old ones tried to explain as well why their fathers and mothers had left their homes. Life was a delicate balance between chaos and order. Only the People could save the world from doom by living a pure and righteous life, by remaining clean in body and spirit. Should they grow corrupt, or perish at the hands of the enemy, the balance would be destroyed and the world would end. There would be nothing but darkness, fog, and swirling, endless chaos. The People were running to save themselves and to save the world. The children listened and believed. Every day they could be seen with their mothers and grandmothers, faithfully trooping back and forth from the river or the streams to wash and purify.[5]

Before long there was trouble again between the many nations, just as there had been on the trail. Some of the Kickapoo had stolen horses from the Children of the Sun. The Alabamas would not camp along the same creek as the Wichitas. A Hillaby had caught his wife with another man and had killed them both; now families of the victims had sworn vengeance. It was all to be expected. The fierce pride that made the many nations and peoples resolute and courageous—able to withstand almost any hardship—divided them also, one against the other.[6]

A warrior stole horses or killed his enemy to gain status and, above all to right a past injustice. Let another wrong him or a member of his clan or town, and he would stop at nothing to redress the balance. It was a matter of honor, of keeping the symmetry between order and chaos. A warrior might retaliate in an instant with a knife or a club. He might seek vengeance the following day, or in a season, or a lifetime, or perhaps after several lifetimes through his children's children. The timing was of no importance; time was a white man's notion. But reprisal would surely come, for his was a world of endless bouts over honor and vengeance. To do otherwise, to shrug off insults and damages and pass through life obsessed with money and property, was to live as a white man. Unpunished crime would destroy the balance in life and result in chaos and the ultimate death of a town and or even a nation.

Perhaps this was the spirit that also drove Daniel McIntosh, however much he might deny it, for he was consumed with the spirit of retribution and honor. It was also the force that compelled

Opothleyahola. Somehow he would save the People, punish his enemies, and prove himself a better man than Daniel and all of the McIntosh.[7]

In the camps there was also mounting trouble with some of the miccos and leaders of the towns and other nations. It was not their way to follow another blindly and in silence for very long. Some began to wonder if Opothleyahola had lost his magic. Others called him a fool who had led them all astray. There would be no help from the North, they said; the Great Father Abraham Lincoln had lied. As the day cycles slipped past, there was mounting confusion over what to do. Some began to speak of digging in for the winter and waiting for Union troops from Kansas. Just as many began to counsel leaving for the North before the autumn rains turned to sleet and snow. The white men from the North, some argued, had never promised to ride into Indian Territory, but only to be in Kansas waiting for them. A few chose to leave, taking their chances in the open country and traveling for Kansas.

Still others began to hitch their wagons and leave, not for Kansas but home. The war was over, they said; the Confederates and the McIntosh were gone. For them the battle at the rounded mountain had been a war. Never in their wildest thoughts could they fathom what was coming, any more than Texas Confederates could grasp the power of the northern industrial giant that was daily gathering strength to sweep them away.

The questions and doubts remained, and some continued to leave for their homes or across the plains for Kansas. Opothleyahola was powerless to stop them. Whenever there were doubts, Opothleyahola was there with his letter from the government. For any who would listen, he had the words read. Those who believed in Opothleyahola remained. The rest departed. Yet for every wagon or family that left, another arrived, and usually with word that there were more farther south who were on their way.[8]

One at a time the riders with Opothleyahola turned their mounts and slowly headed back to camp, wondering at what they had seen, at a plains country so vast and open. But Opothleyahola remained, staring into the wind and the land stretching before him. Why did help not arrive, he wondered? Where were the Union troops? And where were those who had ridden north in search of aid? Where were Sands, Bob Deer, White King, and the others; why had they not returned? What was happening in Kansas?[9]

CHAPTER
❖
TEN

The Promise

There was nothing but open country, clear sky, and a bright Kansas sun. The grass stood tall and thick, bending and swaying in the ceaseless wind. Only a dry creek bed and a single sycamore cut the monotony of the open land. The tree was a remnant from an older, better time when there was more rain. It grew leaning from the bank, over the creek bed, with half its roots dead and exposed. A few more storms and the sycamore would tumble to the ground, swept away from the world of the living. There was nothing more in any direction, only the land, the wind, and the sky—and in the distance, men on horses coming from the south.

From far away they were little more than dark, tiny specks engulfed by the endless country. But as they drew closer the riders grew more distinct. The men rode at a trot, with one of them slightly ahead of the rest. The one in front was E. H. Carruth, a school-teacher and a newly appointed Indian agent. He held the reins of his mount with both hands, trying desperately not to bounce and jar in the saddle. His feet were barely in the stirrups and his legs flopped helplessly with the gait of the horse. He wore a dark suit and high boots. Gloves covered his hands while a straight-brimmed hat and scarf shielded his face and neck. His entire body was cut off from sunlight.[1]

He was a familiar breed on the frontier, Mr. Carruth. He had come west to bring the news of civilization to heathen and savage—and also to improve his position in life. Several years before he had lived with the Cherokees, then the Seminoles and Muskogees, teaching the word of God. When war began, Carruth had fled north, where he landed a job as Indian agent, thanks to U.S. Senator James G. Lane of Kansas. Carruth thought of himself as a kind and caring man, for he truly pitied the destitute wherever he found them. In his own world he was seen as learned, even wise. But he was also hopelessly rigid and condescending, as narrow in vision as the pinstripes in his cheap, dusty suit.

His was a view that was utterly incapable of imagining—much less conceding—that entire nations could happily exist without anything he had to offer. It never crossed his mind that there were peoples anywhere who were not eager to embrace his way of life. And if on occasion he encountered such people and such thinking, to a man like Carruth their attitude could be explained only as ignorance or depravity.

To him the Indians were simple and childlike, something to be protected and nurtured—like pets. He was also one of those who imagined that he "understood the Indian" after a few years among them. He was sure he knew what the red men needed: the Christian message, a proper education, private property, and material progress. Most of all, Carruth was certain, they needed him. Like so many of his kind, he saw himself as a beacon, shining wisdom and virtue. But he also realized as he bounced along that what the Indians required most at the moment was protection from their enemies farther south.[2]

Riding close behind Carruth were other men: three miccos, White King from the Muskogee Nation; the Shawnees Bob Deer and Jo Ellis; and several Choctaw and Seminole leaders. While Opothleyahola organized every town and nation that would listen, they were to ride ahead and seek help from the government. For days they had carefully picked their way north along the Black Beaver Road through Cherokee country, across the prairies and even to the edge of the plains. Always in danger of capture or death, they had traveled mostly at night. Not until they reached the Kansas border had it been safe to ride in daylight and in the open. Once in Kansas the tribal leaders turned east searching for Union officials or the military, or anyone who might come to their aid. After several encounters with government officials that got them nowhere, they finally came upon Carruth. The delegation told Carruth their story, and the white man quickly set out with them to locate the proper authorities.[3]

For two days they rode north and east over the Kansas prai-

❖ NOW THE WOLF HAS COME

ries, stopping occasionally to rest and water the horses and to give Carruth a chance to straighten his legs. At night the Indians sat about their campfires saying little in the presence of a stranger, but the white man talked incessantly, despite his aching muscles and limbs. With a shrill, piping little voice so characteristic of those from his land, he went on and on about secession and slavery—and probably about drinking and gambling and fornication, somehow mixing them all together. He spoke as well about the white man's religion in that strange evangelical way that always combined the sublime with the horrid. In the Christian world that would soon engulf the land, all Indians would be lifted out of darkness and squalor. They would all be one through the body of Christ: imbued with the ways of piety, charity, work, and something called a free market and wage labor. The red men would come to appreciate Original Sin and the everlasting torment that awaited all but the true believers.

On the third day, the riders spotted dwellings in the distance, the settlement of Barnesville. Word had it that Senator James Lane was at Barnesville in command of something called the Kansas Brigade. Along the way Carruth had also told them all about Lane and how he was certain the senator would help. Senator Lane was devoted to the Union and to anyone who resisted her enemies, he explained. When the war began and the Great Father Abraham Lincoln was endangered by rebels, even in Washington City, James Lane had personally guarded his life by posting sentries at the White House. The senator had already called for Indians in the Territory to rise against secessionists. In Kansas he had even organized volunteers to march south to the Texas coast and had talked of arming slaves and unleashing Indians along the way. The senator was a man of action as well as words, Carruth assured them, the type they could count on.

But the senator was not there. He was away with his troops in Missouri, killing or burning out secessionists wherever he found them. No one had any idea when he would return.[4]

Carruth took the delegation next to the settlement of LeRoy. At LeRoy was the southern superintendent of Indian affairs, a government official responsible for the Indians in Kansas and the Territory. The southern superintendent was a man named William Coffin. Once in LeRoy, Carruth and the Indians rode straight to the superintendent's office, a nondescript, two-story building.

At the Indian Office the white man dismounted and straightened his back, then stepped onto the porch and went inside. The

71

building was in reality several offices. The main floor was a large room with desks and file drawers scattered about in no particular order. At nearly every desk sat a bureaucrat, sprawled over papers and writing furiously, as if the world would cease should he fail to finish whatever he was doing. A few looked up when Carruth walked in, but most went on with their work. They displayed a collection of hairstyles, the bureaucrats: shaggy, close-cropped, balding. Some of the youngest were trying desperately to grow beards; others sported muttonchops or long, drooping walruslike mustaches. All of them wore suit coats that were frayed and wrinkled and white shirts with stiff celluloid collars turned dingy yellow. They were typical of their kind, in appearance and behavior.[5]

Carruth soon discovered that William Coffin was nowhere to be found, but there was someone else around—Oliver Coffin, the superintendent's son. His father had put him on the payroll even before arriving in Kansas. In fact, most of the other men working in the room were relatives or personal friends. Even the building they were in belonged to William Coffin; he was leasing it to the government.[6]

Carruth explained what had happened: how the Indians were organizing in the Territory against Confederates; the failed attempt to meet with Senator Lane. Then he asked when he might be able to meet with William Coffin, the superintendent. The answer was disappointing: Oliver's father was not in town. He was away checking on the Indians at several reservations. There was no way to know when he would return or where he might be at the moment.

Carruth inquired about the possibility of help for the Indians who were organizing in the Territory. The Indians would be protected was the answer; everyone knew that troops from Fort Scott or Leavenworth would soon have orders to march south. Furthermore, supplies were being stockpiled in Kansas for the loyal Indians.

Some of the miccos were in the room by then, and one of them raised a question of his own: What about William Coffin going to Indian Territory to confer with Opothleyahola when he returned? Every bureaucrat in the room stopped what he was doing and looked up in horror. Even those who had been writing furiously put down their quills. The suggestion was considered impractical; Indian Territory was far too dangerous for civilians. The whole region was best left to the military, it was said. The Indians turned an icy stare on the bureaucrats.[7]

But Carruth was more determined than ever and took matters

72

into his own hands. He told the Indians to return home and gather their best men to meet again in Kansas for a parley. No matter the cost, he promised, the government would not forget them.[8]

The Indians came back the following month. When they returned to Kansas the land was brown and the wind chilly, but their spirits were high. It had been a long ride, and dangerous. Somehow the Confederates had been alerted and were everywhere scouring the country, determined to keep the miccos from reaching Kansas. But the Indians were safe at last.

Among the delegates riding north to meet again with the government were miccos Sands, White King, Bob Deer, and David Fields from the Muskogee and Shawnee nations, and several Chickasaw and Seminole leaders. They rode once more to LeRoy, site of the planned meeting. But this time it was Carruth who was nowhere to be found and William Coffin the Indian superintendent was away again. There was someone else waiting for them, though, a medical doctor named George Cutler, another white man and also a confidant of Senator James Lane. Cutler was the federal Indian agent to the Muskogee Confederation. Like his patron James Lane, however, or William Coffin, or so many of the white men in charge, he had never entered Indian Territory and had almost no experience with Indians.[9]

Agent Cutler took the miccos to still another location, Lane's new headquarters at Fort Scott, where they could meet personally with the senator. After two days' ride they finally reached their destination. As they rode up, the little party encountered a scattered collection of tents and unhitched wagons. Slowly they worked their horses through the maze.

For the miccos, Fort Scott was a strange and frightening place. Everywhere they looked were white men: ragged, dirty, some crawling with vermin, nearly all of them with beards; they had the same look as the white men of Texas. Some of the men carried shotguns and had long knives hanging from their belts. Others seemed to have no weapons at all.

The miccos passed a group of squatting men talking and desecrating their fire by spitting tobacco juice in the flames. From one of the tents came voices and laughter, from another a woman's scream and the sound of a slap, then whimpering. They rode by other white men as well, some sprawled on the ground in a drunken stupor, a few lying in their own vomit. It was the Kansas Brigade.[10]

Then came the fort, a cluster of sod houses, stone and wood frame buildings, and mud-chinked cabins. The riders finally made their way to the center of the complex and pulled up in front of one of the buildings, general headquarters. But inside it was the same story: the senator was no longer in Kansas. They were told he had left for Washington City to counsel with the Great Father. . . .

For a long, awkward moment there was only silence, then bitterness perhaps, or even rage. A great parley had been called by the government, and none of those who had arranged or were to lead the meeting were around. But this time the story took a different twist. Someone in a blue uniform approached with an idea: the Indians could go to Washington and plead their case to the highest authorities. They could meet with Senator Lane, and even the Great Father. Confronted personally by the Indians, the authorities would have to act. All of the arrangements could be made in advance by telegraph; it would be a simple matter. The Indians could be in Washington in a matter of days; they could take the train.

From Fort Scott, Cutler took the miccos still farther north to Fort Leavenworth, the nearest railhead. The weather turned gray and colder as they rode, the land more rolling, and with more trees. They passed through several communities along the way, all of them nondescript and dingy. Every town was filled with the same kind of people: coarse, bearded, and flashing hatred at the Indians. But in one community they probably noticed as well a cluster of tents and cabins set apart from the town. The tents and cabins provided shelter for runaway slaves from Missouri. Since last summer when the fighting had begun, black people had fled to Kansas in a steady stream. Dressed in little but rags, they huddled about campfires or peered out from cabin doors or tents. But at least they had cabins and tents; and on the fires were large, boiling pots filled with soup, all compliments of the government. It was a good omen.

Fort Leavenworth seemed like any other frontier post at first glance, the same log cabins and unpainted buildings, except perhaps they were greater in number. But there was something more at Leavenworth and it set apart the settlement from any other town in the region. Just across the Missouri River lines of telegraph poles and steel rails extended all the way to Washington City. Leavenworth was the end of one world and the beginning of another. In certain ways it was where the frontier ended abruptly and the reality of U.S. authority and power began. And it was the lines of poles, wires, and steel rails that made the difference. It was wonderful what the railroad and telegraph could do, sending people throughout the country and transmitting messages across the continent in minutes. Some called it a miracle.[11]

❖ NOW THE WOLF HAS COME

As Cutler and the weary miccos rode into the fort, they probably noticed something else that was different. At Leavenworth there was a certain look about the men in uniform. They seemed cleaner and healthier than the Kansas Brigade, and the weapons they carried were oiled and ready. The soldiers had the way of men who knew what they were doing. So did the one the miccos found in charge, General David Hunter.

A grizzled veteran from the old army, David Hunter was Union commander for all of Kansas and Indian Territory. A blunt, nononsense kind of man with piercing eyes and little expression, Hunter listened carefully to the miccos. He quickly approved the mission to Washington and made the necessary arrangements. He also gave the Indians their first accurate assessment of what was happening.

There were not enough forces in Leavenworth or all of Kansas to send into Indian Territory, Hunter told them. Every man was needed to defend against a possible Confederate attack from Missouri. The troops at Fort Scott, the ones called the Kansas Brigade, were a drunken rabble formed by a worthless politician, James Lane. Once Hunter had possessed a high opinion of Lane, but not anymore. Lane not only was worthless, Hunter probably told them, but he was little more than a common bandit, using the war to satisfy his own political ambitions and to launch a campaign of plunder and terror in Missouri. He was a disgrace to the government and to those he served. Nothing could change for the Indians in the Territory until reinforcements arrived or the Confederates were driven from Missouri in the east.

What about the stockpiles of food and tents promised by those at the Indian Office? Or what if Opothleyahola and those with him could somehow get to Kansas on their own: would supplies be waiting? There was no way of knowing. Certainly, Fort Leavenworth could not feed the thousands who were fleeing the Confederates. Provisioning Indians was primarily a matter for the Office of Indian Affairs, and in particular the regional superintendent, William Coffin, the man no one could find.

Hunter could hardly conceal his anger. The entire Indian Office, he believed, was rotten with toadies and incompetents. In all of his years with the military he could not recall half a dozen men at the Indian Office who were worth the powder and lead it would take to shoot them. Their main concern was carving out careers for themselves and their families. None of them could be trusted, and William Coffin was probably as deceitful as they came. Some

75

in the military believed the Indian Office had a network of spies that extended into the highest levels of the War Department, maybe higher. If Coffin could not be found no matter how hard anyone tried, it was evidence he was up to something.

For weeks Hunter had received bits and pieces of information concerning Indians who were trying desperately to organize and fight their way free of Confederates. Now he had the whole story. Thousands of them were staking their fate on promises from the government. And the only ones who could furnish an inkling of support were a mental case of a U.S. senator and a scheming bureaucrat nowhere to be found. Before the miccos left for Washington, though, Hunter made a promise of his own. He would telegraph the War Department for reinforcements to support the Indians. If reinforcements arrived, he would get them into Indian Territory as quickly as possible; but, unlike others, he gave them no guarantees.[12]

CHAPTER
❖
ELEVEN

The Predator Beast

The metal giant, gushing steam and noise and raining ash, soot, and fiery sparks, pulled into the station. Horses bolted, dogs barked, and somewhere a bell clanged. Even before the train had completely stopped, men in dark suits and caps jumped from the cars so they could help down the passengers. A crowd from the station rushed up to the moving cars, then followed the train until at last the locomotive came to a halt with a final metallic jolt and an extra burst of steam. The entire scene was a mixture of chaos, gentility, filth, technical precision, boundless energy, and a grasping, mindless obsession with raw power and speed. It was a perfect image of the age and the culture that had made it possible.

Stepping from the train were men in top hats and others in buckskin. Standing and waiting on the ground were officers in blue and coarse-looking laborers in faded, sweat-stained jackets and trousers. There were missionaries, too, and gamblers and entrepreneurs, all coming or going or searching for something or someone.

A few steps from the confusion stood the Indians and the federal Indian agent, George Cutler. While passengers scrambled off the train and others jostled and pushed to get aboard, the Indians waited in a deliberate, almost secretive, way. At last Cutler led them to a special coach, the last car of the train. One by one, the Indians made their way up the steps of the car, entering another world.

Waiting inside were gentlemen from the railroad. It was the railroad's custom to offer coaches and escorts for special guests, for the railroad officials were nothing if not hospitable. One at a time, each of the gentlemen came forward, extending a hand to the Indians. Such men radiated power and cultivated tastes with their tailored suits and waistcoats dangling watch fobs, their silk shirts and silk ties, and their diamond-studded stick pins. Every hair on every head was properly combed; every whisker lay in place. When they greeted the Indians with a handshake, each of them bowed graciously as well. Their words were always deliberate, well chosen, and reassuring, their smiles quick and natural. They were the kind of men who inspired confidence and trust in everyone around them. Everything about such men seemed perfect, everything, perhaps, but their eyes. No matter how warm the smiles or reassuring the words, their eyes remained empty.

The special railway car would carry the Indians to Washington City to meet the Great Father. All of the arrangements had been taken care of; everyone had been wired and was expecting them. They would travel to Washington in a roundabout way, however: first to New York, Philadelphia, and Baltimore, so the Indians could fully appreciate the magnitude and power of the nation that would save them from ruin. The railroad gentlemen led Cutler and the miccos to their seats. Soon there was a blast from the locomotive whistle, then a jerk, and the coach car began to creep ahead. Before long, they were racing overland toward a world of farms, fields, cities, industry, and war.[1]

The train pushed into Missouri, following the Missouri River and moving across a half-wooded countryside. Occasionally, the Indians spotted a cabin and the brown ragged remnants of an old cornfield, and even a house or two with siding. But mostly the land seemed empty and endless. There was no indication that Confederate forces were only a few days' ride away.

Farther south, near the Arkansas border, battles had already been fought. So far the results were not encouraging, for the enemy had driven back the Union army at a place called Wilson's Creek. At one point Confederates had advanced as far north as the Missouri River. Mostly, though, the state seemed open to marauding forces—Confederate or Union—or to any outlaw using the excuse of war to practice murder and theft. There were rumors, too, of another kind of enemy that was every bit as frightening and deadly. It was said that clever, manipulative men had bought up rifles when the war had begun, then held them from the govern-

78

❖ NOW THE WOLF HAS COME

ment, which was desperate for weapons, until their price was met. While good men died on battlefields, those they defended were debating terms.[2]

The train crossed the Big Muddy at the city of St. Louis. The river was filled with craft of every description: paddle wheel steamers, barges, rafts. It was the first time the Indians had seen the river since they were driven from the old country years before. Once they crossed the river, the farms seemed to grow more plentiful and more prosperous in appearance. Cabins gave way to painted homes of clapboard and even latticework. Rail fences cut across the land, neatly separating pasture and field. Everywhere the land was cut over, rooted up, tilled, and terraced. The white man believed that nothing should remain as it was—as surely as the Indian believed that nothing was as it first appeared, that there was more beneath the surface or just out of sight, if only one could understand.

On the farms were coarse, hardworking families who rose before day and worked until dark, putting their lives into the land. Few of them could imagine the changes that were coming. Fewer still could understand that the same force that was gathering strength to fight a war and destroy the South could put an end to their world as well. The officials from the railroad pointed out an occasional home or a point of interest as they passed, but it was too much to remember. Everything seemed to blur in an endless procession of fields, homes, and more fields.

Along the way were many towns: gritty, glum, forgettable little places with shops made of brick or sandstone and clapboard homes in shades of gray or whitewash. Along the streets were inexpensive buggies and residents in cheap suits and plain dresses. Usually on a hillside or a rise nearby stood one or two other structures as well. Large and often gaudy, they were the homes of the local industrialists—the owners of a mine or a mill. Every community had them: one or two families who lived in large drafty dwellings, drove splendid carriages with blooded horses, and imagined that they were the most influential citizens in their state. And ten miles away would be another town, just as forgettable, and another wealthy family or two, just as pretentious and parochial.

The inhabitants of the towns thought of themselves as cultured and learned. Their belief system revolved around linear logic, cause and effect, and Newtonian physics, though few or none would have recognized it as such. Heat flows, gravitational fields, stresses and strains, diffusions of liquids and gases: it was all a part of their daily routine. And overriding all was a self-assuredness in themselves and their culture, and in what they called "the future."[3]

The good residents of the towns loved nothing more than to speak of tolerance, brotherly love, forgiveness, and their abhorrence of slavery. But in truth, every community was largely a pecking order bonded together by envy, hypocrisy, and sanctimonious venom. The Methodists hated the Baptists and the Baptists responded in kind. And they all loathed anyone who smacked of Romanism or rebellion or who was a stranger who did not know his or her place. The industrialists sneered at the merchants, while the merchants looked down on those in the trades and crafts; and everyone despised the unfortunates who worked their lives away at the sawmills, or the mines, or on the railroad. Hillbillies, the townspeople called them, or clay eaters, or white trash, for the miners and the mill hands came mostly from the hard scrabble farms of Kentucky or western Virginia. Everyone always had a pleasant "good morning" or "good evening" at the tip of prim, tightly drawn lips, but intolerance and bigotry were as finely honed as the blades and gun barrels produced at their mills.

The better sort could be found in Sunday school, where they prayed for the Union and lashed out at slavery and intemperance and sin. Never mind that they also ran the mills and mines where crippling accidents were a common occurrence, or where coal dust filled the lungs, causing a man to cough out his life before he was forty. Never mind that some of those who prayed the loudest had earned money as slave catchers and had even enticed a few unfortunates to escape plantations in Kentucky in order to apprehend them and claim a reward. And never mind that a few of the wealthiest and most sanctimonious had secretly made fortunes through an illicit slave trade that had flourished for decades.

The train stopped briefly at most of the towns for passengers or to stoke up on water and wood for the locomotive. At every community there were soldiers on foot or horseback. Usually when they stopped, the locals would stare and gawk in disbelief at the Indians in the coach car. Occasionally, too, their faces held that look of hatred that the Indians had seen so many times before.

As they traveled still farther east, the train sometimes passed towns late at night where the miccos spotted buildings open at one side and filled with a fiery glow. Often sparks could be seen erupting to the metal rafters or pouring onto the floor, as if a lid had been removed from a giant cauldron or a door had opened from the white man's hell. Within the buildings were grimy, sweaty men

80

forging the tools of war, turning out cannon, rifle barrels, wagon rims, and swords.

And it was only the beginning. The mills and factories could earn more money in thirty days than in the previous three years. The war promised vast opportunities in every business for those with know-how, venture capital, and audacity. Soon there would be wigs and facial compounds to cover the scars of unfortunates from the battlefields. Next would come something called "plantation pills" or Drake's Bitters, medicine to ward off the many fevers that lurked about the South. Embalming services would spring up in every town, promising to preserve any loved one from battlefield to home, no matter the distance: fifty dollars for an officer, half as much for a private; bodies could be made to look as if they were asleep. An entire industry would arise devoted to the manufacture and sale of artificial limbs. They came in wood or metal, the artificial limbs, specially shaped for the left or the right arm or leg, produced in the exact ratio that men lost either member—the northern people were nothing if not precise. And if weapons misfired or uniforms came unstitched, if shoes were worthless after the first long march, if Drake's Bitters proved a fraud, no matter, for it was the age of iron, steel, shoddy, and fraud. There was no one with time or power enough to call anyone to account.[4]

For several days more the train continued east, passing towns and factories, until at last it crossed a river named the Hudson. Once across, the train turned south with the Hudson, following the river toward the sea. Greenish gray palisades rose above the train and the river like sentinels. Sometimes the miccos caught a glimpse of grand homes, glistening gray or white, half hidden among trees and terraced gardens, on top of the precipice. More homes and buildings came into view as they traveled farther south. Some were large and beautiful—almost ancient in appearance—others less imposing, and a few dingy and dilapidated. There were more towns, too, with strange-sounding names like Poughkeepsie, Peeksville, Tarrytown, and Yonkers. The river swarmed with ships of all sizes and description, many with sails and others with smokestacks belching black soot. There were flatboats, steamboats, sailing ships, and barges as well. Finally, they crossed a narrow channel and the view from the train windows changed into a swirl of stone buildings, iron railings, horse carriages, and countless numbers of white men. Then came other coach cars and locomotives sitting on side tracks, warehouses, heaps of coal and rusty metal, and rows of crates sitting beside the tracks. The train began to slow and

81

eased into the great Hudson railway station. They were in the city of New York.

Everywhere hung limp and lifeless bunting colored red, white, and blue. On the roof of the station were three enormous American flags. Soldiers were everywhere, too, boarding nearby trains, some of them laughing, joking, and shoving one another, others somber and withdrawn.

The young men boarding the trains were the types who were always first to rush to the colors, and the first as well to drench the land with their blood. They were neither poor nor rich. All of them were boundless, self-assured, and certain of the justness of their cause, for they saw all of life in stark black and white. Yet they were hopelessly confused and forever limited by the very idealism that made them good and great. Like their enemies forming in armies to the south, they never imagined there could be other reasons for war but to defend a way of life or to right a terrible wrong. They never considered that a war for union had anything to do with land titles, mineral rights, timber rights, patents, contracts, and markets, to say nothing of borrowed money. Even the motives of their enemies they could not attribute to such. They never realized that southern planters were in debt to the North by $200,000,000, or that secession sentiment was strongest where the debt ran deepest, and where prospects for paying off grew dimmer every year. For the young men boarding trains, war could only be about a mystic Union, a flag, home and hearth, and the girl left behind.

On the platforms nearby, older men in suits of broadcloth or wool raised silk hats or tipped canes in salute and farewell. Teary-eyed young women and stoic mothers in hoopskirts, cloaks, and furs waved white scarves and perfumed kerchiefs. A few of the women were at the train windows exchanging some personal memento or a last few words with those inside.[5]

In every direction were crowds: soldiers, civilians, messengers, laborers. Adding to the pandemonium were bells, whistles, the chug of engines arriving and departing, and in the distance, perhaps, the faint notes of martial music and a band. And rising above it all was the constant buzz that accompanies huge numbers coming and going. To the Indians it was a deafening, alien world of chaos and confusion, a suffocating experience void of meaning.

The delegation of Indians, along with Cutler and their hosts from the railroad, made its way through the crowds and the station. They passed women still sobbing over departing loved ones and men speaking in anxious tones about news from Virginia or

82

tariff rates, or the price of bonds. The very air was thick with anticipation and excitement, not the normal excitement of a station where crowds met and departed daily, but the eagerness that comes from quick riches and war. Most of the white men and women barely noticed the Indians as they passed; the few who did quickly resumed their conversations.

Outside the air was chilly, the sky a mixture of autumn haze and smoke so thick the sun could barely cast a shadow. As far as the eye could see stretched drab, soul-less three-story buildings colored brown and gray and coated with coal soot. Hanging from the buildings were still more flags and bunting. Horsecars, coaches, cabs, carriages and wagons of all kinds filled the cobbled stone streets. The air was filled with their sounds: cracking whips, neighing horses, and the rattle of wheels on stone. Quickly, the railroad gentlemen called carriages for their guests. Some of the coaches were dark and drab, others were magnificent glistening vehicles colored red, yellow, or black, with cushioned seats inside and Irish coachmen on top.

The coachmen, like the police at every corner, were men who had fled their native Ireland. For centuries their kin had been robbed, starved, brutalized, and murdered by the English who had seized their land. Half a million of the Irish had been starved to death in the past few years by crop failure and a British government that wanted nothing more than to see them all dead. Those with strength enough to escape had come across the water, hoping for another chance at life in America. They had filled the shantytowns, the factories, the mines, and cities like New York. Often they were turned away and kicked out on the streets by native inhabitants who looked with hatred and contempt on what they termed howling mobs of beggars and Irishmen. When wanted at all, it had been for the most dangerous and revolting work at the mills and slaughterhouses. Now there was a war and they were filling the armies as well. For the first time in America a good Irishman was in demand.[6]

As the Indians rode through the streets, they noticed the constant procession of inhabitants along the sidewalks: men in suits colored brown or charcoal, women in velvet and furs, all of them oblivious to the comings and goings of the others. In the shadows near the buildings hovered little children of no more than five or six, selling candies, pickled meats, and worthless trinkets. Dirty-faced and gaunt from sickness or abuse, they held up their baskets, hoping the busy, well-dressed men and women would notice. Nearby and competing with them were adults sitting on the sidewalk, some minus an arm or a leg and clutching tin cups and staring ahead in glum resignation. It was a strange, wild, exotic place, the city of New York, with its opera, high fashion, and theater, its ward bosses, racketeers, and crime lords; with museums, publishing houses, parks, newspapers and opinion molders, and religious leaders, slum lords and slum dwellers, anarchists, prostitutes, pickpockets, degenerates, cutthroats, and thieves. Everywhere was motion, noise, and the vigor of a rising nation mixed with the pungent smells of horse sweat and manure—and for the Indians, the sickening sweet stench that always seemed to accompany white men. In every direction were busy, pushing, desperate city dwellers consumed with a single overriding thought: to gather as much wealth as possible, and to keep the wolf from the door. All of them—even the well dressed and professional—were trapped in a system that required every man and woman to struggle or be ruined, to eat or be eaten, some said.

Perhaps that was why so many supported the war. They actually believed they would soon overcome every problem and injustice, that human nature would be refined and humankind would no longer be subject to the same old problems, foibles, jealousies, and hatreds. Just one more war, just one last righteous cause, and all would be everlasting peace and benevolence, and there would no longer be fear. With their sciences and factories, with their armies in blue, many dared imagine they were ushering in a brave new world.

The Indians stayed in one of the better hotels, the type with oversized tables and chairs, red or green carpeting, shiny spittoons, and oil paintings that lined the halls along with hissing and flaming gas lamps. In a lobby that reeked of cigars, chandeliers hung from high ceilings covered in garish fixtures. Underneath the chandeliers gentlemen and ladies sipped tea and cast disapproving looks at the strange, dark-complexioned figures who were guests of the government and the railroad. It was the way of the government and the railroad to treat their guests, especially those who might be overawed by everything they saw, to the finest in material niceties. And had the Indians remained in New York for any time, they would have been treated as well to a tour of the city.[7]

New York was more than the largest city in the United States; it was the soul of the white man's America. From New York money rushed in and out to the rest of the nation—like blood through a heart—giving life and purpose to everything else. More cash and paper transactions occurred every day in the city than anywhere

84

else in the Western Hemisphere. It was New York, not Washington, not the mill towns, nor the farms, not even the countless numbers of young men in blue assembling in train stations, town squares, and city streets across the North, that would play the crucial role in the great war for union. It was the city of New York that was all-important, with its finance capital, its money markets, its international connections, and, above all, its own peculiar breed of aristocrat and entrepreneur.

The Indians could have only wondered at the austere, imposing structures that lined the financial district, even more at the men inside, for they were the captains of finance, these men; they were America's answer to the "old regime." They could fashion fortunes from underwriting a government that would put a million men under arms. Regal and opulent was the life they enjoyed, surpassing by far the most lavish displays of slaveholders in the South. Their many mansions were filled with furnishings and works of art that would have been the envy of museums. They dined on silver plate and bathed in tubs of marble and gold. Their servants, their hirelings, their stables of blooded horses, and their stables of mistresses, all succumbed to their every whim. Touring the continent every year, they were lionized by kings, popes, and prime ministers, and at home by senators, governors, and, most of all, the public. They draped themselves in the finest of broadcloth and silk and were weighted down with diamonds and gold chain. Strutting peacocks of fashion they were, shuttling back and forth from avenue to beach. Such men thought nothing of spending more on a dinner party than most could earn in twenty years of hard labor. They were the pillars of society, the leaders of a whole new order based on industry, science, and, above all, money. Often they made a bold display of their devotion to the Union and what they termed "our boys." Repeatedly they contributed to military hospitals or charities for war orphans and widows. Yet behind the massive doors of their marble-columned world, away from the idolizing crowds, there was a darker dimension to their dazzling lives.

Every day and sometimes into the night they could be found betting and wagering against the very nation they professed to love. As the blood began to flow in Virginia and Tennessee and young idealists gave their last full measure of devotion, the princes of Wall Street would reap huge sums speculating in stocks, bonds, gold, and their country's fate. As Union prospects rose, then dimmed, so did the speculative frenzy. The otherwise poised and dapper gentlemen resembled demons transformed and possessed—

85

buying and selling, snorting and ranting, shrieking and howling, standing on chairs and waving their arms. In the back rooms they gathered for the latest information from the Rappahannock or the Mississippi. Bets on the price of gold hung on how many boys lay mangled at Bull Run or Wilson's Creek. Even a battle in faraway Indian Territory did not escape their attention. Even the movements of an obscure Indian leader were on their minds. A Union advantage on the battlefield could bring on the deepest despair. A Confederate victory might cause them to burst out in "Dixie," for it meant the war would continue, that bonds would fall, gold would rise, and the North would have still greater need of guns, uniforms, and borrowed money. Never mind that the president wished such men lined up and shot; it mattered not that an outspoken handful could see them for the threatening and manipulative beings they were. Their wealth had bought them status, respect, and even the love of a gaping and adoring nation that admired nothing so much as money.[8]

Such men understood that with flux and uncertainty comes the chance for riches, and that nothing is so fluid, or so lucrative, as war. Often they could be found championing popular causes: revolution, union, secession, the rights of man, or whatever movement promised upheaval—not because they believed in such things, for they believed, ultimately, in nothing but power, dialectic history, and their own duplicity. They were neither northern nor southern, these men, nor even American. They saw themselves as gentlemen of affairs, above the petty regional or national loyalties that directed the behavior of lesser men, providing a service and seizing every opportunity. Despite what was professed in public, they feared and hated peace, stability, and liberty and were terrified at the thought of a rising, self-sufficient middle class. They stood for chaos, war, debt, money panics, shadowy deal making, anything that would cause markets to soar or plummet. Above all, they sought an ever-more-powerful, credit-starved government that was dependent on them.

They frequented the leading Episcopal churches, patronized the arts, endowed university chairs, and would have been shocked to think that anyone considered them sinister or evil. But sinister and evil they were by the standards of any culture or any race, for as surely as they helped finance and equip the Union, such men were not beyond doing the same for the South. Swift ships on moonless nights would slip away from New York loaded with guns and powder, sailing first to Halifax or the British Bahamas, then to their ultimate destinations: Wilmington, Charleston, and Mobile. Helping to make such things possible was a corps of army and navy officers—an army within an army. They were paid, these officers, to look the other way or even to haul supplies to southern armies.

Sometimes working in tandem with the gentlemen of Wall Street were others from across the water, men who, if possible, were even more detached and calculating. The gentlemen from Europe, it was rumored, made or broke kings and prime ministers by turning on or off the money spigot, and even war or peace, according to how it served their purposes.

They were evil, sinister, and ingenious, these kind, the ones in America as well as Europe, and largely accountable to no one. They were servants only to themselves and to their own insatiable hunger for money and power. That such men lived and breathed only a few dared imagine; fewer still dared challenge them. Perhaps no one could truly envision the magnitude of their evil, no one but a desperate faraway people with the gift for prophecy and visions and the burden of vivid, blood-chilling dreams.[9]

THE MONTH OF BIG WINTER

(December)

CHAPTER
TWELVE

A Vision

The night was clear, still, and frosty. The only light came from shimmering stars. Nothing stirred; utter silence reigned. Yet all around there was life and spirit, just out of sight, poised and waiting. The whole world was holding its breath and waiting. Then, magically, the earth changed in some mysterious way. Life and spirit overcame the darkness. In the distance a single bird chirped, then another. Nearby an animal moved, rustling the fallen leaves. Soon a faint glow appeared in the east.

More birds began to sing, and a squirrel scampered amid the hickories and post oaks. A possum lumbered off, deeper into the woods. Then a deer moved, raising its head and sniffing the air. Stars began to vanish and darkness fled to the land of shadows and death. The glow in the east grew brighter, changing colors from pinkish gray to orange, while a single fleecy cloud became emblazoned in gold. Rays of light shot up from the horizon, fanning out and heralding the miracle that was to come. And in a clearing facing the light stood a solitary figure dressed in leggings and wrapped in a blanket. His arms were raised with palms outstretched. Standing motionless with eyes shut, he prayed and he waited.

At last it appeared—the symbol of the living god: brilliant and blinding, filling the world and the soul with warmth and life; rays of sunlight bathing the land, the trees, and the outstretched arms and wrinkled face of Opothleyahola. For a few sacred moments he stood in utter solitude, showered in golden sunlight and in a swirl of visions—magical visions filled with wisdom.

Then a warrior approached, leading a horse. He brought ominous news: the enemy was forming once more and preparing to move. Soon they would come again for the People. The Texans and the McIntosh were camped to the east, toward the Arkansas border. But this time there was a second army as well, Confederate Cherokee warriors farther northeast, near Talequah. According to scouts, the two armies would soon break camp. If they both moved toward Opothleyahola, the People could be caught in a giant snare and the warriors outnumbered two to one.

For days scouts had reported on Confederate activities and warned of how the enemy was massing again in large numbers. For just as long Opothleyahola had wondered what to do. If the People remained camped on the banks of the Arkansas River and Union troops did not arrive soon, they would be overwhelmed. If they fled north or west for the Kansas border, they would enter the plains and the lands of the deadly Komantsi long before reaching safety. It was the same choice they had faced when war first began: to remain in their homes and face annihilation, or to run for their lives, knowing all the while they might be ridden down. And every night the horrid, recurring dreams, the nightmares of mankillers and of bodies wrapped in shiny ribbons, had continued. Each morning before light Opothleyahola, searching for an answer, had come to the little clearing in the post oaks to pray for guidance. But there had been no answer; the gods had remained silent. Fasting and praying, the Old One had waited for a sign, yet there had been no sign—at least until now.

At last there had been a vision, with the first rays of the sun. Opothleyahola had seen a forest, a creek, the rabbit, and the bear; he knew now what to do. The People would neither flee across the plains nor cower on the banks of the Arkansas River. Like the rabbit trickster, they would do the unexpected, and like the mighty bear they would attack—straight into enemy territory to the east, at both armies, before the Confederates realized what was happening. The Muskogees would no longer be hunted; they would become the hunter. And while the warriors attacked, the women and children could slip away.

Between the People and the enemy, Opothleyahola had learned, lay a narrow finger of hills, timberland, and creeks stretching all the way to Kansas. While the warriors struck the enemy, the women and little ones could make their way north, half hidden amid the hills and trees. There would be no more waiting for help from the Great Father or his government. Instead, the People would go to him, or at least to his government in Kansas.

It would seem good and natural to be traveling again amid the creeks and timber. It would never have been right for the People to have crossed the open country; it was not their way. Neither was it their way forever to run or hide. Perhaps the warriors could catch the enemy by surprise and slaughter him. If nothing else, they would buy time for the mothers and children to get away.

Not everyone would follow. There would be those who would choose to remain on the Arkansas River. Others would hitch up their teams and turn south for home. Nothing could prevent it, for it was the glory and curse of the People that every town should choose its own path in life. Only the miccos or the war captains in battle could give orders. Those who went with Opothleyahola would follow from choice—out of faith, love, respect, or the sheer beauty of his words—but never from orders. A Muskogee would endure almost any hardship for a cause or a leader he believed in. Pain, cold, hunger—he would suffer it all for an eternity. He would follow those he trusted and loved even to where the land ended on the turtle's shell and the earth touched the sky. But a Muskogee warrior could never be ordered by a speaker.[1]

There was a reason, though, that would entice most to follow. For the People it was a reason as important as the blood that stirred in their veins. The ones they would attack included the McIntosh: traitors who had led half of Muskogee civilization into a world of corruption and impurity; creators of massacre, treachery, and mayhem; the cause, it was believed, of every evil that had befallen the People for a lifetime. Countless spirits from the other world screamed out for vengeance: the aged and the little children left dead and unburied on the Trail of Tears; mighty warriors betrayed and murdered on the banks of the Tallapoosa. With a single, haunting voice they called upon the People and Opothleyahola to raise the club of war. Now at last, someone would answer their cries.

The sun had risen over the post oaks. The warrior with the horse was waiting, and so were thousands more camped along the Arkansas River. They were waiting for their leader, his story of a vision, and word of what they must do. The time had come; it was time again for war.

CHAPTER
❖
THIRTEEN

The Trickster

The sun was retreating behind the ridge of hills to the west. Overhead, blackbirds charged to their nightly destination like cavalry in ragged, broken lines. Slanted rays of sunlight washed the land and the campsite of tents, men, animals, and wagons. But the sunlight offered scant warmth and little comfort from the growing cold. Before the next morning a thin sheet of ice would outline the banks of the nearby creek. Standing in the golden, chilly light was a tall, brooding figure with long, dark hair and a beard. He had on the duster and the wide-brimmed hat that had become his trademark. Oblivious to the cold, he was staring at the distant ridge and the setting sun; his growing anger warmed him. The man was Daniel McIntosh.

Yet another day had passed and the men had not attacked Opothleyahola. It had been three weeks since the bloodletting at the rounded mountain. For days, the troops had been resupplied and ready; the wagons stood packed, the horses were rested and reshod; and still everyone waited. For just as long Opothleyahola and thousands with him had been scattered in camps along the Arkansas River, headed nowhere so far as anyone knew. Yet no orders had come to march. At one point, for several days the Confederate commander, Douglas Cooper, had hardly left his tent. An orderly would report each morning that the colonel was ill. But even the most dull-witted private in Daniel's regiment had come to understand what that meant; everyone but the Texans understood.

Cooper was either too drunk or too hungover to raise himself from his cot. So another day would slip away, then another. Cooper had tried to excuse it all with an explanation that his force had been ordered to stand by as reinforcements against an expected Union attack from Missouri. But there had been no Union attack; for Daniel McIntosh and the men who rode with him, there had been only the frustration that comes with dashed hopes and the realization that nothing was getting done.[1]

Finally, the Confederates had begun to stir. Over the past few days southern forces had begun to converge and move on Opothleyahola. John Drew's Confederate regiment, the First Cherokee Mounted Rifles, was camped only a few minutes away; they had ridden in earlier from the north. The Cherokees and Cooper's command were to combine forces at Bird Creek, then push northwest to get between Opothleyahola and any chance of escape to or aid coming from Kansas.

All day rumors had it that orders to march and attack would come before another dawn. Some of the troops were so hopeful that they had spent the morning packing their gear and cooking rations. But now there was other news and it was more than just a rumor. A courier had ridden in from John Drew's Cherokee camp with a report that Opothleyahola had made contact and wanted to talk. Cooper had obliged, promising to send a delegation into the hills to the west to meet with the enemy.[2]

Squinting into the last feeble rays of sunlight, Daniel could hardly contain the rage within. Once more hopes and plans for action were being shelved by a commander who was either unfit for duty or, at the least, obsessed with persuading Opothleyahola to surrender. How many times would Cooper allow himself to be deceived, Daniel wondered? For the past several days reports from some of Daniel's scouts had indicated something was happening in Opothleyahola's camps: much coming and going from one camp to another, councils far into the night, drums and songs of war. There were also confusing rumors of warriors fanning out in several directions, of pro-Confederate farms being looted and torched. Something was about to happen, of that Daniel was certain, and it wasn't peace or the surrender of Opothleyahola.

What was Opothleyahola planning? Had he found some unknown or uncharted trail to slip away to Kansas? What if there had been treachery; could the Cherokees be trusted as an ally? What about the leader of the Cherokee Nation, John Ross; had he made a secret pact with Opothleyahola? Everyone believed that

John Ross had been compelled to ally with the Confederates only out of fear for his life from archrival Stand Watie. The Cherokees were nearly as divided as the Muskogees by hatreds new and ancient. And what of the troops in Drew's Cherokee regiment, only minutes away; were they reliable? Inside of the Cherokee Nation was a secret society named the Keetoowah, an organization dedicated to the United States, abolition, and, no doubt, Opothleyahola. No one knew their strength or even the names of their leaders. Were any of the Keetoowahs with Drew's regiment?

These were serious questions all, and their answers could prove decisive. But for the moment, Daniel McIntosh worried increasingly about a single concern: What would occur tonight when a delegation rode off to parley with Opothleyahola?

Nighttime at the camp of John Drew found everything in order at first glance. Scattered campfires outlining nearby wagons and strings of horses flickered throughout the woods. A small cluster of tents marked field headquarters for the nearly five hundred men. Hickory smoke filled the still and chilly night. All was quiet—too quiet. Something was wrong, for not a soldier could be seen: campfires were deserted; no one was tending the horses; not even sentries or pickets were in sight.

Inside one of the tents was John Drew, a dark melon-faced man with ruddy complexion. He was also a man of substance, and one of those who had allied early with the Confederates. As a reward he had received command of the First Cherokee Mounted Rifles. Earlier in the day some of his scouts had reported that large numbers of Opothleyahola's people were approaching from the hills to the west. Later, a messenger from Opothleyahola had ridden boldly into camp. He had come to offer a chance for peace, he said. If Confederates would come to Opothleyahola's camp that evening, bloodshed could be averted. Any who came to speak with Opothleyahola would be guaranteed safe passage.

Drew did not trust the messenger, much less his leader. Like Daniel McIntosh, he knew Opothleyahola was a master of strategy. He understood Opothleyahola's habit of using words and councils as a way to stall for time or mislead those who threatened him. But Drew feared as well that he might have little choice but to accept a meeting. Too many of his own men were only mildly interested in warring with the Muskogees. Like so many Indians, most of the Cherokees saw the war between North and South as little more than a chance to renew old blood feuds with rival factions and clans within their own nation. Just as important, some of his regiment no doubt were Keetoowahs, looking for a chance to turn the entire command against the Confederates. If the Confederates refused to attempt a peaceful settlement, it might furnish the Keetoowahs with an excuse to seize control. Also, Drew was not in charge. He passed along the invitation to parley to his commander, Douglas Cooper, and Cooper quickly accepted, spotting another chance to influence Opothleyahola. Cooper selected a delegation of four men to meet with Opothleyahola that evening.[3]

Just after sundown, the delegation, leaving the campsite of John Drew's Cherokees, headed out toward a range of hills and a still-glowing western sky. For the next hour or so all seemed well in the Confederate camp; sentries standing post, men cooking or squatting about the fires. It was nearly seven o'clock when everything changed. Drew stepped from his tent and looked around; the entire regiment had disappeared. Everyone had deserted, except for the few orderlies and officers in the other tents and a scattering of privates. No more than sixty men were left in camp.[4]

Meanwhile, the Confederate delegation that had ridden to Opothleyahola's camp had found anything but a chance to talk peace. Everywhere were warriors streaked in paint. There were hundreds of them, maybe thousands. Everywhere, too, were roaring campfires, the sounds of drums and war chants, and huge numbers of men waving weapons. The whole wild scene had an overwhelming power that charged the air. And Opothleyahola was nowhere in sight.

The meeting was a ruse. While the Confederate delegation stood surrounded and overawed, the Keetoowahs in Colonel Drew's regiment had made their move. For months they had been planning a way to destroy Confederate power in the Cherokee Nation. So had Opothleyahola, ever since John Ross had betrayed him and joined the South. For days Opothleyahola and the Keetoowahs had been in contact. That night the Keetoowahs spread a rumor that Drew's Cherokee regiment would be attacked and overwhelmed. The only hope was to join Opothleyahola or die: Opothleyahola had powers and magic that his enemies had never imagined, the Keetoowahs told the others; no one could stand against him. Before Drew or any of his remaining officers realized what was happening, nearly the whole of the Cherokee Mounted Rifles had melted away into the night, most of them going over to the other side. With nothing to offer but a leader's reputation for magic and skill, the Keetoowahs had persuaded an entire regiment to dissolve. Not a shot had been fired and total Confederate forces in the area had been cut by a third.

Moments after Drew stepped from his tent, the Confederate delegation to Opothleyahola returned, some of them breathless and nearly panic-stricken. Opothleyahola would attack before dawn, they gasped. The only way they had been able to escape was by convincing warriors that Confederates, like the Muskogees, carried women and children in their camps, women and children who needed to be sent to safety. John Drew ordered what was left of his command to hitch up the wagons and flee to Douglas Cooper's camp. Cooper had to be alerted. Otherwise, he might be overwhelmed by a night attack he did not expect, and the disaster would be complete.[5]

Cooper was stunned. Since the fighting at the rounded mountain, Opothleyahola's forces had sat in camps along the Arkansas River. The Confederate commander had hoped it was a sign that Opothleyahola was weary of the chase and considering peace; that perhaps an understanding could be arranged—that maybe he could at last get his hands on the treasury of the Muskogee Nation. Even when scouts reported movement in the Indian camps, Cooper had not given up, especially after the offer to talk peace. Yet hours later Opothleyahola had suddenly massed for war. And now Colonel Drew had ridden in to report that Confederate forces had been cut by nearly five hundred men, that an entire regiment had vanished and Opothleyahola would attack before dawn.

How could it have happened, Cooper wondered? Why were the Indians attacking at all? And how could a whole regiment be persuaded to walk away from their posts and join the other side? There was simply no place in Cooper's understanding to make sense of what was going on. That hundreds of men could be trained as a unit and pledged to support a nation at war, then in an instant shift sides, and by virtue of nothing more than a leader's reputation for magic: it was too much to grasp. That the same leader and thousands with him would suddenly commit to battle because of a vision that had come with the sun would have been beyond belief. The more the white man thought, the more confused he grew. What had gone wrong? What should he do?[6]

Standing in the shadows, though, was another man who understood what was happening. He had never underestimated Opothleyahola. And never for an instant had he imagined the outcome would end in anything but blood. Daniel McIntosh knew what had to be done too—attack and kill Opothleyahola as soon as possible. Otherwise, he would escape to Kansas or, even worse, seize all of Indian Territory for himself. Daniel saw that Opothleyahola was growing stronger by the day, even the hour. If the Confederates delayed much longer, Opothleyahola's forces would be too large for Cooper or anyone else to subdue, then the whole of Indian Territory would be his. Indian Territory was still essentially up for grabs to anyone who could prove himself the strongest leader—to anyone who proved he had the strongest magic. Daniel knew as well that if something was not done soon, the chance to avenge his father might be forever lost.

The warriors did not attack that night. Every Confederate remained in arms, facing into the dark, deployed and waiting until dawn, but the attack never came. Opothleyahola was playing a game with disastrous results for the Confederates: feigning peace then war, promising battle then not attacking. And still Douglas Cooper did not fully grasp the situation. The following morning, Cooper broke camp and moved south. He hoped to join Confederate reinforcements several miles away before Opothleyahola could strike or anyone else deserted. His route would take him across a wooded ravine onto a prairie and along a tree-lined creek bank shaped like a horseshoe.[7]

CHAPTER

❖

FOURTEEN

Vengeance

They came out of the woods and into the tall grass, hundreds of them, moving in ragged, meandering columns. Not a word was spoken; not a sound was uttered. Every warrior carefully stepped into the moccasin prints of the one in front as he moved along. Some carried rifles and shotguns, others, bows and arrows. They all had knives, a few carried hatchets and war clubs tucked into sash or belt. Dangling from some belts were scalps—the mark of courage. Their shirts were buckskin, cotton, even silk. Their colors were red, white, green, and homespun brown. Fringe and embroidery decorated shirts; in their hair were feathers and cornhusks. A few had on headgear made from the skins of deer or bears or cougars. Every one of them had his face streaked or covered with paint: part red, part black.

The warriors moved to the bank of a stream the white man called Bird Creek. Carefully, they waded into the freezing waters and picked their way across. On the other side the bank was tall and steep, but up they scrambled, nearly to the top. Then with knives or bare hands the men began digging and scooping away dirt. Soon there was a long, narrow shelf trench carved into the bank, a place where a man could stand or kneel. Along the top of the bank other warriors scattered limbs, vines, and tree trunks. Before long they had a nearly perfect defense. Protected by the creek bank and brush, a warrior could fire into the open country in front, exposing nothing but a rifle barrel or maybe the top of his head.[1]

To the left of their line a wooded ravine jutted into the prairie. Some of the warriors moved into the ravine and hid in gullies and underbrush. Still farther to the left was an abandoned farm, a mud-chinked cabin and corncrib. Around and inside the cabin other warriors took shelter or dug in. Following the bend in the stream, the entire battle line formed a gigantic horseshoe, except for the wooded ravine. It was no accident; the war captains had chosen their ground carefully. It had always been the way of the People to battle near water if they could, to use the banks, streams, and timber to their advantage. And just beyond the creek bank, stretching across the prairie and nearly touching the wooded ravine, was a narrow road, the way the enemy would come. Before long, from the tip of the wooded ravine came the sound of a warrior hooting like an owl. Something was coming down the road.[2]

The Confederates came in double columns. In front rode Daniel McIntosh, with several of his kin, and Douglas Cooper. Then came the rest of the Creeks and, close behind, the Texans. The wagons and what was left of Drew's Regiment followed, and finally the Choctaws and Chickasaws. The entire force strung out for nearly a mile.[3]

The men were ready for a fight but anxious, too, every one of them. They were still shaken by the night before: an entire regiment—troops they were counting on—had simply vanished. As they rode along glancing left and right, the Confederates knew that every bend or dip in the road might send them smashing into Opothleyahola. No one seemed to know where the Indians had gone. No one had heard from any of the scouts since yesterday. Still, the Texans, at least, had little doubt of the outcome. After all, they reassured one another, they were only dealing with "Injuns." They would need that reassurance.

More anxious than any, perhaps, was Daniel McIntosh. All of his life Daniel had seen Opothleyahola rally and manipulate others with words. In the old days in Alabama, Opothleyahola should have been put to death for advising the sale of tribal lands to the federal government, then signing a treaty to make it happen. But he was able to talk his way free before the Council. Those who condemned the McIntosh as traitors never seemed to remember that Opothleyahola had signed a treaty giving away millions of acres to the United States, that he was as guilty as anyone of handing over the ancient lands to the white man. They seemed to forget as well that the lands he had signed away belonged only to the people of the Lower towns, people like the McIntosh. Always, it was Opothleyahola who had organized the Upper towns and any who would follow, challenging the authority and position of the McIntosh for his own selfish ends. It was Opothleyahola, more than anyone, who was behind resistance to Confederate forces: visiting every town or farm; whipping up bitterness wherever he spoke; dredging up the old hatreds, and ripping apart Indian Territory. Above all, Daniel could never forget, it was Opothleyahola who had publicly condemned his father to death, then shamed the Council into ordering the execution. He was a dangerous, deadly man, Opothleyahola. There was only one way to deal with such a man. As he rode at the head of his men, Daniel swore on the memory of his father that he would find and punish his enemy. He would hunt him down, no matter how long it took, and put an end to his life. And he would personally cut out the tongue of Opothleyahola.[4]

The head of the Confederate column was just beyond the trees, where the road entered the prairie, when it began. Two riders came racing in at full speed; they were from an advance party Cooper had sent out as a precaution. Opothleyahola was ahead in force, they reported, dug in along a bend at Bird Creek, not a mile away.

Daniel drew his revolver, ready to order his column to advance; somewhere ahead waited his blood enemy. The clan McIntosh and the others with them would have another chance to even old scores. But before anyone could act there was a stir to the rear: shouts and confusion, then the pop of rifles. It was Opothleyahola's warriors; they were in a ravine that Daniel and his men had passed moments before. There were more shouts, then more gunfire, and, finally, a volley.

Douglas Cooper decided to attack on all fronts. Taking off his hat, he raced back the way he had come, waving his men into line. At the rear, Choctaw and Chickasaw troops, already dismounted, would charge the ravine. The Texans in the center were to advance on horseback into the timber, between the Choctaw and McIntosh units, keeping Confederate ranks together. Daniel McIntosh and his men would also charge on horses, across the prairie and straight for Opothleyahola's warriors in front. The entire force would sweep the land, cutting across prairie and ravine like a scythe, moving toward Bird Creek.

The Texans and the McIntosh regiments dressed ranks, forming two mounted lines of men, the second line reinforcing the first. Near the center of the Texas line waved a brownish red flag with a

102

crescent moon and stars. Gunfire was rising in volume on the right, where the Choctaws and Chickasaws were already fighting. Then a voice rose above the din in front of the mounted lines: "Forward!" With a jolt the entire command lurched ahead, two advancing lines stretching from the woods onto the prairie.[5]

They rode with caution, not wild abandon. Fighting at the rounded mountain had taught them better. Yet, despite their caution and plans, Confederate lines began to break apart almost from the beginning. Most of the Texans drifted toward the heavy timber or the ravine, where the Choctaws and Chickasaws found enemy fire growing hotter by the minute. The Creeks were on their own in the open country. As Confederates advanced, it became clear that Opothleyahola's warriors were in scattered pockets along an entire line, from the ravine and the woods to Bird Creek and the open country. Increasingly, each Confederate unit focused only on the threat to its immediate front or flank; the fighting became several isolated battles instead of one.

Some of the Texans galloped all the way to the creek, finding no one. But for most it was a different story. The Texans began to encounter gunfire from the woods. Mostly it was to the right, isolated and scattered at first, then more intense. Suddenly, a portion of the Texas line was staggered by a volley from the right flank. A rider fell to the ground; horses went down as well. Then came another volley from the same direction. It was the Keetoowahs from John Drew's old regiment, fighting with Opothleyahola; the white men were easy targets on horseback. But there was no panic among the Confederates, not this time. The Texans dismounted then pressed their enemy on foot, determined not to run again from Indians.

The McIntosh moved across the open country, straight for the line of trees and vines that marked the edge of Bird Creek. Opothleyahola's warriors were waiting. When the men on horseback came within a hundred paces, the warriors opened fire. Then from behind the creek bank rose the sounds of panther screams and turkey gobbles—the war cry of a Muskogee.[6]

Daniel's men answered in kind, with guns and war whoops. For the first time since the whole affair had begun, both sides of the Muskogee Nation were facing one another in combat. Some of Daniel's men dismounted and formed a battle line. Standing in the open, they fired and reloaded as fast as possible. A few leaped from their mounts, then rushed the creek bank with guns raised and knives drawn. Shouts and screams mixed with the sounds of gunfire and galloping and whinnying horses. Others still on horseback moved to the left of the heaviest fighting, toward a cluster of trees, hoping to get on the flank of the warriors.

The Confederates on horseback rode to the edge of the trees and brush before dismounting. Firing and shouting, they rushed the timber, but again the warriors were waiting. Several of them stepped from behind trees; others rose from the ground, firing guns and arrows. It was close in, then hand to hand—firing, slashing, clubbing. Men, stumbling and coughing, fell to the ground. One lay with his eyes rolled back till nothing but the whites showed, his lids still fluttering; then came the jerking death spasm. From another came the gurgling sound of someone choking on his own blood. Wild, bloody vengeance it was, and raw courage, and the blackest hatred.

It was too much for either side to stand; one had to flee. Suddenly, the warriors pulled back from the trees. Then all along the creek bank they fled, jumping into the icy water, some struggling to swim to the other side with the wounded.

The Creek Confederates mounted and reformed for an all-out assault across the stream, for Opothleyahola's warriors were on the run. But just as Daniel was about to order a charge, a hard-riding courier came up with news: the other Confederates were heavily engaged and in need of reinforcements.

Daniel glared at the courier, then at his enemies across the creek. The warriors were in clear view, scattered and dazed, and for the moment nearly helpless. They could all be run down on horseback, trampled or shot. Everything Daniel hated and had pledged himself to destroy lay before him like an exhausted wild animal, finally brought to bay. Perhaps Opothleyahola was with the scattered bands retreating through the grass. One final blow and his father's spirit could rest, and Daniel's code of vengeance would be appeased. But there was yet another code to which Daniel and his father before him had pledged themselves, and now it beckoned— the code and the world of the white man. If Daniel truly wanted to be a part of that world he would have to put aside old hatreds and personal feelings. He would have to ride away, for the white man was calling. For a long, lonely moment Daniel stared across the creek, looking perhaps for Opothleyahola. Then he wheeled his horse and ordered the rest of the command to follow, toward the rising sound of gunfire in the smoky woods.

The warriors who had first attacked from the wooded ravine had been driven back. Confederate Choctaws and Chickasaws had finally rooted them out of their ditch, fighting it out nearly tree to tree, each side taking scalps as they killed. One Choctaw Confederate shot a man and scalped him. Then he rose up just in time to shoot another warrior who was about to attack. But the battle was no longer in the ravine. It had moved to the abandoned farm, to the log cabin and corn crib.

Both cabin and crib sat in a clearing nearly surrounded by woods, and behind the woods was Bird Creek. Around the little farm and in the woods on either side, hundreds of warriors were poised and ready.

The Choctaws and Chickasaws could see the cabin in the distance. Quickly, they mounted and formed to charge without waiting for reinforcements. Sensing victory after the fighting in the ravine, they would waste no time. Near the center of their line an officer motioned forward; the Confederate Indians dashed ahead. When they came within range, the warriors opened fire.

With the sound of gunfire, Confederate Indians dismounted and formed a line along a rail fence. Then they unleashed a volley of their own. A moment later, dead or dying warriors littered the ground ahead. Some of the warriors drifted back from the corn crib and into the cabin yard. The Confederates fired another volley and still more warriors dropped, but the rest stood their ground.

The Choctaws and Chickasaws moved forward over the fence. The lines were fewer than a hundred paces apart, then only fifty. Warriors firing bullets and arrows clustered around the cabin. Inside, others fought from doors and windows. It was close in and lethal, the sort of combat in which a pistol or an arrow was as good as a rifle, and a shotgun was the deadliest of all. Smoke filled the air, cutting vision. The closer the two sides drew toward each other the louder and more confused it became, and the more deadly, too. Every man was shouting; gunfire was constant, no longer in volleys.

The Confederate Indians kept moving forward, firing fast. One of them caught an arrow. Another dropped to his knees, clutching his stomach; still another grabbed his face. But the jumbled line of men kept advancing. Into the yard they came, the warriors falling back but still fighting. Suddenly the Choctaws rushed the cabin, and the warriors fled across the clearing toward the woods. The Confederates gave chase, driving them into the timber before they stopped. But it wasn't over.

Other warriors had formed to counterattack. Shouting and whooping, they burst from the woods on the right, then the left, driving the Confederates back toward the cabin. Within minutes the Choctaws and Chickasaws were nearly surrounded. But Confederate reinforcements, more Choctaws and Chickasaws, arrived just in time.

With fresh troops the Confederates dressed ranks and charged again. Once more they drove the warriors through the clearing and the distant woods, even into the creek, before they stopped. But still more warriors began to form for battle, massing just to the right of Confederate lines.

This time the warriors made a dash for Confederate horses far to the rear. The Choctaws and Chickasaws had no choice but to rush back past the cabin, running to save their mounts. It was a foot race and the warriors were winning. If they scattered the animals, it could be disaster; the Confederates might end up cut off and surrounded.

The warriors had nearly reached the horses; it was nearly over for the Choctaws and Chickasaws. That was when Daniel McIntosh and his Creek units rode up. Daniel's men dismounted and formed into line. They charged the warriors and drove them away, this time for good.

All afternoon there was sporadic fighting. Whenever they could the warriors fought with their backs to the sun, forcing Confederates to squint into the light. The Texans, it seemed, were victorious wherever they fought, driving warriors from field or ravine, from one to the next. But the longer it lasted, the more the white men sensed something was wrong, until at last the panting Confederates were exhausted.

It was no longer a white man's battle. A warrior cared little for holding a position in combat, be it a creek bank or a cabin clearing. What counted was enemies killed and deeds of valor. The longer it went on, the more the fighting became a matter of warriors showing bravery and prowess by standing in the open, mocking and taunting their enemies or waving scalps, then darting away whenever the white men charged. The gunfire would slacken, at times grow heavy, then die away again. By dusk the Confederates had nearly exhausted their ammunition; had it lasted much longer, some units would have been forced to withdraw.

But suddenly, as if by magic, it was over. The warriors disappeared through the woods and across the creek, into the growing darkness. Nothing remained but the sounds of the wounded and a rising northeast wind. Riding across the field was Colonel Cooper, already claiming victory. In the days ahead he would speak and

❖ NOW THE WOLF HAS COME

write of hundreds of warriors killed. He would speak as well of facing thousands of the enemy in battle. Perhaps it was so; perhaps he was fighting not only warriors but spirits of the dead. The white men would try to convince anyone who would listen, and most of all themselves, that Bird Creek was a victory.[7]

It was night when Daniel McIntosh finally rode across the clearing and by the cabin where so much of the fighting had taken place. Overhead low, heavy clouds were quickly filling the sky and a few flakes of snow had begun to fall, the first of the season. The Confederates had spent the day fighting an enemy and nearly exhausting their ammunition. How many warriors were killed? Daniel and his men could count no more than twenty-seven. Some claimed that the warriors had dragged away many of their dead, but that was small consolation. Already there were rumors that more Keetoowahs had put on the cornhusk and were on their way to join Opothleyahola.[8]

Ghosts surrounded Daniel as he picked his way across the field: ghosts of the fallen and the ghost of his father, William, still crying out for vengeance. No matter how much he tried to rationalize in the fashion of a white man, Daniel could not escape the sense that he had failed. He kept thinking of how his men had driven the warriors from Bird Creek, and how easily they might have been ridden down—and how he might have been able to kill Opothleyahola. Most of all, he kept thinking of his father.

Soon everyone would learn of the Battle of Bird Creek. White men might speak of taking possession of the field, but every Indian, no matter how much he denied his heritage, would understand what had happened. Again the Confederates had failed. Everyone would be watching and waiting to see what followed. One more setback for the Confederates, and all of the nations in the Territory would rally around Opothleyahola. Then the McIntosh would be the ones seeking to escape.

Daniel pulled up his horse, then turned against the wind. Squinting through the snow he could barely see the light of countless flickering campfires in the hills to the west. At one of them was his darkest enemy. Somehow an old blanket Indian had managed to get his people through more than a hundred miles of country, fighting and winning battles against all odds and logic as he moved. Somehow, some way, he had to be stopped.

CHAPTER

FIFTEEN

The Spirits

The snow soon went away, but it began to rain again, not the heavy shower of a single storm, but a slow, constant, soaking drizzle. Campsites sank into mud and every road became a pond or stream. The season had come for rain or snow and ever-stronger blasts of cold sweeping in from the plains. Shades of brown and gray colored the land while brooding clouds shrouded the sun and turned the middle of day into a dreary twilight. It was the time of mournful colors, deep shadows, and cold, endless nights. Some said, too, that it was the time of death. A few more warriors, mostly from the Cherokee Nation, came to join the People in their rain-soaked camps. But the other nations were still waiting and watching to see what would happen next. There would be no general uprising.

The enemy slowly withdrew to the east for ammunition and supplies following the battle. For the ones with Opothleyahola, though, there would be no more ammunition or supplies unless they came from Kansas. There was just enough powder for one more battle. The warriors would have to make every bullet and dram of powder count. For several risings the People hardly moved at all. Their wagons, laden with everything they owned, could not move through mud. As they waited, their herds of cattle and horses stripped the country of grass, and soon the animals grew weak. Huge numbers had to be released onto the open range, forever lost to their owners.

Finally the rain ended and the weather turned warm. The People broke camp and the wagon parties began to move again, heading north. They were still too few in number to remain where they were; even after Bird Creek the enemy was too strong. Always the People followed the hills as they traveled; rolling, rock-strewn hills covered in scrub oak and guiding them northward. Somewhere beyond the hills was Kansas.

There was no sign of Union troops, and still no word from the miccos. The People could not help but wonder and worry. Where were Bob Deer and Jo Ellis; where was Sands? Why was there not at least a message? Still, they remained hopeful. Any day, they told one another, northern troops would arrive. The Great Father could not afford to lose a land so rich and great. Rumor had it that John Ross might join them as well, bringing the whole Cherokee Nation. His heart had never been with the Confederates, it was said. But so far there was no one. All day, as they struggled along, the People scanned the horizon, looking for a sign that friends were nearing.

Then the rain came once more, another cold, constant winter drizzle. And the mud. Wagons bogged down, some to the axles. The more everyone worked to free them, the deeper they sank. In places the mud turned into little more than a dark, watery ooze. Some days the People barely traveled out of sight of their last camp because of the weather. Other times it was so wet they could not move at all. It seemed it would never end: rain, mud, a brief clearing, then more rain and more mud; and the People plodding and struggling or stuck. Always, too, there was Opothleyahola, pressing them to push ahead. He was growing weaker and his cough was getting worse, for the weather and the many nights outdoors were taking a toll. But there were other and more important matters to consider. It was only a question of time before the enemy would come again.

Finally, the clouds went away and the sun returned. The mud dried and puddles vanished. Once more the wagons moved freely. For the moment the People put aside their worries and fears: children laughed and played as the wagons creaked along. And every night in camps there were songs and chants and stories of valor in war. An entire civilization was moving across the land; riding, walking, camping. All that they had ever been, all that they had ever known or handed down since their beginning, they carried with them. In the wagons, on the horses, or trudging along on foot, they were the last remnant of a way of life that was ancient and even timeless. They were still many risings from Kansas, but

109

for the first time since leaving home there was nothing between the People and federal territory but the hills and open country—or so it seemed.

It happened at the end of a long, weary day of travel, just as the main wagon party was making camp in a half-hidden meadow in the hills. Scouts rode in with news for Opothleyahola: to the east, Stand Watie's Confederate Cherokees were getting ready to move. There were no Keetoowahs with Stand Watie. His men were loyal to the South and the Keetoowahs were their blood enemies. Stand Watie's troops would come as one against the People. There was something else, too, perhaps much worse. Scouts reported that a fresh Confederate column had been spotted riding out of Arkansas. The column was heavily armed and larger than anything the People had faced before. Along with forces under Cooper and the McIntosh, the Confederates would outnumber warriors three to one. If they all chose to attack together, the People could be overwhelmed.[1]

Opothleyahola sent runners northward fanning out in every direction, searching for reinforcements. A real Muskogee warrior on foot could outdistance any horse. At first a horse would quickly race ahead and out of sight. But by the end of the day a Muskogee runner would pass the animal. If Union troops were ahead, the runners would find them. Still other runners raced north toward the Delaware Nation in Kansas, seeking help from other warriors if possible. The Delawares were a large party in Kansas, and many believed they would support their brothers, the Muskogees. Then Opothleyahola turned his attention to those in camp. He reminded them of the fate awaiting any who fell into the hands of the enemy, how the southern white men with the clear eyes and the smell of death would show no mercy. Around campfires he read again the letter from the Great Father promising help. Most of all, he spoke of the old ways and the ancient beliefs, and of the gods who would shield their children if only they would remain brave and true.

There was little rest for anyone in camp that night. Some of the People began hitching teams and loading wagons, with plans to move before light: women and children would go first, as always. The warriors would follow later, forming a shield between the wagons and the enemy. Others mounted up and rode into the dark to alert the other camps. There were countless numbers, spread across the hillsides and neighboring meadows; the sooner everyone understood their danger, the better.

Through the next several days and nights the People streamed out of the camps, their wagons choking the single winding road to the north. Yet nearly half of them still remained, waiting their turn. Too long had they waited on the weather. And even when the weather was fair and the roads dry, for too long they had only crept ahead, depending on an inner sense that would tell them when to hurry. Too much, as well, had they counted on the help of others. Still in the meadow waiting to leave were James Scott and Lizzie. James could see the worry and fear in his mother's face, and though his father tried to reassure him, he sensed that something dangerous or dreadful was nearing.

Every day Opothleyahola sent ahead more runners to search for help, but none returned with news. Growing numbers of wagons and families left for the open country without waiting for a place on the road. In desperation, many abandoned their wagons, bundling up what they could, walking away or riding off on horseback. And all the while, as they packed or fled, the large deadly column of white men kept drawing closer.[2]

They rode with the same easy gait as the other white men from their country, every one of them. There was something, too, about the way they carried themselves in the saddle: fiercely proud and utterly self-confident, as if every man were certain he could defeat any enemy in his path. They had earned that confidence. Some had already won renown on distant battlefields. Their commander was Colonel James McIntosh, no relation to the Creek McIntosh. His methods of warfare were simple: attack and keep attacking, no matter the odds. Brave and ambitious, even foolhardy, in many ways he was a symbol of the men he led and the nation he served.

Like the other white men, they came mostly from the pine barrens and sandy bottoms of East Texas, or from the Arkansas hills. They went by names such as Lane, Neal, Ferguson, and McDonald. Their world revolved around family and clan, the land they worked, and their own peculiar codes of honor and vengeance. They were more a band of individuals than an army, their homeland a collection of farms and villages more than a nation. Though they never would have understood, in certain ways the white men on horseback were no different from the ones they had come to destroy. And like every army of invasion, they would not hesitate to do what at home would have been unthinkable.

They wore the familiar uniforms: homespun brown and butternut, sweat-stained, ragged and tattered, even greasy. No two were alike except for an emblem of the Lone Star on the hats or belt buckles of most. All of them carried an array of weapons, and no man fewer than two: rifles, shotguns, revolvers, knives, swords. Their personal appearance, if possible, was even more striking. Many had long, stringy manes that touched the shoulders and scraggly beards coated in dust or spattered with tobacco juice. Except for the weapons and what passed for uniforms, they were a perfect image of their Celtic ancestors from a thousand years before.

James McIntosh and his men rode from Arkansas to Fort Gibson, stronghold of Confederate authority in Indian Territory. There he got in touch with Douglas Cooper, who was at the fort as well. He quickly recognized Cooper as an incompetent, but just as fast, James McIntosh began to map out plans to smash Opothleyahola.

Cooper's troops, including his Indians, would follow the Arkansas River northwest for three days, getting behind Opothleyahola. Then they would turn due north, into the hills and toward Opothleyahola's camps. At the same time, James McIntosh and his white men would ride up the Verdigris River, then west toward the hostiles, creating a giant pincer. Outgunned and outnumbered, weighted down with wagons and families, Opothleyahola would have little choice but to surrender or die at the hands of Confederates closing in from two directions.[3]

The day after his meeting with Cooper, James McIntosh issued orders to his units: cook rations and be ready to move by morning. Cooper sent similar orders to his forces camped several miles away and also made plans to gather munitions. Bearded white men cooked bacon and cornmeal, then cleaned guns and molded bullets by the light of campfires. And Confederate Indians, in particular the McIntosh of Coweta, hoped and prayed that this time they would succeed.

Another day and the Confederates with James McIntosh moved out for the Verdigris River. Cooper's troops, scattered in several locations, began to assemble for their march along the Arkansas River, as planned. The southerners made good time that day, at least the ones with James McIntosh. Even though it turned cold and began to snow, they rode hard all afternoon before making camp. That night a frosty moon broke through the clouds. Some of the Confederates mentioned that the moon had been setting to the northwest, with its light side tilted up like a bowl receiving water. A few believed it was an omen. Then someone else remembered that in three days it would be Christmas and they would not be home.

The following day the weather warmed and the snow melted. Before dawn the Texans with James McIntosh were in the saddle. Their plans were to rendezvous with Stand Watie's Cherokees before reaching Opothleyahola, but James McIntosh was anxious for a fight. He pressed his men and horses for the next three days, waiting for no one until he was within sight of the hills where Opothleyahola was camped.[4]

Christmas Day seemed to end for James McIntosh and his troops like any other in the field: soldiers making camp and trying to stay warm, men cooking, others tending to the horses. But it was not a typical day. The weather had turned colder again, much colder. The wind was rising from the northeast and clouds were streaking in, mixing with a frozen red-orange twilight.

Then came danger as well. A line of men appeared on horseback, not half a mile away. Sentries raced in, pointing back toward the riders and the fading twilight. The Texans, some of them still wrapped in blankets and bareheaded, jumped up from around their fires and seized weapons. Others raced to steady the horses and saddle up. A ragged line of mounted Confederates quickly began to form. It was nearly dark, but the white men could still see the figures on horseback, maybe two hundred of them—some of Opothleyahola's warriors.

The Confederates threw out a picket line, followed by a regiment of several hundred men. Slowly they rode forward into the darkness and the cold, groping for the enemy. Then an officer called a halt and moved ahead by himself—nearly halfway to the enemy line. Finally, he, too, would go no farther; it might be a trap. This time Opothleyahola was up against more than a drunken incompetent for a rival. He faced determined, clear-headed leaders and some of the finest cavalry anywhere.

The Confederate officer signaled for the warriors to send someone forward, and several Indians complied. For a few anxious moments each side tried to communicate, but it was pointless. Neither could hope to understand the other. The warriors whirled about and galloped away, back to their own kind. The white man did the same, returning to his world. Then the entire line of warriors vanished into the dark.

Still later one of the Texas scouts rode in. He was an old Indian fighter and he had information. Campfires had been spotted in the hills to the west; it was Opothleyahola. The white men began squaring away gear and putting their weapons in order. Then orders went out to cook four days' rations and be ready to move by daybreak.[5]

It was a bitter wind that swept through the hills and camps of the People: a howling, mournful wind that came with the clouds. And the night was the blackest of nights. By tomorrow the Confederates would reach the hills. Yet there were many women and children still in the camps. Another day and the enemy would be upon them all. The white men would come as in the past, like savages: shooting, burning, pillaging. The little ones might be run down with horses, the women raped and gutted. It could end in a slaughter like Tohopeka in the old country, maybe worse. Once again a recurring dream was closing in on the People and the old man who led them. All around, the world of darkness and chaos crept closer, and the cold bitter winds continued to moan.

Opothleyahola, alone with his thoughts, squatted beside a fire. Wrapped in a blanket, he stared into the wind-whipped flames. With every gust sparks swirled around his face and hands, but he paid them no mind. At last, he pulled something from beneath his blanket and out of his coat pocket. It was the letter, yellow and wrinkled from the touch of so many hands. He looked down at the letter and the ink-smeared writing, thinking about who had written, thinking also of the worth of a white man's promise. Then he slowly opened his hand and the scrap of paper blew away, into the night.

In the past he had always found a way for the People to survive, no matter what they faced, but no more. He was sick and exhausted; sometimes his cough was so bad it left him too weak to stand or even to sit. Now there were chills and fever as well. But most of all, he was sick from worry, for he was out of ideas. It was too much for one so old, too much for any man. Why had the gods deserted him, he wondered? Why had they turned away from the ones who loved them and had remained so true? The enemy could not be tricked into another ambush, and they would come with the first light. If the People tried to scatter in small bands, they would be hunted down. If they stood and fought they would be overwhelmed, for the warriors could not fight a white man's battle. It was one thing to lie in ambush, to strike and run or to melt away in the dark. There was no one more skilled or courageous at such fighting than a Muskogee warrior. But the kind of battle that would

114

come tomorrow was another matter. Battle lines and massed volleys—only the white man had stomach for such killing. And even if there was a way to trick the enemy into another ambush, it hardly mattered. Dampness and rains had turned the gunpowder into worthless paste. War captains advised there was little more than a barrel of dry powder left. And the scouts reported that only a short distance away were still more of the enemy: Stand Watie, Douglas Cooper, and Daniel McIntosh. They were closing in, all of them. So too was fate. Perhaps it was Opothleyahola's fault, the disaster that seemed to be coming. Maybe he had been a fool, trusting in Union officials and even his own visions. Maybe his hatred for the McIntosh had blinded him to the truth. Many risings had been lost fighting at Bird Creek then getting bogged down in the weather that followed. If he had pressed ahead from the Arkansas River instead of fighting, the People would be in Kansas. But his wish for blood and vengeance had absorbed him; now the People would pay for it with their lives.

Trapped in a swirl of worries, perhaps Opothleyahola drifted away to other times and better places: the old country and the falls at Tuckabatchee; or maybe the life once shared with his long-dead wife. He had known but one wife and had never remarried, even though she had been dead for years. She lay buried on the hillside near his home; her spirit was with the gods. Perhaps he thought of his daughters, who were somewhere in the wagons farther north. But the world of bitter winds and cold soon returned, driving away his personal cares. Stiffly, Opothleyahola rose to his feet, then straightened himself and looked about. Around him were the faces of his people: mothers, fathers, the little ones. They were standing in the firelight, staring and waiting for him to decide what to do. And in the dark behind them were the spirits and faces of the dead, watching and waiting. . . .

There was but one chance. Some would have to die so that others could live. The warriors would stand their ground, fighting to the death, buying time with their lives so the rest could flee. It would be desperate and close in, mostly hand to hand. There were no other options. The outcome was certain, too, for the warriors were outnumbered and hopelessly outgunned.

The rest of the night wagons kept moving from the campsites, fleeing north. In every direction, frantic parents were packing, bundling up, and abandoning camps, many holding children by the hand or in their arms as they hurried away. Everywhere, too, was Opothleyahola, moving about his camp, clutching the barrel of his rifle and using the weapon as a walking stick. Keep to the hills, he told them. Even if off the road, follow the hills and move always toward the Kansas border. If traveling by night, follow the star that never moves. As he spoke with one then another, he made them a promise as well—that he would be in Kansas waiting for them. If only they would remain true to the old ways and the old gods; if they would but humble themselves before the Master of Breath, they would be shielded from harm. And somehow, some way, he would be with them in Kansas. He had never betrayed the People, he reminded them. He had never broken a promise. If they remained true to one another and to the ways of their fathers, the People would live. And he would be waiting for them, like a grandfather awaiting his children.

Finally, Opothleyahola turned and went into the darkness, vanishing like one of the spirits. The warriors were forming along the ridge and gullies, facing the direction of the enemy. The wind picked up and it began to spatter rain, then sleet. And in the east, it was getting light.[6]

CHAPTER

❖

SIXTEEN

To Die Well

It is hard to kill a nation or a way of life. Faced with death, a nation, just as any animal of the forest, will struggle to live. Its people will starve, freeze, or sleep out in the open, enduring almost any hardship before allowing an end to all they know. Leaders will buy time through statecraft or cajolery. Captains will lead the weak and innocent to a place of hiding. Many are those who will sacrifice their treasure, and even condemn themselves to a life of wandering before casting off everything they are. All of this and more a nation will do to survive. But if finally trapped or cornered, if forced to pick between death or slavery and the end of all they cherish, a last, determined remnant will often choose to die. Like an old buck or a bear, still proud but nearly exhausted, they will turn to face their tormentors and make a final stand. And they will come to their end with a single grim consolation, that the gods who see and know all will forever say: they lived and died well. So it was for the warriors of the Muskogee Nation on a rocky, windswept hillside.

The war captains placed their men on the crest of a ridge covered in boulders and stunted post oaks. Behind every rock and tree they took position. Some of the boulders were separated by crags and passageways, terrain where a single determined warrior could hold off five times his number—at least for a while. Farther down the slope, in the direction of the enemy, was a line of Seminole warriors. At the bottom of the ridge was open country, and still farther away a narrow tree-lined stream called Chustenahlah.[1]

In feathers and paint they waited, some of them whispering prayers and ancient chants to ready themselves, everyone scanning the gray horizon. One wore the feather of the eagle, painted red. Others had faces streaked with the marks of the snake or the sun. Hanging from necks were pouches with bones and powders and, in a few, even bits of the tie snake. Still others clutched sabia stones— magical stones that could change colors or dart across a room or campfire. A warrior could draw power and courage from magic powders, and always from the stones and bits of the snake.

The warriors, especially the young, were eager despite the odds. Once again their weapons burned in their hands. Some were certain they would be invisible to the enemy, for the holy men had prayed and made magic all night. The holy men were ready, too, wearing the fox skin and the feather of the horned owl or the buzzard, ready to minister to the wounded.

It grew colder and the winds blew stronger. All morning drizzle and sleet kept falling, peppering the land and the warriors. Before long, sleet began to cling to hair and feathers and stack up on rifle barrels. Icy winds turned faces and hands numb, but the men endured—and waited.

In the distance the enemy finally appeared. They came out of the frozen mist like something dark and sinister, three long, winding columns. Ahead of the columns and on the flanks rode mounted pickets. The entire command carefully made its way for the tree-lined creek, slowly and irresistibly. The enemy knew the warriors were in front of them in the hills. This time there would be no surprises.

The mounted pickets converged at the icy stream. Then one by one they picked their way across a rocky outcropping that stretched to the other side. Once across, the white men worked their way through the trees then fanned out again in a thin, ragged line and carefully nudged ahead. They were hardly out of the trees when one of them raised an arm, calling a halt. In front was a narrow strip of open country, then the hills. The pickets looked up at the top of the rise. There was nothing in sight but rocks and brush. Suddenly the hills came alive with a blast of gunfire, then the sounds of panthers, turkeys, and crowing roosters.

The enemy columns moved up fast, dashing across the stream to join the pickets. The Confederates quickly formed a long line of mounted men at the bank of the stream, straightened, and prepared to charge. Once in ranks they stood motionless, staring at

❖ NOW THE WOLF HAS COME

the ridge and the prairie they would cross, their eyes focused toward the point of attack. A strange stillness gripped the land, for the warriors were no longer firing. For a long, lonely moment, the only sound was that of the wind and the sleet. Then a Confederate rode a few steps out from his line. He turned toward the men and said something to an officer in the ranks. The officer spoke to another. A bugle call split the frozen air, and the mounted line of white men plunged ahead.

The line moved for the hill like an enormous sidewinder. From the middle of Confederate ranks a cry arose, quickly spreading up and down the line, a wild, eerie cry that would soon rise on a thousand battlefields to the east. It was the same terrible sound the warriors had heard in another battle in another land long ago. With the howling, the mounted column broke into a run, surging across the open ground, with horses dashing for the slope and men wild for blood—screaming, shouting, and panting for breath. At the foot of the hills the Confederates leaped from their mounts. Some of the men held the reins of the animals, but the rest charged ahead. Scrambling over rocks, bursting though bush and thickets, they rushed on as if possessed.[2]

The line of Seminoles fired a ragged volley, then slowly retreated up the hill. At first they withdrew, still facing the enemy and walking backward, showing contempt for the huge line that was moving closer. Some even stopped to reload and fire again. But the Seminoles began to sense the fury of those who were drawing near. Some of them turned and ran for the top of the ridge.

The Confederates were already firing at the rocks and trees along the ridge; minié balls threw up dirt and bits of rock around the half-hidden warriors, but they paid no mind. The enemy came closer and the howling grew louder, yet the warriors at the crest of the ridge held their fire, waiting. Carefully, every warrior picked a target and took aim, most with bows, the rest with guns. The enemy was fewer than fifty steps away, then thirty. Every warrior fired . . .

Hardly a white man went down. There were not enough guns, and too few arrows had found their mark. For too long the People had come to rely on the white man's weapons, forgetting the old ways of war. Some of the warriors stepped from behind rocks and trees to fire arrows again, hoping to get a better shot in the open. The result was the same. Others simply drew knives or hatchets. Only the ones with the power and skill to fight with a bow had a chance to keep the enemy at bay—and also the Seminoles. Every

Seminole held a gun and was reloading and firing as quickly as possible.

The white men drew closer still, deadly and determined, shouting and howling. They never delivered a single massed volley. The Confederates, standing, crouching, charging, came in firing and fighting at will.

It was the same with the warriors; they, too were ready to kill. Along the ridge they fought it out face to face and hand to hand. Every man was an army, fighting his own battle. Warriors fell riddled with bullets; white men dropped or limped away bleeding from arrows. One warrior, slashing and stabbing with a knife, leaped from a boulder onto the white men below. Another stepped into the open when the Confederates approached, then calmly waited for a fight to the death. Others put their backs to rock walls, drew knives, and stood their ground. Every man chose his own way to kill and to die.

The grass caught fire, even with the sleet and rain. Soon no one could see more than a few steps in any direction. From out of the smoke a warrior with a knife rushed several Confederates, taking one with him before he fell. Another Muskogee appeared; he was shot to pieces before he took a step. Gun blasts, gurgling screams, smoke, moans, boulders, and blood: it was a blind, desperate struggle. And rising still above the din of battle was the cry of the white man at war.

As the fighting raged, another column of white men made their move. Not all of the Confederates had charged the ridge; a reserve unit had remained behind at the creek. When the fighting began, they mounted and rode north along the base of the hills. Their plan was to move north, veering away from the battle, then turn into the hills, getting between Opothleyahola and a retreat for Kansas. But when the white men finally cut into the hills, there was someone waiting to challenge them.[3]

The war captains had already guessed the Confederate plan. They knew the white men probably had a reserve unit; so did they. Muskogee reserves rode over the crest, straight for the white men galloping up the slopes. Quickly, the Muskogees dismounted and took position among the rocks. The two sides exploded at one another, men and charging animals clashing, swirling, tumbling. It was guns and arrows, point-blank—in the face. One warrior leaped onto the back of a Confederate, dragging him to the ground. A shower of arrows brought down riders and horses; a blast of gunfire took even more warriors. Within moments bodies littered the ground. Some of the fallen rose to their feet dazed and bloodied; a few pulled knives or revolvers and kept fighting.

For a moment it was rounded mountain all over again. Confederates fell back surprised and stunned, but not for long. The white men dismounted, formed ranks, and came again with a vengeance. The warriors stood their ground. It was even more savage this time: knifing, clubbing, shooting, each side struggling to annihilate the other. Two warring races were at each other's throats, locked in combat and everlasting hatred.

A Muskogee clutching a rifle stepped from behind a tree; he was as old as Opothleyahola. Calmly he began loading and firing at the enemy, determined to kill as many Texans as possible. Confederates ordered him to surrender, but he kept on fighting. The old man had picked his spot to die. A moment later he was riddled with bullets. He fell to his knees, then slumped to the ground, his body lifeless, his spirit in the hands of the gods.

For the rest of the day it went on, killing and dying in the smoke and cold. Once the warriors rallied, driving back the Confederates. But the guns and wild fury of the white men began to tell. The ridge and slopes lay strewn with dead warriors, some still clutching bows or knives. Survivors, broken and bleeding, began to fall back from the hills and gullies, back to the campgrounds. But the killing wasn't over; the worst was yet to come.

There were still women and children in the camps. Many were waiting for their men fighting in the hills, believing they would somehow drive back the enemy. Others were still packing; and there were those too sick or old to flee. All day growing numbers of warriors straggled into the camps, some streaming blood, others simply walking, glancing over their shoulders as they moved along. One warrior carried another in his arms. Another came in stooped and clutching his side, blood trickling down his buckskin leggings.

A blanket of smoke hung over the meadow at the main camp, blocking out the surrounding hills, but everyone could hear the fighting. They could tell, too, that it was drawing closer. Suddenly, warriors on horseback burst through the smoke and into the campsite, then came more warriors on foot. For the first time, some of them were running.

That was when it began, with the sight of warriors running. Most in camp dropped what they were doing and rushed to the wagons or the horses. Others simply ran. James and Lizzie Scott were with their mother in one of the wagons, racing for the road at the end of the meadow. They passed a little baby frantically waving its hands, the mother and father either dead or lost. There were others, too, the lame, the stooped, the aged, all struggling to escape. Runaway horses and cattle joined in the rush, trampling the hapless. Some tried to keep order and help the weak, but it was impossible. The People no longer ran just for the road; they scattered in every direction to escape, scrambling into the hills alone or in groups. It was wild, runaway panic, and it was growing, the urge to survive crowding out all else. Every person and animal sensed instinctively what was about to happen.[4]

The fighting grew closer and louder and more distinct: the rattle of rifles, the shouting and yelling. Then it ended. The gunfire stopped and a strange quiet settled across the smoky meadow, but only for a moment. The sounds of war came again, rolling over the camp. And this time they were far more ominous: first a bugle, then hoofbeats, and finally the cry of a thousand voices—the chilling howl of evil closing in for the kill.

At the edge of the campsites, nearest the enemy, twenty warriors crouched behind rocks and trees—twenty Hillaby warriors facing an army. They were the chosen ones, the ones who would fight to the death, trading their lives for a few more moments so others might escape. Every one of them had rifles or shotguns, most taken from enemy dead. Their powder was dry, their guns poised and ready. Peering into the smoke, they waited for the thundering host of men and horses that was drawing closer.

The enemy rode out of the smoke in a solid line, riding straight for the warriors hidden in the rocks and trees. When the white men came within twenty steps, every Hillaby rose to his feet and fired. Shotguns and rifles roared, tearing a hole through the line of Confederates. Horses reared or rolled to the ground; several with empty saddles raced away. Mounted men fought back, firing wildly into the smoke. The entire Confederate line was stopped, but only for an instant. The white men withdrew and closed ranks, then charged again. The warriors, most of them waiting in the open, met them with guns and knives. Both sides began firing. The Texans closed in, nearly surrounding them. It was desperate, but hopeless. And quickly it was over. Every Hillaby but one lay dead, riddled with bullets. Somehow a warrior pulled a Confederate from the saddle and leaped on the horse, all in a single motion. Spinning the horse and firing a revolver, he shot his way free of surrounding Confederates and fled.[5]

It was nearly dark when the Confederates burst into the mea-

❖ NOW THE WOLF HAS COME

dow and the main camp. Darkness came early with the clouds and winter weather. But the campfires lighted their way—and burned away perhaps a thousand years of civilized behavior. The white men came at a gallop with weapons drawn, shouting and firing. Before them were scattered bands of the People: the old, the blind, the sick—some of the ones left behind in the panic and too weak or feeble to fend for themselves. When the white men came close, some, groping with arms outstretched, barely able to walk, struggled to their feet to get away. The Confederates rode them down, shooting and trampling.

Fanning across the campsite, the white men struck at will, running down or shooting anything that moved: women, children, cattle, dogs. It wasn't war or even murder; it was slaughter. Here and there a few fought back; mothers turned with pestles and knives to protect their young. But it was all in vain. Mothers, babies, warriors, they were run down or shot to bits. Other white men roamed the meadow, shooting or clubbing the wounded. Some of the People tried to hide in abandoned wagons, but the wagons caught fire and their only choice was to run and be shot or to die in the flames. The screams of little ones, bodies quivering and jerking, babies with bashed heads, lifeless forms everywhere: it was the nightmare of Tohopeka once again . . .

No one knows how long it lasted. Darkness put an end to it, darkness and exhaustion. The gunfire grew sporadic and died away. The white men began taking prisoners. Soon bonfires made of wagons and the scattered belongings of the dead lit the night. And around the fires bearded white men feasted on fresh beef, their eyes gleaming in the light.

Colonel James McIntosh stood beside one of the fires with his officers. Huddled nearby were some of the prisoners. No one had noticed, but the sleet had changed to snow; already it covered the ground. Colonel McIntosh, perhaps by design, had not been in the meadow to see the killing. Early reports were that hundreds of Indians lay dead on the hills or across the meadow. There were nearly two hundred prisoners as well: women, children, and slaves. Not a single warrior was taken prisoner, not one. They fought to the death or, if wounded, were butchered. So far there was no account of what had happened to Opothleyahola. No one knew if he was dead or with the ones still free and running.[6]

Then came the sound of hoofbeats and riders and the sight of a column coming in from the dark. It was Stand Watie and his regiment of Cherokee Rifles, three hundred men. Stand Watie was a dark, squatty man with long hair, a granite jaw, and a fierce, determined look. His troops were as well equipped as the white men, with rifles and revolvers, and they had the look of soldiers ready for battle. Like the Muskogees, they were fighting their own civil war. Their enemies were Keetoowahs, the Cherokees with Opothleyahola. The Keetoowahs, they said, had taken some of their women. But it was much more than that. Their feud was also one that harkened back to the old days when the Cherokees lived in the East. It was a blood feud, too, and it could have only one ending. Colonel Watie reported to his commander and the two began to plan for the following day. Tomorrow, Stand Watie promised himself, he would dip his sword in the blood of the enemy. The Keetoowahs and any who rode with them would die: the Muskogees, the Seminoles, and, if he were still alive, Opothleyahola of Tuckabatchee; all would die.[7]

That was when a soldier brought something to Colonel McIntosh, something found in camp. It was a wrinkled, ink-smeared letter promising Union troops and help for the Indians with Opothleyahola. Perhaps James McIntosh handed the letter to Stand Watie. If so, Stand Watie would have shown utter contempt, wondering how Opothleyahola could have hung his fate on such a promise. Did he not know who had written the letter? Did he not understand that the author was a liar and cheat who had leeched a living off the Cherokee Nation and other nations in the Territory for years? The letter was the product of the worst sort, the type who feigned compassion and concern but would sell his soul or the soul of any person or any nation for money and position. The letter was written by a teacher and missionary—E. H. Carruth.[8]

124

CHAPTER
❖
SEVENTEEN

A World of White

The People struggled all night, groping through the snow and cutting winds. Many were dazed and in shock from what had happened. Blankly staring into the dark, they staggered ahead, placing one foot feebly before the next, as if in a trance. Their dreams had been shattered in the meadow and along the hillside at Chustenahlah, but their nightmare had only begun.

There was no time to rest. Too soon it would be light and the enemy would return. Many struggled ahead in large parties with wagons. The lucky ones had a few head of cattle and extra horses. But large numbers were scattered across the land with nothing: no wagons, no stock or food, nothing but the clothes and blankets on their backs. In the panic they had lost all they owned. Others traveled in small groups: a few families bundled in blankets, the men leading horses carrying women and children. Opothleyahola was with one of the parties. He was still alive, but sick with fever—and dread.

The People were hopelessly scattered across the hills and even onto the prairie to the west. With first light they could be seen in every direction, trailing off into the gray, snowy mist. They looked like tiny birds struggling in a world of white ice and white death, a white man's world.

It was colder and the snow was growing worse, much worse, as the day cycle deepened. Pushed on by the winds, it came down in lateral sheets, sometimes cutting visibility, to a few steps. All the while they had lived in the Territory, the People had never seen anything like it. In the gullies and draws the snow piled up in drifts to the waist, then higher than a man's head. Wagons bogged down, parties became stranded or separated in the blinding white. The cattle got away and turned south, putting their backs to the winds. One party had to stop for another reason; half hidden in a thicket of black-jacks, they waited. Underneath a wagon a woman was giving birth with only straw for a bed and pinned-up blankets to keep out the wind and ice.[1]

Still later, those with Opothleyahola heard gunfire somewhere in the snow and fog to the left. Then it ended. The People could only hope and pray they would not be next. As the enemy approached, many of the fearful and disillusioned tried to surrender, hoping for the best. Some became prisoners; others were butchered. There was no pattern or reason to it. In an instant a prisoner might be lying in the snow, riddled with bullets, or with his throat slit ear to ear, his scalp missing. A prisoner's fate hung on his captor's whim or fancy of the moment.

Growing numbers of the weak and dispirited began to fall behind. Some of the grandmothers and grandfathers said good-bye forever to family and quietly walked away, vanishing into the storm. A number of warriors picked a spot to die. They stopped in their tracks, raised their arms, and began to chant the songs of death and war, calling on the spirits to join them. Then turning south, they squatted down with bow or war club and waited for death, either from Confederates or the cold.

By the end of the day, the real enemy was no longer the Confederates but the weather. The wind had slackened at last and the snow was coming to an end, but not the cold. It was deepening. For a night and a day the People had struggled to escape the white man. But they had spent their energy, and the frigid air was closing in. Already, many with exposed hands and faces were showing the first signs of freezing: the tingling and numbness and, soon, the pale ashen color of dead skin.

Most of them made camp before night. Whenever possible, the People camped half hidden in ravines and thickets. Some stripped bark from the south side of trees or snapped off limbs from rotting logs, anything they could find that was dry and would burn. A few pulled bird's nests from beneath their coats to use as kindling. Soon there were smokeless, little fires scattered throughout the thickets and icy ravines, with groups of hungry, half-frozen survivors huddling close to stay alive.

126

That night the sky began to clear, and in the east an icy sliver of moon appeared, skirting the clouds. The moon and stars gave the snow a soft bluish tint. A last rush of raw wind swept the thickets, causing ice-coated trees to creak and pop; then came the silence—cold, bitter, and dreadful. Tomorrow the day would be clear and bright, the type of weather where anyone could be spotted in the snow. There were still no Union troops in sight; perhaps they would never come. Most of the People were out of food, and Kansas was at least seven risings away.[2]

All day the Confederates had tried to follow bundled up in anything they could find to wear—overcoats, dusters, jackets. Some had jammed straw inside their clothes to keep warm. Many tied strips of leather or cloth over the crown of their hats and under their chins to keep headgear from blowing away. Others had wrapped themselves in the blankets of the Indian dead. Scarves pulled up over nose and mouth, strips of rags wrapped around hands: they did everything they could to keep out the cold, and still it wasn't enough.

At first the Confederates were in a single unit, but with the weather it became impossible to keep so many together. Finally, the white men and Stand Watie's Cherokees divided forces. For the rest of the day all of them picked their way north into the wind: horses plodding through the snow, men holding onto their hats. It was easy to trail the Indians for a while by following the camp litter and personal belongings, the guns thrown away, the bodies. But the snow soon covered everything, even the dead.

Stand Watie's men happened upon one party of wagons and a large band of the People, hundreds of them. The warriors were huddled together on a hillside under cover of rocks and trees. They outnumbered the Cherokees, but had no guns or powder. As the Cherokees closed in, the warriors waited with knives drawn. It was desperate, bloody, and brief. The Cherokees struck without mercy, killing as many as they could; one was the war captain Alligator. The rest of the People ran for their lives into the wind and snow.

For the rest of the day the Cherokees and the Texans, nearly as miserable as the ones they chased, struggled through a frozen world of swirling white. By nightfall some of the white men had seen enough and were openly talking of turning back. So was their commander, James McIntosh. In the morning they would fall back to

Arkansas and winter quarters, he decided. Stand Watie's Cherokees would retire as well.[3]

But not far away, at another Confederate campsite, it was a different story. Warming his hands by the fire was Daniel McIntosh. His men had been riding all day as well, coming up fast from the south, and he had no plans for turning back. Daniel had not even begun. He and his commander, Douglas Cooper, were making plans for the next day and the following week, and for tracking down survivors no matter how brutal the cold. Opothleyahola had not been found, they had learned. He was not among the dead or captured at Chustenahlah. He was ahead somewhere, and they would find him. The winds died and the skies began to clear above Confederate camps. Everyone in the McIntosh clan understood what tomorrow would bring. Opothleyahola and his followers would be largely in the open, unable to hide and leaving tracks in the snow if they tried to flee. Soon the McIntosh would finish what had begun in the hills and the meadow near Chustenahlah. Soon Opothleyahola would be within their grasp.[4]

❖ NOW THE WOLF HAS COME

CHAPTER
❖
EIGHTEEN

The Hunted

The man eased through thicket and snow, clutching a bow that was set with an arrow. Slowly he raised then lowered a foot, careful not to make a sound in the snow. He lifted and lowered the other foot the same way, and all the while his crouching body slipped ahead like a spirit. His head never glanced left or right, never jerked or bobbed; always his eyes remained fixed on something ahead in the shadows.

For what seemed like most of a morning the man slowly stalked the animal in the shadows, his hunger sensing out the game. The animals had hardly stirred since the blizzard; they would have to be tracked down if hunted. Stalking downwind and pushing aside his cold, the hunter moved at angles and zig-zag patterns, drawing closer. When the animal raised its head and sniffed the air the man stopped, standing still, as frozen as the icy landscape. Then the animal would look away and he would resume his stalking. At last the man was forty steps away. Slowly he drew back the string of his bow and took aim. For a heartbeat man and weapon were one, poised and taut in the stillness and the cold. Then came a swish and a pop. The animal leaped from the shadows: it was a large buck with an arrow sunk deep behind the shoulder. The deer jumped and raced into a clearing, then staggered and fell, its blood mixing with the snow. There was a jerk, a quivering spasm, and it was over.

The hunter straightened and walked to his prey. He squatted beside the deer and placed his hands on the antlers. "I commend you for your strength and courage," he said, "and honor all that you were when you lived. And I beg your pardon for ending your life, but the little ones and the women are starving and will die without food." The man whispered a prayer of thanksgiving to the One who breathed life into every creature and made all things possible. Then he bled and gutted the deer, the warm pools of red melting the snow. Next he grabbed the animal by its legs and in a single motion slung it across his shoulders as he rose to his feet. He turned and retraced his steps in the snow, through the thicket and back to the ones who were waiting.

It was sunny and brutally cold for the next several days, and all the while the enemy prowled the land, in the hills and the flatlands below. The Confederates fanned out in every direction, searching far and near for the People. The white men and Stand Watie's Cherokees went away, and for a moment the People hoped they could flee. But others came to take their place. No one could be sure from the distance, but it looked like Cooper and the McIntosh. Everywhere it seemed there were Confederates on horses, squinting into the icy horizon, searching always for dark, distant forms moving in the snow. It was utterly remorseless the way they worked, sweeping across one section of country, then another.

The People were hopelessly scattered in bands large and small, in every direction. A lucky few, perhaps, were only a rising or two from Kansas. The rest were far away. Many were still hiding in the ravines and hills near the battlefield at Chustenahlah. In desperation some tried to break free and race for the Kansas border. The Confederates tracked them in the snow, hunting down and killing on sight. Mostly the scattered survivors remained in the hills, crouching in the shadows and praying they would not be found; coming out after the enemy had passed, only to find the lifeless, bullet-riddled bodies of those who had tried to escape.

At first the People survived by killing and eating most of their remaining animals, sometimes devouring the meat raw, for smoke and fire would give away their hiding places. Cattle and oxen they ate, then the dogs, and finally some of the horses, the only animals that could get them north to safety. But it was not enough, for most of the animals had been lost in the fighting and the storm. In the end, some of them tried to survive by picking through horse droppings for undigested kernels of grain. To keep the remaining ponies alive, they scraped back the snow so horses could get at the grass, or they fed them bark from trees. The ponies died anyway, just like their owners.

130

There were others with no animals at all. They turned to the thickets and the land to survive, scratching through the snow for roots, nuts, wild grasses, whatever they could find. Some tried to make a drink from the bark of trees. Still others tried to cook and eat leather straps or bridles, then the fringe from their shirts, anything that could keep them alive. But their hunger consumed them, crowding out any other thoughts and made worse by the bitter weather. In some camps the weak and wounded were the lucky ones. They would roll up in a little lump of frozen flesh, numb to the hunger and pain, simply waiting for the cold to work its will. When there was nothing left to eat and the screams of the little ones would not end, haggard mothers could only sit and watch in hollow-eyed stupor and pray for death to end their babies' misery. Some of the little ones even begged their mothers to let them die. The mothers killed their babies first, then themselves. Others went mad and wandered into the open country, longing to be shot.

Only those who remembered the old ways had a chance to survive. Hunters with bows and arrows could stalk and kill an animal in silence without alerting the enemy. They might bring in a deer or even a buffalo. Another with a snare might trap a rabbit or a bird. But for those who had lived too long by guns and metal tools, for those who knew only the ways of the white man, there could be but one result: their choice was to starve or freeze in the hills or stake everything on a merciful capture and a life of submission and slavery. It was as Opothleyahola had foretold.

Even in the best of camps the People began to grow weak and sick. It was too much, living in the open and the bitter cold: the game was not stirring, and the enemy was always too near to venture far for food. Sometimes the Confederates came nearly in sight of the camps. And every day there was the distant pop of gunfire and a reminder of what might await them all: some unfortunate had been discovered, someone had tried to surrender. Every day, too, a growing number of the sick and wounded breathed their last, giving up the life spirit. Always the most pitiful and innocent were the ones who suffered most. Some of the dead were babies only a few days old. The dead were stripped of clothes for the living. But there was no way to bury them, for there were no tools and the frozen ground was as hard as flint. The People could only cover the bodies of their loved ones with snow, knowing that at night the frozen forms would be food for the wolves.

Desperate to keep warm, the People huddled together, half naked or in rags. Some tied bits of cloth to switches, forming pitiful little tents, but they gave no shelter. Mothers cut up horsehides to sew into crude moccasins for the children. Yet they had nothing but knives to fashion and string together hides. The footwear quickly began to unravel, and soon the little ones were again standing barefoot in the snow. Another day of hideous cold passed, and then another. The sun shone brightly, but it gave no warmth, and the enemy continued his relentless searching. Every night the People gathered close with backs turned to tiny fires, staring out into the darkness and the cold, watching and listening for danger. Even the young and strong grew weak, their faces gaunt. In some camps the cries of the little ones slowly ebbed and softened to exhausted, piteous whimpers. It seemed as if the agony would never end, that there was nothing left for them all but to starve or freeze.[1]

CHAPTER
❖
NINETEEN

The Gods

It was the clearest of weather and the deepest of cold. The sky was bitter blue; the air was frozen crystal. In every direction the land was a dazzling, overpowering white, so bright it nearly blinded. Every creek and stream was frozen over, the ice thick enough to hold a man or a horse. A single wayward pine stood in the open, split and broken at the top, its sap frozen. It was the worst cold the country had seen in nearly a lifetime.

Coming through the cold was a column of men on horseback, snow flying from hooves, breaths of steam shooting from men and animals. It was Douglas Cooper and Daniel McIntosh, followed by their command. All of them wore heavy coats or dusters or were wrapped in blankets. They were covered from head to foot. Most had scarves pulled up to protect the face and hats pulled low, leaving exposed only slits for the eyes. Despite their headgear and the overcoats and blankets, they were all clearly in misery. None of them had ever felt anything like the bitter cold. In Texas and the Territory there was usually snow and cold every winter, but nothing like this. They had heard of such weather in Kansas and farther north in Nebraska Territory, but for them it was unbearable.

Adding to their misery were old frustrations, creeping in like the cold. Soon after parting with James McIntosh, Douglas Cooper had called together his troops as planned, to march along the Arkansas River and get behind Opothleyahola. But there had been problems concentrating all of the units and acquiring munitions.

Next there was a shortage of provisions. Then the teamsters had deserted the wagons. Instead of abandoning wagons and pressing ahead, Cooper had stalled. While James McIntosh and Stand Watie closed in on Opothleyahola in the hills and meadows at Chustenahlah, Douglas Cooper had barely moved at all. And Daniel McIntosh, along with the other Confederate Indians, seethed in frustration. Whether Colonel Cooper was again holed up in his tent in a drunken stupor, no one would say. At last, Cooper had pulled out with his column, moving across the snow-covered ground. But he no longer traveled for the frozen Arkansas, for word had arrived of the battle with Opothleyahola. The only chance to join in the fighting was to march due north by the straightest possible route.

For the next day or two, Cooper and the McIntosh made good time, considering the cold. The country was mostly frozen prairie and hills. Along the way they met James McIntosh and Stand Watie. They, but not Cooper's Texans, and certainly not the McIntosh of Coweta, had given up the chase and were returning to winter quarters.

Cooper and Daniel McIntosh combed the land for several days after passing Chustenahlah. Everywhere were tracks in the snow, scattered bits of camp gear, abandoned wagons, and bodies. Sometimes they encountered whole families returning south, those who had given up on Opothleyahola and were going home. It was from the stragglers and refugees that Cooper and Daniel learned for certain that Opothleyahola was still alive. The Confederates took a number of prisoners. They killed their share of stragglers as well, especially those who tried to run, turning it into a sport, tracking and running down victims as if they were rabbits or wild turkeys. It was from the prisoners, too, that they learned of many families scattered to the west across the open country. Perhaps Opothleyahola was with them. Taking no chances, the Confederates turned west into the plains, searching.

They found more tracks and abandoned wagons, then starving, emaciated cattle limping along on frozen stumps, and finally more bodies, frozen human forms half covered in snowdrifts, eyes open and staring into the bitter sky. One of the dead lay with forearm raised, as if reaching out for help or mercy.

At one point they noticed several figures in the distance. The figures turned and began to run. In an instant the Confederates went after them, horses kicking up the snow. At the head of the column was W. E. McIntosh, a relative of Daniel. Young, thin, and fuzzy chinned, he wanted desperately to prove his manhood and be the one who killed Opothleyahola. The Confederates bore down on the ones ahead. The figures on the ground were women as well as men; they were scattering in every direction. Then one of the men, resigned to his fate, suddenly stopped and turned. He stood waiting for the Confederates who were closing in. A shot rang out, and he fell to his knees, then slumped face down into the snow. Young McIntosh leaped from his horse, his pistol still smoking. He raced up to the body and rolled it over. Maybe he had killed a war captain; maybe it was Opothleyahola . . . The dead man was a Cherokee. Probably he was a Keetoowah from John Drew's old regiment, hoping to sneak home before anyone noticed he was missing.[1]

Opothleyahola had to be close, maybe less than a day's ride away. Yet there was still no sign of him. The Confederates decided to fan out in every direction and hunt him down. Leading the Confederates were two men, each in his own way driven to find Opothleyahola. Cooper, still hoping to get his hands on Indian gold, needed him captured alive. Daniel McIntosh wished him dead.

The southerners began to suffer frozen hands and feet. And despite precautions, they began to run low on food. But Cooper and Daniel would not let up. The men began to roast slabs of Indian ponies they had seized along the way. The smoke in their camps smelled like sweaty horse. For four bitter days they remained in the open country, hunting and scanning. Yet even as they continued their relentless searching, pausing only to rub life into frozen hands and feet, there was another development.[2]

No one could say for sure when they first noticed what was happening. The animals were the first to sense it. Along the creek banks and in the faraway hills, deer moved even farther into the thickets and small animals burrowed deeper into the snow. The air seemed to grow heavy and thick, and from the northeast a faint wind, cold and wet, began to stir. Icy tree limbs and branches began to move and pop. Then came the clouds, dark and fast-moving, blotting out the sun. Sleet started to fall and the rising winds began to moan and wail; another blizzard was coming. For a second time an icy blast was roaring off the plains.

The next morning the Confederates awoke to a blanket of fresh sleet and snow and winds as savage and bitter as the first storm. The men, all but one, slowly rose to their feet, still clutching the blankets they had slept in. One of the Texans failed to stir. An officer walked over and kicked at the sleeping Confederate's boots then stooped down and shook him, but nothing happened. The

135

officer rolled the man on his back before he understood what was wrong. The sleeping Confederate lay perfectly still with eyes half open staring into the swirling snow. He had frozen to death.[3] That was enough for the southerners. Cooper ordered the entire command to break camp and be in the saddle within an hour: they would return to winter quarters before everyone perished from the cold. Nothing human could live in it; not even the Indians. Shivering and half frozen, men stiffly saddled up and mounted, then wheeled their mounts and headed south. The Texans moved out first, then the Choctaws and Chickasaws, and finally the Creeks. One of the last to leave was Daniel McIntosh. He sat on his horse, still proud and erect, still wearing his duster and hat, with a blanket wrapped about his shoulders. Even in the ice and bitter cold his eyes blazed. He kept staring north into the wind and the swirling snow. Somewhere out there was Opothleyahola, still alive. Daniel could feel it. He looked up into the falling snow, then into the distance.[4]

To Daniel it seemed as if Opothleyahola was forever just beyond his grasp. Whenever the Confederates closed in, there was always something that allowed him to slip away. At the rounded mountain it was darkness; at Bird Creek it was a call to break off fighting and reinforce another part of the line; now it was the weather. It was as if Daniel and his family were caught in a cyclic web; as if it were forever their destiny to track and chase their enemy, but never to finish the kill.

The weather would have to do the job. The bitter cold and merciless winds would avenge his father, Daniel told himself. There would be nothing left of Opothleyahola but a frozen carcass for the wolves and the crows. Then Daniel turned and rode off through the snow to catch up with the column.

The Confederates were wrong, all of them. They did not see the truth. The white men, Stand Watie, and most of all those like Daniel McIntosh, who had long since rejected their blood—they could not begin to understand what was happening.

The storm was not a curse; it was a gift and it came from the gods. The mighty wind swept the land clean. Sacred symbol of breath and life, it swept away every trace of where the People had been, quickly covering with snow their tracks, their baggage, even their dead. The swirling snow and clouds shrouded the hills, making them vanish, shielding and hiding the innocent and the faithful. The white man imagined that, with his guns and machines, he was master of the earth, but he was a fool. His power was nothing compared to that of the gods. He could not control the weather. He could not make the earth shake or the heavens fall. There was but one master of the earth and the heavens: the One who gave and took all life and breath. The true gods were the gods of wind, snow, rain, stars, and fire; the goddess, Mother Earth, and the goddess of the moon; the grandfathers who were the trees and the hills and the spirits of the animal world and the dead. And they came now, all of them, each in their own way, to shield and guide their children the Muskogees, and to lead from harm the one who had always been true—the one called Opothleyahola.

The McIntosh had never understood the power of Opothleyahola. Even some of the People did not truly see. He had powers that no one had imagined. Opothleyahola had called down the storm.

For the first time in days the People were free to move. Across the hills and ravines, even in the open country they would be safe from the Confederates. No one would see them in the blinding storm, and there would be no trace of where they had been. Every track would fill with snow; every campsite would become a drift. They would be as ghosts moving in the wind. Some of the People, those too weak or sick, would not survive it. They would perish in the storm as the weak must always perish. But the strong would live and the Muskogee Nation would survive, if only the People would rise up and move into the face of the winds.

And so it came to be. Somehow the People called up their last remnant of strength. Gaunt men hitched half-starved ponies to wagons. Others bundled up whatever they were strong enough to carry in blankets slung over their backs. Many simply rose to their feet, turned into the wind, and began the long walk, clutching nothing but a ragged blanket or a shawl wrapped about the shoulders. And each of them took something else as well. In their hearts they carried the words of their leader, remembering how he urged them to trust in the old ways and in one another. They remembered, too, his promise, that he would be in Kansas waiting for them. Somewhere to the north there were warm fires, blankets, and food. Somewhere in the distance was another chance at life. And they would find it even if they had to march across the state of Kansas and camp before the gates of Fort Leavenworth.[5]

CHAPTER

TWENTY

The Great Father

The miccos were peering out the window as they approached the station. They passed black men in work shirts and ragged trousers lugging crates onto wagons. Then came more crates, an enormous stack of them higher than a man's head and longer than several coach cars, placed neatly by the train tracks. Next were soldiers and, finally, on the platform in front of the station, a veritable menagerie from the white man's world. There were vendors and hucksters, army sutlers and prostitutes, civil servants, animal acts, diplomats, liquor dealers, men with shell games, and those seeking government contracts. There were pickpockets, wire pullers, con artists, and one or two elected officials surrounded by their toadies and sycophants. All of them were mixing and jostling, filling the platform as well as the station, even spilling into the muddy street. The Indian delegation had arrived in Washington.

From New York the Indians and their railway hosts, following the route of Abraham Lincoln after his election the year before, had traveled south through Philadelphia and Baltimore to the capital city. In New York the financier was lord of the realm, in other cities and towns, the industrialist; but in Washington the trickster and egotist were king. Mostly Washington was a gathering place of egos: the vain and the vindictive, the pietistic and the petty. Above all, it was a city filled with those for whom nothing was too low or foul if the price was right. Along the Potomac everything was for sale—weapons contracts, jobs, lives, integrity; only the conditions and terms were a matter of dispute. Other cities were larger and more refined, many were more attractive, but no other place was so greedy or grasping.[1]

There were good men in Washington, leaders who were brave and true and even a few who were great, but always they were the exception. In certain ways Washington was hardly a city at all, for it produced little or nothing of substance: neither food, nor clothing, nor tools, nor even weapons. If the entire metropolis had vanished from the earth, along with the Confederate capital in Richmond, both North and South would have gained. Some considered Washington the symbol of all that was hopeless in human nature. Its most celebrated citizens were often dregs of the land, men whose only talent was deception and cajolery and a will to claw to the top of a dung heap no matter how many lives they wrecked along the way. Others looked upon the city as a tribute to those who could not distinguish between philosophy and fraud, policy and theft, or even self-defense and murder. It was a place where anything went—as long as leaders couched their acts in moralistic language. For it was the habit of the English-speaking everywhere, particularly those who fancied themselves democratic and free, to engage in self-deception.

It was cold when the Indians arrived in Washington. Stepping from the coach, they could barely make their way through the station for the crowd, but they would not be detoured. The miccos had been away from their families and homes for too many days and were anxious to meet the Great Father. From the station they traveled to a hotel by carriage. They saw more slaves, lugging carts or walking with tubs or bundles; and there were white men on horseback, as well as others in carriages and horse trolleys, all coming or going. Wandering in no particular direction were stray cats, dogs, drunks, organ grinders, sneak thieves, and even an occasional hog rooting through the scattered garbage. There were soldiers, too, at every intersection, directing traffic and pulling over carriages and wagons whenever large units of troops passed. The entire city was part armed camp, part circus.

At the hotel another crowd, children mostly, with a sprinkling of adults, soon formed when the Indians arrived. They stood in the street looking up at the windows, hoping for a glimpse of the "savages." Not satisfied, some of the adults went inside, then upstairs to the rooms, peeking around open doors or through keyholes. It was a common occurrence. Every time a delegation of Indians arrived in Washington the curious gathered. They were fascinated that anyone so "alien" and "bizarre" could live in America. Indians could barely walk into the lobby before they were confronted by white men, who touched their garments and fingered their ornaments. Let an Indian show himself at the window of his room and those below would step back in fright. In Washington as elsewhere, the miccos were treated to whatever they desired. Food, tobacco, liquor, and women were theirs for the asking—and often without asking, for a town like Washington was awash in liquor, and prostitutes were as common as lobbyists. One of the madams said it best: it would be impossible to carry on government without her. The girls for the Indians were hand-me-downs from the army camps, but that was of no concern. Besides, the Indians had a medical doctor for an escort in George Cutler; he could always check the girls for disease. Repeatedly the miccos were showered with gifts: nuts, candies, clothes, uniforms, cheap watches, and cheaper jewelry. Long before, the white man had learned that gift giving was a symbol of friendship and civility to Indians, and the quickest way to their hearts. Before they could meet with the Great Father, though, the miccos received a tour of the city. It was always the custom to give Indians a tour of the town.[2]

In appearance Washington had an unkempt and half-finished look. The buildings were mostly red brick or brown. In front of some, small barren trees sprouted up through broken sidewalks. The streets were either dust or mud, except for the few that were ineptly paved with ill-fitting stone. A gigantic crane jutted up through an unfinished capitol building, and not far away great blocks of stone lay scattered about the base of what was to be a monument to the first president. Wherever space permitted, it seemed, there were military encampments. Tents colored white, green, and brown were scattered about in every park and on a distant ridge beyond the fetid marsh and muddy waters that formed the Potomac River.

The miccos visited the Federal Arsenal first. At the arsenal they inspected what seemed like a forest of rifles, stacked in endless lines and awaiting distribution to armies farther south. They saw as well rows of cannon and enormous shore guns—the type that shook the ground when fired and hurled thousand-pound projectiles at unseen enemies miles away. But what impressed them most was a military camp on a ridge called Arlington Heights.

The air at the camp was pungent with the smells of kerosene, saddle wax, and burned gunpowder. In every direction were tents, field cannons, horses being shod and curried, couriers coming and going, and, above all, men marching and drilling. On that single ridge were more men in uniform than warriors in all of the Muskogee Confederation. And as the Indians considered everything in front of them and all they had seen or heard—the endless countryside, the towns and cities, the industries, the technical wonders, and the countless promises—they came to grips with a simple truth. The white man was great and powerful not because of his weapons, his God, or his government; neither was he great because of his money; the white man was a mighty force, above all else, because there were so many of him.[3]

They saw the immense stone palace of a treasury building, standing squarely between the White House and the Capitol. They might have noticed, too, a bronze statue of Thomas Jefferson holding the Constitution. The statue was covered in green mold, the work of the weather and the years, some said. Then came the War Department. It was altogether fitting that a department devoted to war had been in charge of Indian affairs through most of the nation's history.

At the War Department as elsewhere, the miccos encountered earnest looks and reassuring words from bureaucrats and officers in blue. Help would be forthcoming, they heard repeatedly. The government would spare no expense: men, money, supplies, whatever it took to provide for those who were loyal to the Union. Wherever they went the miccos heard or saw evidence of Union support and power: marching troops, beating drums, cavalry passing. Surely, they reasoned, such a mighty nation could spare troops to save friends on the western frontier. Everywhere, too, they saw bureaucrats and assistants to bureaucrats, and still more assistants to assistants. The bureaucrats and assistants made their lives in shadowy offices and file rooms that were covered in mounds of paper. They rarely left what they called their work until the last glint of light had left the western sky. They never saw the grass or touched the ground. They were the whitest white men the Indians had ever seen. And always, at the side of the miccos or discreetly in the shadows wherever they went were their escorts from the railroad: the men with tailored suits and tailored smiles and lifeless eyes.[4]

And if the Indians were by chance in town on a Sunday, they would have been treated to a special sight as well, for there was no place more pious or pompous than Washington on a Sunday morning. Bloated statesmen smelling of bourbon and rosewater; bejeweled ladies carrying the scent of perfume, powder, and occasionally laudanum; officers in blue; hatchet-faced clerks; petty officials and

THE GREAT FATHER ❖

petty swindlers—they all filled the streets in carriages and cabs, flocking to church to hear fine sermons on sacrifice, loyalty, valor, and devotion to duty. Another battle or two and the congregations would be joined by soldiers limping in on crutches or with empty sleeves. Soon the wounded and dying would fill the churches, day and night, using them as hospitals. The same would happen to museums, art galleries, public buildings, and even private homes.

The Indians toured the unfinished capitol building with its marble chambers furnished in red, bronze, and gold. Yet even at the capitol building the miccos did not find James Lane, the senator from Kansas. After all the many miles and many faces, they would never see him. Perhaps it was unavoidable. There was someone else, though, who knew all about the Indians in Washington and who was eager to meet them at last.

The miccos were whisked away to an out-of-the-way chamber of a nondescript building where they would meet the Great Father, Abraham Lincoln. They walked into the room and found the Great Father sitting alone and waiting. Like everyone else, he assured the miccos he would not let them down, that his red children would be saved from harm. Soon troops would move south, he promised, to destroy Confederate armies and to protect Opothleyahola and restore the land. He knew all about the plight of those in Indian Territory. At the missions and the forts in Kansas, and at the Interior Department were those who kept him informed.

It was all very impressive; it was designed to impress. It was also a lie. The man the Indians met was not the president. The real Abraham Lincoln never knew the miccos were in town. All of the ones the Indians had met—at the Capitol, the treasury, and the arsenal—all of those who had come forward with a handshake or a reassuring word, they were all part of a monstrous fraud. Technically, they worked for the government, but in truth they were the kept creatures and hirelings of others. Outside of government were men with ideas of their own for Indian Territory and plans as well for the ones aligned with Opothleyahola. They had largely influenced events in Kansas and Washington since the miccos had first ridden north from the Territory pleading for help.[5]

Indian Territory was a bounty of pasturelands, timberlands, coal and iron ore, and along the rivers some of the finest farmland in America. As settlers poured west and good land grew scarce, growing numbers had begun to look with envy at the forested hills, the bottomlands, and the prairies stretching between Texas and Kansas. So had the railroads.

142

Even before the war, railroad survey crews were swarming over Indian Territory, noting the vast resources and potential wealth. Some of the rail companies had even applied for rights-of-way and permission to buy lands. For nearly a decade political hacks and puppets of the railroads had spoken of Indian Territory as a plum to be seized, and of its inhabitants as little more than obstacles to progress—no different from buffalo or gypsum weed. Besides, as was often said, the railroads and white civilization would be good for the Indian. For years in nearby Kansas, other worthies presumably promoting the abolition of slavery had served as agents for the railroads and quietly slipped across the border to examine possibilities for constructing lines. If only the government would allow construction, the companies could acquire enormous holdings as a right-of-way, and fortunes could be made selling timber, minerals, or property to land-hungry settlers. It could be the chance of a lifetime.

The war for the Union would furnish such a chance. No matter that Indian Territory had been given to someone else for "as long as the grass shall grow and waters run." Never mind that the land was already settled with homes, towns, and farms by the Muskogee Nation and twenty other nations. Never mind that the inhabitants had started with nothing but bare hands and stone tools, surviving drouth, starvation, plague, cold, and despair. It was of no importance that Indian Territory already had a civilization. The railroads saw only a land that was rich and fertile, and if the land held homes and fields, so much the better. They would have it all; the railroads would pick it clean.[6]

After the war the Indians who had sided with the South could be stripped of their lands for committing treason; it would be easy to justify. Enormous tracts of the richest land could be handed over to the railroads in the name of punishing the guilty and promoting progress. Following a war with southern agrarians, terms like "industry" and "progress" would be synonymous for a hundred years. But what of the Indians who were loyal to the Union, men like Sands, White King, Bob Deer, and Jo Ellis? And what of the thousands with Opothleyahola? They were sacrificing their homesteads and possibly their lives for the sake of the northern cause. Their only crime was loyalty and courage in the face of overwhelming odds. How could they be stripped of their lands, too? And how could it be done in a way that would mollify the legalistic and even the kindhearted? The gentlemen from the railroads knew how. They had a plan.

WINTER'S LITTLE BROTHER

(January)

CHAPTER
❖
TWENTY-ONE

The Cycle

The sun was low in the west, breaking through parting clouds. The last few flakes of snow sifted down through the sunshine and onto the icy landscape. Everywhere the land was colored in shades of white: the sparkling white of late afternoon sun on snow and the bluish white that comes with lengthening shadows. The winds had stilled but the cold was deepening. It would be another terrible night.

A party of wagons and famished, broken-down ponies creaked along through the snow, heading up a gentle rise. There were other horses, too, with just enough strength to carry sick, emaciated forms. For days they had struggled along, all of them: the sick, the wounded, and the starved. Alongside the wagons and ponies were thin, haggard figures in blankets and rags. Some of them left a trail of blood in the snow as they walked or limped along, the sharp ice cutting into frozen feet. There was no formation or order as they moved; the wagons were in no particular line. Every wagon and person moved at their own pace as if in a trance, unaware of the rest of the world. Faces peeking through rags and blankets seemed more dead than alive: the ashen and frozen skin, the eyes sunken and hollow. On some ice crusted around nostrils and lips. Behind, in the distance, other wagons and scattered groups on foot stretched as far as the eye could see. And somewhere farther back were the war captains who were still alive: Holata Micco, Halleck Tustenuggee, and maybe Little Captain. It was growing late but everyone kept plodding, bound for the open ridge in front.

Several days before, a runner had found them as they were traveling north. Half-starved and nearly frozen, the runner had returned from the Delaware Nation in Kansas. Gasping for breath and warmth he told his story: there were no troops in Kansas on their way to help. Northern forces were threatened by Confederates in Missouri and had no units to spare. The Delawares were armed and ready to march to the aid of their Muskogee brothers, but none could leave without permission from Union authorities, and so far no one in power would allow it. There was other news as well. Officials at the Indian Bureau had been reached; they understood what was happening. They knew Opothleyahola and thousands with him were struggling to reach them. An appeal had gone out to every farmer in the region for food, blankets, anything they could spare. Also the military was stockpiling tents and rations. And soon additional supplies would arrive from the east by mule train or rail. If only the Indians could fight their way free from Confederates and the weather, there would be food, blankets, and warm fires waiting in Kansas.[1]

For the next three risings the People had pressed ahead, putting their last bits of life and belief into the promise of aid. At last they were in Kansas. Behind them was only death and sadness, but on the ridge in front they would be able to see far north—into the new land and their new home. In one of the lead wagons was Opothleyahola. He was burning with fever and often delirious, and there was a tightness in his chest that was growing worse. In another wagon was someone else he had met along the way, someone he had not seen for months, one of his daughters. She was coughing up blood and gasping and wheezing for air. Her days were numbered.[2]

Just before reaching the top of the rise, the wagon with Opothleyahola came to a stop. Two younger men walked over to help their leader out of the wagon to the ground; he no longer had the strength to stand alone. The younger men carefully assisted him from the wagon, then, holding his arms, they slowly walked a few steps to the crest of the ridge and a view of the future.

In the distance, looking north as far as the eye could see, was a vast, frozen plain, open and endless—nothing more. There were no forts or settlements, no farms, no fires, no waiting tents, no blankets, or food; there was nothing . . . It had all been a lie: the promises of troops and support, and the promise of supplies. It was another hideous white man's lie. There was only a wasteland locked in ice, without any sign of life or hope. For Opothleyahola it was too much to bear, and he turned away. But just as he moved he caught a vision of something in the distance to the north. He lifted his head and peered again into the gathering frozen twilight. What he saw chilled the blood more than any storm or blizzard.

Ahead he could see the dim light from a cabin window. Inside the cabin was a man sitting on the floor, staring into the embers of a dying fire. Glowing coals struggled to outline cabin walls and overhead beams. Somehow the very air carried a presence that was sinister and threatening, and just out of sight. Occasionally, the coals popped and hissed, spitting flame and sparks. Images of light and shadow would appear—dancing, magical forms that filled the room with their power. Light and motion would drive away the dark, and the spirit world would come to life. But the flame would die down and the images vanish. Back would come the night. And outside the cabin there were other forms as well, faint shadowy images gathering in growing numbers. They huddled in the darkness, underneath the brush and trees, staring at the window and the man inside. Finally, one of them standing away from the others came forward and raised his head, and an eerie mournful cry rose into the frozen night. It was the wolf pack gathering for the kill.

EPILOGUE

Nearly nine thousand people from more than twenty nations fled north with Opothleyahola in the winter of 1861–62. Remarkably, of that number possibly seven thousand starving and freezing wretches finally staggered into Kansas. The rest lay dead in the frozen mud and bloody ice of Indian Territory or were in the hands of Confederate forces. But once the survivors were in Kansas, their misery was far from over; in certain ways, it had only begun. Over the next four years many more would perish. Herded into death camps called federal compounds and security centers as well as onto reservations, they would die by the hundreds from disease, exposure, and even starvation. Above all, they would die from treachery and neglect.[1]

Government contracts and promises of supplies would never be honored. The few tents and blankets that arrived were paper thin, moth-eaten, or ripped. New clothing and footwear were practically nonexistent. Before long, many with frostbitten feet could be seen in the camps dragging themselves about by their hands and arms. Others with both frozen hands and feet simply lay in the snow, helpless to move. Standard rations were condemned flour and, once a week, a tiny portion of rotted bacon still covered in hog bristle. With no cooking utensils or even axes for cutting firewood, many were forced to consume their food raw, just as when hiding from the Confederates. Some of the ponies began to sicken and die from disease, but federal authorities would not allow the

Indians to move to safer, cleaner ground. Carcasses of dead animals littered the campsites and even the nearby creeks where the Indians took their water; soon they, too, began to sicken and die.[2]

Though people perished in huge numbers, there were never more than one or two doctors available. One of them was Samuel Coffin, another relative of William Coffin, the superintendent for Indian affairs. The good doctor would quickly examine a patient, declare him incurable, and move on to the next. And in a day or two there would be more bodies and fresh graves to dig in the frozen ground. At one point, smallpox broke out, killing hundreds perhaps. After days of delay, the government finally supplied some vaccine, but it proved inert and still more lost their lives. To prevent the disease from spreading, many had to burn their last scraps of clothing and were left literally naked in the snow. Vast supplies of food, clothing, medicine, and even delicacies were stockpiled farther east to be shipped, but somehow the supplies rarely arrived, or mysteriously disappeared.[3]

Wholesale fraud became the normal manner of business in dealing with provisioning the Indians. It was easy to do, easier still to excuse. There was a war on to save the Union and make men free; no one in Washington had time to worry over the details of feeding a bunch of Indians in Kansas. Just as tragic, a veritable army of private citizens, federal agents, and military personnel systematically looted Indian Territory of its cattle and horse herds through four years of war, reducing the land to a picked-over wilderness. Probably chief among the rustlers was William Coffin and also a gentlemen named Perry Fuller—an attorney specifically empowered to provision the Indians and look after their legal affairs. Even federal agents admitted that the greatest depredations against loyal Indians and their property came from northern cattle rustlers, not Confederates. Hundreds of thousands of cattle were stolen and driven east, where they brought exorbitant prices from a government in need of beef. Sometimes the herds passed nearly in sight of the very ones who owned them.

But the half-starved and disease-ridden Indians would never learn of what was happening, shut away as they were in camps. While boys in blue grew strong and lean dining on Indian-raised beef, Muskogee women and children died almost every day from any number of maladies brought on by malnutrition. At the same time, Indian agents defrauded their wards of even the scant supplies that occasionally arrived. Agents engaged in the sale and speculation of hides and tallow from beef sent for starving refugees. In desperation, the women and little ones tried to augment their diet by planting crops; but the soldiers came and helped themselves to the harvest, then took away the rest.[4]

It was not a deliberate conspiracy by the white man to kill them all, at least not a conspiracy in the conventional sense. It was never necessary to conspire, for an entire nation believed fundamentally that another nation had no right to exist. It was more like an unofficial policy: unwritten and usually unquestioned, but nevertheless a policy, very real and very deadly. Above all, perhaps, it was a matter of the strong devouring the weak. And if an occasional government official dared pry into such matters, there were ways to handle the problem; there was always money to go around for those who would look the other way. The wonder was not that men could be bought; the marvel was that their price was so low.

When they realized it was hopeless to remain in Kansas, the Indians begged to return to the Territory. All they asked was that weapons be supplied so they could fight their way home. Even if there were no weapons, they said, they would be willing to return and take their chances with the enemy. But the government would not let them go until it finally moved the Indians to Fort Gibson in the Cherokee Nation after reestablishing federal control there.

At Fort Gibson it was the same story again: another federal compound with disease, starvation, and more death.[5]

Who was responsible for the whole affair, the fraud and the theft, the treachery, the false promises, and the thousands of blighted lives? No one could ever say for sure, for that was the nature of the white man's system of justice. No one was ever truly responsible for anything, least of all those with influence. Anyone who saw the horrid camps and reservations was outraged. Everyone agreed that it was a tragedy, that something should be done and the guilty held accountable, but nothing happened and no one could ever quite determine who was to blame.[6]

Was E. H. Carruth the guilty party, the man who wrote a letter making promises he had no power to keep? Was he a moralistic fool or a scheming accomplice for someone else? In addition to working for Senator James Lane, he was also an agent for the southern superintendent of Indian affairs, William Coffin. Was it the fault of James Lane, the mercurial politician who was never around when needed? He urged the Indians to rise in arms against the South without any way to help them. Or were the guilty simply an array of gross incompetents or petty cheats who were looking for a way to make a fast buck from the war, men like William Coffin and Perry Fuller? There was one other possibility, however, and another set of individuals to consider. And their tactics and motives were much darker and more sinister.[7]

The gentlemen from the railroads had always coveted the lands of Indian Territory. Even before the war was over, discussions ran in a casual way about railroad land grants and Indian possessions. They were mighty figures, the railroad men—in the White House and the halls of Congress. But behind the railroads and controlling them were other men even more powerful and grasping, the financiers who supplied the capital and greased the rails with money and, some said, with blood. Their influence could only be imagined, never fully measured. Like ever-widening rings in a pond, the impact of the financiers in London, New York, and other money centers spread farther and farther.

Some of the moneylenders were linked to a web of business interests with ties to the South as well as the North in the Civil War. After the conflict they were looking for ways to recoup their losses in the South, especially after the Fourteenth Amendment was passed forbidding assumption and payment of Confederate debts. When the war was through, such men would see that treaties stripped huge portions of Indian lands as punishment for so many having sided with the South. The Indians deserved no better, it was said; they were guilty of treason. Much of the land would go to railroads controlled by the financiers. The land was given as a right-of-way to construct their lines—and to reimburse or augment the fortunes, others would say, of the ones who had played both sides against the middle in the greatest tragedy in American history. And that was only the beginning.[8]

The financiers and their lobbyists saw to it that tribal funds were invested by the government in securities of the very railroads that had been given Indian lands. Even the funds for orphaned Indian children were channeled into railroad stocks and bonds. Ultimately, a collection of financial and corporate moguls—some of them the same individuals—along with an army of lobbyists and political toadies would open all of the Territory to the white man and reduce every Indian head of household to 160 acres of land. Even before the work was done, business journals around the world were speculating on the worth of Indian farms and ranches that would soon be seized. Always the justification for it was couched in the most high-minded and pietistic language. It was all done in the name of justice, progress, democracy, civilization, and Jesus. And always, of course, it was done for the red man's own good.

And when there was little left of the old nations and the towns and clans but picked-over bones and carrion for crows, still the financial and industrial elites were not finished. They sent their agents among the unsuspecting who were still alive on their few paltry acres to buy up mineral and timber rights—whatever that meant—for pocket change or a bottle of whiskey or a promise to build a church. It ended only after there was so little left it was no longer cost-effective to steal.[9]

But what of the loyal Indians like Opothleyahola and the thousands who followed him to Kansas? They were not traitors or rebels; they had sacrificed all for the sake of the United States. How could the federal government justify seizing their lands as well? The answer was simple: it couldn't. But a solution was just as simple. There could be no problem with loyal Indians if none of them were left alive. Let them all starve, freeze, or die from disease in overcrowded camps through four years of war. Let the women and children eat rotted meat and sleep in the cold and snow with hardly a shawl or sheet. Let the men be organized into military units and sent off to battle. Let them all be swept from the earth. No gentlemen of affairs in faraway New York or London need even discuss the issue. The war and the long, brutish winters would take care of the matter, along with avarice and greed, and perhaps an occasional bribe to the proper officials to make sure that the Indians were never properly supplied.

Even as the People were hounded from their homes and slaughtered by Confederates farther south, the trap was being set for their extermination in the North. There was a raw, primordial quality about it all, despite the trappings of civility and legality. As Muskogee civilization seemed to be nearing death, the predator beasts closed in from all sides. It was as the wolf pack hunts. And only in their most horrid nightmares and lurid visions did Opothleyahola or the ones with him ever grasp what they were facing.

After the war, land near Opothleyahola's old home went to one of the railroads, the Missouri, Kansas & Texas. The MKT was a financial appendage of the house of Rothschild in London as well as of J. P. Morgan of New York, John D. Rockefeller, and, later, Jay Gould. A section of track came nearly within sight of the very land that once lay in pasture and field for Opothleyahola. One of the first locomotives to ride the new rails was a special train filled with railroad and financial dignitaries, some from as far away as Europe. None of them knew or would have cared that their route would ultimately pass near lands that once were Opothleyahola's. Perhaps no one on the train or anywhere else understood or ever guessed at the truth and the full story of what had happened—except a handful of gentlemen with evil, translucent eyes.[10]

There was one flaw in their plan, however; not everyone died. Despite bitter cold, rotted food, disease, war, and, above all, treachery and neglect, somehow the People endured, as they had always endured. Somehow, some way, they were protected, and half of them, at least, survived it all. Even in the death camps there was magic. For they had been created by the Master of Breath and were to live forever, no matter the hardships or the powers against them. Always in times of trouble, a champion or a leader would be sent to guide and protect. They would live on as a symbol and testament against the forces of treachery and evil. In the present, in the future, and in the past, the People would never die.

What became of some of those whose lives were touched by the great trek to Kansas, Indian as well as white man? Their fates were as varied as their ways of life. James Scott and his sister Lizzie survived, though not their mother. James lived a long life and had a family of his own. But like so many of his generation who lived into the twentieth century, he was forever lost between two worlds: one Muskogee, the other white. And he would never wholly adjust to either.[11]

Soon after the Indians arrived in Kansas, E. H. Carruth became special agent to the Wichitas and other smaller tribes. Before long, accusations arose concerning his status as a "go-between" or middleman in the cattle-stealing business. The evidence suggested he was using his wards in cattle raids into the Territory. Before the accusations could be proved, however, Carruth, the good teacher and missionary, would die. George Cutler, Indian agent and escort to the miccos in New York and Washington, supervised one of the death camps in Kansas when he returned. He, too, was later implicated in cattle rustling before fading from the scene. Afterward, he made another life as a journalist and newspaper editor, then as a doctor in California. William Coffin proved that there was no correlation between virtue and longevity; he lived to be ninety-three. Though notorious for scheming, defrauding the Indians, and loading up government payrolls with family members, he was never formally charged with anything. One of his many relatives ultimately became president of the Atlantic and Pacific Railroad, one of the first railways to build into Indian Territory. After the war William Coffin practiced law and also, incredibly, continued to serve as a representative in Washington for Indians until two years before his death. Near the end of his days, he would write of himself: "I think I can safely say . . . I have not been a great success or total failure at anything."[12]

James McIntosh, the Confederate commander at Chustenahlah, died within a year of his victory over the Indians. As befit his nature, he died leading a wild charge against Union forces at the Battle of Pea Ridge in Arkansas. Following the war, Douglas Cooper managed somehow to get appointed again as Indian agent to the Choctaws, despite his Confederate loyalties and incompetence. After taking his post as Choctaw agent, he tried to profit from a kickback scheme that defrauded his Indian charges, but not for long. He died soon afterward, penniless and a hopeless alcoholic.[13]

Fate was kinder but even more ironic for the Muskogee McIntosh, in particular, Daniel. Although leaders of Confederate forces, they emerged in postbellum Indian Territory as major political figures, successful lawyers, gentlemen farmers, and also as investors in the railroads. They had long since learned how the game was played. Daniel lived to a ripe old age: respected, prosperous, Christian, and thoroughly convinced that his family's decision to walk the white man's path was the only hope for the Indian.[14]

Stand Watie also had a full and colorful life. He rose to the rank of brigadier general before the war was over, the only Indian to hold such a rank—North or South. His hit-and-run guerrilla raids became the scourge of Union forces. He was also the last Confederate general to surrender. After the war he was a prosperous farmer and respected leader of the Cherokee Nation.[15]

And what of Opothleyahola, the man who as much as anyone had led the Muskogee people for nearly a lifetime? What was his fate? He was one of the many who perished in Kansas during those dreadful years in the camps. Army doctors said something about pneumonia or consumption as a cause of death. The Indians had their own story. They said he lost the will to live when he saw how they had all been betrayed and when his work was done. He gave up the breath spirit, as they put it. It was not his fate to see or know that the People would survive, not in this world, at least. His was to be a life cycle of sacrifice and suffering so others might live—and a life cycle, too, of greatness.[16]

No one knows where they finally buried Opothleyahola. Some say it was at the Sac and Fox Reservation in Kansas, while many speak of Fort Leavenworth as his final place of rest. Still others claim he was buried alongside his daughter on a windswept hill near old Fort Belmont. But there are stories that endure—fragments of legends, really—about this man who is now mostly legend. There is a story still told around the hearths of Muskogee homes when the weather is cold and stormy, as it was so long ago when Opothleyahola and the old gods saved the People. When he died, the story goes, the Indians carried the remains of their beloved leader into the hills of eastern Kansas. And somewhere amid the post oaks and blackjacks, at the top of a ridge, they laid him to rest. They buried him with his horse and facing east, it is told. For on the final day of judgment, when every wrong is made right and evil is forever swept away—once again Opothleyahola will lead the People for a final time as he rides out to face his gods.[17]

NOTES

CHAPTER ONE. GRANDFATHER

1. E. H. Carruth to Hopoeithleyahola and Oktahahassee, Sept. 10, 1861 in U.S. War Department, *War of the Rebellion: A Compilation of the Official Records of the Union and Confederate Armies*, Series 1, vol. 8: 25; Charles M. Hudson, *The Southeastern Indians*, 121, 128, 155–56; William P. Dole to Secretary of War, Annual Report of the Commissioner of Indian Affairs for 1862, U.S. Cong., House, Executive Document 1, 37th Cong., 3rd sess., Serial 1157, 180–81.

2. The references to Muskogee beliefs and mythology come from many sources, including oral interviews with members of the Muskogee Nation, 1985–86; Jack Gregory and Renard Strickland, *Creek Seminole Spirit Tales*; Hudson, *The Southeastern Indians*; George E. Lankford, *Native American Legends*; Ake Hultkrantz et al., *Seeing with a Native Eye: Essays on Native American Religion*; and John R. Swanton, "Religious Beliefs and Medical Practices of the Creek Indians"; Colonel Douglas H. Cooper to J. P. Benjamin, Secretary of War, Jan. 20, 1862, in Opothleyahola File, Oklahoma Historical Society, Oklahoma City, 1 (hereafter "Cooper's Report," Opothleyahola File); James Scott interview, Indian-Pioneer History, WPA Project, Oklahoma Historical Society, vol. 7: 172–76 (hereafter James Scott interview); Angie Debo, *The Road to Disappearance*, 142–50.

3. The best primary account of the Creek War of 1813–14 can be found in Theron A. Nunez, Jr., "Stiggins Narrative, Creek Nativism, and the Creek War of 1813–1814," 1–47, 131–75, 292–301; Swanton, "Religious Beliefs," 615.

4. Good accounts of early Creek-white relations can be found in David H. Corkran, *The Creek Frontier 1520–1783;* Michael D. Green, *The Politics of Indian Removal: Creek Government and Society in Crisis;* and

Thomas S. Woodward, *Woodward's Reminiscences of the Creek, or Muscogee Indians, Contained in Letters to Friends in Georgia and Alabama;* and Debo, *The Road to Disappearance.*

5. The Muskogee people believed that the heavenly plates were a gift from the Master of Breath, the Supreme Deity. Modern archaeologists suspect they came from pieces of armor plating, perhaps from as early as the time of De Soto. The concept of a sacred fire dates from at least the Mississippian cultural tradition, perhaps from even the paleolithic period. The sacred fire was also a gift from the gods. Should it ever die, it was believed, the People and all that was good and righteous would perish. See: E. S. Greer, Jr. "A Tuckabatchee Plate from the Coosa River," *Journal of Alabama Archaeology* 156–58. Creek removal documents can be found in the National Archives, especially Record Group, 75, Records of the Bureau of Indian Affairs, Correspondence of the Office of Indian Affairs, Letters Received (M234) 1824–81; and letters Sent (M21) 1824–81, Rolls 222–23; as well as U.S. Cong., House, Executive Document 276, 24th Cong., 1st sess., Serial 292. Firsthand accounts and good secondary sources include Gloria Jahoda, *The Trail of Tears* and Grant Foreman, *The Five Civilized Tribes* and *Indian Removal.*

6. For accounts of the rebuilding in Oklahoma, see Ethan Allen Hitchcock's report in U.S. Cong., House, Executive Document 219, 27th Cong., 3rd sess., no serial set no., Hitchcock Report; William W. Savage, Jr., "Creek Colonization of Oklahoma"; Andre Paul Du Chateau, "The Creek Nation on the Eve of the Civil War."

7. Technically, the name Opothleyahola means good shouter, good whooper, or good child whooper—a reference to his position as Speaker of the Muskogee Nation. His name has always been spelled a variety of ways in the English-speaking world. Sometimes it is Hopoeithleyahola, other times Hopui-herre Yahola. There are other variants as well. The spelling we chose is the one most commonly used by historians.

8. There are only a few articles on Opothleyahola and no books. See Blue Clark Carter, "Opothleyahola and the Creeks during the Civil War"; Kenny A. Franks, "Operations against Opothleyahola, 1861"; John Bartlett Meserve, "Chief Opothleyahola"; Mrs. Clement C. Clay, "Recollections of Opothleyahola"; Thomas L. McKenney Report, Opothleyahola File, Oklahoma Historical Society; Clee Woods, "Oklahoma's Great Opothele Yahola"; T. F. Morrison, *A Forgotten Hero: A True Story of a Creek Indian Chief of Civil War Times.*

9. There is only one painting of Opothleyahola, by Charles Bird King. Other descriptions come from James Scott interview; Simon Jackson interview, vol. 62: 340–41, Indian-Pioneer History, WPA Project, Oklahoma Historical Society (hereafter Simon Jackson interview); oral interviews with members of the Muskogee Nation.

10. Debo, *The Road to Disappearance,* 146–50.

11. A gun identified as belonging to Opothleyahola is on display at the Creek Council House Museum, Okmulgee, Oklahoma.

12. Swanton, "Religious Beliefs," 482.

CHAPTER TWO. THE OUTSIDER

1. The lack of geographic place names in depicting the exodus of Opothleyahola is intentional. Many Indian cultures attached a single name to any number of geographic features that shared the same characteristics. The contemporary reader would be hopelessly confused encountering the same name for different rivers, hills, or rocky outcroppings. Thus, we have largely avoided geographic place names. Instead, we have focused on accurate description of the terrain. James Scott interview; Hudson, *The Southeastern Indians*, 121, 128; Swanton, "Religious Beliefs," 489.

2. Swanton, "Religious Beliefs," 99, 489; Hudson, *The Southeastern Indians*, 121, 128, 155; Debo, *The Road to Disappearance*, 153.

3. Swanton, "Religious Beliefs," 243, 454; Debo, *The Road to Disappearance*, 153.

4. James Scott interview; "Cooper's Report," Opothleyahola File, 1; Swanton, "Religious Beliefs," 313, 454; Debo, *The Road to Disappearance*, 151–53.

5. The term "Lower Town" derives from traditional Muskogee political structure, coupled with the English/European encounter. For centuries the towns of Coweta and Kasihta served as political leaders for roughly the eastern half of the Muskogee Confederation. Communities under Coweta and Kasihta were directly in the path of the English-speaking frontier advance and were the first Muskogees encountered by these white men. Hence, the English-speaking dubbed them the Lower Towns of the Muskogee Nation, as opposed to the more remote Upper Towns controlled by Tuckabatchee and Abihka, farther west. Swanton, "Religious Beliefs," 308–10; Debo, *The Road to Disappearance*, 4, 33–36; Green, *The Politics of Indian Removal*, 28–30; William N. Fenton, "Factionalism in American Indian Society," 330–32.

6. The Redstick War, which culminated with Tohopeka, or the Battle of Horseshoe Bend, was a civil war caused by Redstick threats to the McIntosh family and the Lower Creeks. Initially, Tuckabatchee was not among the Redstick towns and indeed was attacked by them. Ultimately, Tuckabatchee became a Redstick ally, thus pitting Opothleyahola of Tuckabatchee against his hated rivals, the McIntosh. For a detailed description of Tohopeka, see Nunez, "Stiggins Narrative."

7. Eunah Hobiya interview, Indian-Pioneer History, WPA Project, Oklahoma Historical Society, vol. 85: 72; Green, *The Politics of Indian Removal*, 182; T. R. Fehrenbach, *Lone Star: A History of Texas and the Texans*, 452–53.

8. Swanton, "Religious Beliefs," 366, 547; Hudson, *The Southeastern Indians*, 121, 128, 155–56, 173, 232.

9. Woodward, *Woodward's Reminiscences*, 33; Nunez, "Stiggins Narrative," 146–52; R. David Edmunds, *The Shawnee Prophet*, 118–19.

10. Daniel McIntosh and others, "Statement relative to the exodus of Ho-poith-la-yo-ho-la and his followers from the Creek and Cherokee country in the fall and winter of 1861 and '62," Opothleyahola File, Oklahoma Historical Society, 2 (hereafter McIntosh, "Exodus Statement").

CHAPTER THREE.
THE TUCKABATCHEES

1. McIntosh, "Exodus Statement," 2.
2. Phillip McNac interview, Indian-Pioneer History, WPA Project, Oklahoma Historical Society, vol. 106: 439 (hereafter Philip McNac interview).
3. Dean Trickett, "The Civil War in the Indian Territory," 17: 316; Muriel Wright, "Colonel Cooper's Civil War Report on the Battle of Round Mountain," 383; Annie Heloise Abel, *The American Indian As Slaveholder and Secessionist*, 136–37; Debo, *The Road to Disappearance*, 144.
4. Debo, *The Road to Disappearance*, 144; Meserve, "Chief Opothleyahola," 445; Jerry Gill, "Thesis," Opothleyahola File, Oklahoma Historical Society, Oklahoma, 19–20 (hereafter Gill, "Thesis").
5. Kenny A. Franks, "An Analysis of the Confederate Treaties with the Five Civilized Tribes," 458–59; Ohland Morton, "Confederate Government Relations with the Five Civilized Tribes," 299–307; Kenneth McNeil, "Confederate Treaties with the Tribes of Indian Territory," 412–13; Jay Monaghan, *Civil War on the Western Border*, 1854–1865, 219–20.
6. John Ross to "Opothleyahola and Others," Oct. 8, 1861, Annual Report of the Commissioner of Indian Affairs for 1865, U.S. Cong., House, Executive Document 1, 39th Cong., 1st sess., Serial 1248, 538 (hereafter Annual Report, 1865).
7. McIntosh, "Exodus Statement," 1–2; Loyal Creek delegation to the Fort Smith Commission, Sept. 12, 1865, Annual Report, 1865, 328–29; Muriel Wright, "General Douglas H. Cooper, C.S.A.," 165; Swanton, "Religious Beliefs," 111–12; Debo, *The Road to Disappearance*, 150.
8. James Scott interview; Gill, "Thesis," 42–43.
9. Leadership among American Indian tribes has been studied by many anthropologists. See, for example, Jessie Bernard, "Political Leadership among Native American Indians"; Robert F. Berkhofer, Jr., "The Political Context of a New Indian History."
10. Cooper to Benjamin, in U.S. War Department, *War of the Rebellion*, vol. 8: 5; A. W. Sparks, *The War between the States as I Saw It*, 30; Monaghan, *Civil War on the Western Border*, 222; Swanton, "Religious Beliefs," 481–84.

CHAPTER FOUR. THE BOY

1. James Scott interview.
2. *Ibid.*; Barney Deere interview, Indian-Pioneer History, WPA Project, Oklahoma Historical Society, vol. 22: 168 (hereafter Barney Deere interview); Gill, "Thesis," 42–43.
3. Carruth to Hopoeithleyahola and Oktahahassee, Sept. 10, 1861, in U.S. War Department, *War of the Rebellion*, vol. 8, 25; Gill, "Thesis," 42–43; Debo, *The Road to Disappearance*, 151.
4. James Scott interview; Swanton, "Religious Beliefs," 409, 454, 478–82; Gill, "Thesis," 42–50.

5. McIntosh, "Exodus Statement," 1; Debo, *The Road to Disappearance*, 151–52; Wright, "Colonel Cooper's Civil War Report," 383–86.

6. McIntosh, "Exodus Statement," 1; Debo, *The Road to Disappearance*, 151–52; Wright, "Colonel Cooper's Civil War Report," 383–86; Edwin C. McReynolds, *The Seminoles*, 292–96; Franks, "Operations against Opothleyahola," 187; Kenneth W. Porter, "Billy Bowlegs (Holata Micco) in the Civil War," 391–95.

7. Gill, "Thesis," 47–56; Wright, "Colonel Cooper's Civil War Report," 376; Orpha Russell, "Ekvn-hv lwue: Site of Oklahoma's First Civil War Battle," 401–407.

8. Debo, *The Road to Disappearance*, 115; M. Thomas Bailey, *Reconstruction in Indian Territory: A Story of Avarice, Discrimination, and Opportunism*, 76.

9. James Scott interview; Gill, "Thesis," 47–56; Wright, "Colonel Cooper's Civil War Report," 376; Russell, "Ekvn-hv lwue," 401–07.

10. W. Craig Gaines, *The Confederate Cherokees: John Drew's Regiment of Mounted Rifles*, 21–24; Gill, "Thesis," 47–56.

11. Wright, "Colonel Cooper's Civil War Report," 364–65; Russell, "Ekvn-hv lwue," 405–406; James Scott interview; Gill, "Thesis," 47–56.

12. Monaghan, *Civil War on the Western Border*, 222; McReynolds, *The Seminoles*, 296.

CHAPTER FIVE. THE CHASE

1. Gill, "Thesis," 53–54; Cox's map in Wright, "Colonel Cooper's Civil War Report," 371, 386; Russell, "Ekvn-hv lwue," 404–405.

2. McIntosh, "Exodus Statement," 2; Gill, "Thesis," 53–56.

3. Sparks, *The War between the States*, 27; Swanton, "Religious Beliefs," 406–36; Hudson, *The Southeastern Indians*, 380; Gill, "Thesis," 53–56.

4. Cooper to Benjamin, in U.S. War Department, *War of the Rebellion*, vol. 8: 5; Wright, "Colonel Cooper's Civil War Report," 378–79.

5. James Scott interview; Russell, "Ekvn-hv lwue," 403–405; Swanton, "Religious Beliefs," 494–95; Hudson, *The Southeastern Indians*, 132.

6. Gill, "Thesis," 53–56; Cox's map in Wright, "Colonel Cooper's Civil War Report," 371.

7. Cooper to Benjamin, in U.S. War Department, *War of the Rebellion*, vol. 8: 5; Russell, "Ekvn-hv lwue," 401–407; Swanton, "Religious Beliefs," 313; Hudson, *The Southeastern Indians*, 240–41, 249.

CHAPTER SIX. THE McINTOSH

1. Sparks, *The War between the States*, 14–15; George L. Griscom, *Fighting with Ross' Texas Cavalry Brigade, C.S.A.* 2–5; S. B. Barron, *The Lone Star Defenders: A Chronicle of the Third Texas Cavalry, Ross' Brigade*, 327–73.

2. McIntosh, "Exodus Statement," 1; picture in Wright, "Colonel Cooper's Civil War Report," 355; John Bartlett Meserve, "The Mac-

Intoshes," 310–25; Monaghan, *Civil War on the Western Border*, 219–20; Christine White, "Opothleyahola, Factionalism, and Creek Politics," 61–158; Sparks, *The War between the States*, 26–29.

3. McReynolds, *The Seminoles*, 293–99; Porter, "Billy Bowlegs," 391–401.

4. Cooper to Benjamin, in U.S. War Department, *War of the Rebellion*, vol. 8: 5; "Personal Reminiscences of Captain June Peak," Opothleyahola File, Oklahoma Historical Society, 1 (hereafter Capt. June Peak); Sparks, *The War between the States*, 22–32; Griscom, *Fighting with Ross' Texas Cavalry Brigade*, 4–5.

5. Confederate movements are difficult to ascertain following the division of their forces. Primary source materials on this matter are contradictory and even garbled. We have constructed an account of Confederate movements from a review of all materials and our own conclusions. Sparks, *The War between the States*, 23–32; Griscom, *Fighting with Ross' Texas Cavalry Brigade*, 4–5; Wright, "Colonel Cooper's Civil War Report," 381–82.

6. Wright, "Colonel Cooper's Civil War Report," 383–87.

7. Sparks, *The War between the States*, 30–33; Griscom, *Fighting with Ross' Texas Cavalry Brigade*, 4–5.

8. Sparks, *The War between the States*, 30–33; Griscom, *Fighting with Ross' Texas Cavalry Brigade*, 4–5; Swanton, "Religious Beliefs," 414–25.

CHAPTER SEVEN.
FIRE AND BLOOD

1. Primary sources are unclear concerning the location of the Battle of Round Mountain. Historians are still debating the issue. See Angie Debo, "The Site of the Battle of Round Mountain, 1861"; idem, "The Location of the Battle of Round Mountain"; Dean Trickett, "Ad Interim Report on the Site of the Battle of Round Mountain"; Wright, "Colonel Cooper's Civil War Report"; and Russell, "Ekvn-hv lwue." Confederate reports from the Battle of Round Mountain as well as the next engagement, at Bird Creek, depict hundreds of Indian dead and only a handful of southern casualties. We view these figures as utterly unreliable, since the source is Douglas Cooper, a man renowned as a swindler, a drunk, and a habitual liar. During the war charges were brought against Cooper for gross incompetence. Cooper to Benjamin, in U.S. War Department, *War of the Rebellion*, vol. 8: 5–6; M. J. Brinson to William Quayle, Nov. 25, 1861, in ibid., 14; Sparks, *The War between the States*, 33–35; "Capt. June Peak," 2–3; Griscom, *Fighting with Ross' Texas Cavalry Brigade*, 5–6.

2. Angie Debo, "The Site of the Battle of Round Mountain, 1861"; idem, "The Location of the Battle of Round Mountain"; Dean Trickett, "Ad Interim Report on the Site of the Battle of Round Mountain"; Wright, "Colonel Cooper's Civil War Report"; Russell, "Ekvn-hv lwue"; Cooper to Benjamin, in U.S. War Department, *War of the Rebellion*, vol. 8: 5–6; M. J. Brinson to William Quayle, Nov. 25, 1861, in ibid., 14; Sparks,

The War between the States, 33–35; "Capt. June Peak," 2–3; Griscom, *Fighting with Ross' Texas Cavalry Brigade,* 5–6, Swanton, "Religious Beliefs," 414–25.

3. Cooper to Benjamin, in U.S. War Department, *War of the Rebellion,* vol. 8: 6; Sparks, *The War between the States,* 33–35; "Capt. June Peak," 2–3; Griscom, *Fighting with Ross' Texas Cavalry Brigade,* 5–6.

4. Cooper to Benjamin, in U.S. War Department, *War of the Rebellion,* vol. 8: 6; Sparks, *The War between the States,* 33–35.

5. Cooper to Benjamin, in U.S. War Department, *War of the Rebellion,* vol. 8: 6; Sparks, *The War between the States,* 35–36; Griscom, *Fighting with Ross' Texas Cavalry Brigade,* 5–6; R. A. Young to Cooper, Nov. 30, 1861, in U.S. War Department, *War of the Rebellion,* vol. 8: 14–15; "North Texan to Editor," Nov. 24, 1861, *Paris Press,* in Opothleyahola File, Oklahoma Historical Society, 1–3 (hereafter "North Texan").

6. "Capt. June Peak," 2–3; Griscom, *Fighting with Ross' Texas Cavalry Brigade,* 5–6; Sparks, *The War between the States,* 34–35; Cooper to Benjamin, in U.S. War Department, *War of the Rebellion,* vol. 8: 6.

CHAPTER EIGHT. COOPER

1. Griscom, *Fighting with Ross' Texas Cavalry Brigade,* 6; Sparks, *The War between the States,* 36–37; Cooper to Benjamin, in U.S. War Department, *War of the Rebellion,* vol. 8: 6–7.

2. Photograph in Wright, "Colonel Cooper's Civil War Report," 355; Monaghan, *Civil War on the Western Border,* 213, 221, 224–25; Wright, "General Douglas H. Cooper, C.S.A.," 142–66; Annie Heloise Abel, *The American Indian As Participant in the Civil War,* 181, 198; idem, "The Indians in the Civil War," 283; Albert Castel, *A Frontier State at War: Kansas, 1861–1865,* 155.

3. Douglas Cooper to Major Elias Rector, May 1, 1861, Indian Office, General Files, Southern Superintendency, 1861–63, I 435 in Annie Heloise Abel, *The American Indian As Slaveholder,* 107, 188, 254–55.

4. Debo, "The Site of the Battle of Round Mountain," 206; Wright, "Colonel Cooper's Civil War Report," 391.

5. Cooper to Rector in Abel, *The American Indian as Slaveholder,* 107, 188, 154–255; idem, "The Indians in the Civil War," 283; Cooper to Benjamin, in U.S. War Department, *War of the Rebellion,* vol. 8: 6–7; Sparks, *The War between the States,* 34–35.

6. Unlikely as it seems to us, one source reports wounded Indians left behind and taken prisoner after the Battle of Round Mountain. All other primary materials depict a deserted Indian camp. Cooper to Benjamin, in U.S. War Department, *War of the Rebellion,* vol. 8: 6; Sparks, *The War between the States,* 36–37; Griscom, *Fighting with Ross' Texas Cavalry Brigade,* 6; "North Texan," 3; Monaghan, *Civil War on the Western Border,* 219–24; Swanton, "Religious Beliefs," 406–36.

7. Sparks, *The War between the States,* 36; Griscom, *Fighting with Ross' Texas Cavalry Brigade,* 6; Cooper to Benjamin, in U.S. War Department, *War of the Rebellion,* vol. 8: 6.

8. Sparks, *The War between the States*, 36–37; "North Texan," 3; Monaghan, *Civil War on the Western Border*, 223; Hudson, *The Southeastern Indians*, 128–29.

CHAPTER NINE.
THE END OF THE EARTH

1. Swanton, "Religious Beliefs," 481–89; oral interviews with members of the Muskogee Nation; Gregory and Strickland, *Creek Seminole Spirit Tales*; n.p.; Hudson, *The Southeastern Indians*, 128, 173, 194.
2. A micco is a local leader, not unlike a city council member. Debo, *The Road to Disappearance*, 144; Gill, "Thesis," 19–20.
3. Grace Kelley interview, Indian-Pioneer History, WPA Project, Oklahoma Historical Society, vol. 4: 298; Stephen R. Lewis interview, in ibid., vol. 109: 179–80 (hereafter Stephen R. Lewis interview); Cooper to Benjamin, in U.S. War Department, *War of the Rebellion*, vol. 8: 7.
4. William G. Coffin, Superintendent of Indian Affairs for the Southern Superintendency to William P. Dole, Commissioner of Indian Affairs, Oct. 2, 1861, Annual Report of the Commissioner of Indian Affairs for 1861, U.S. Cong., Senate, Executive Document 1, 37th Cong., 2nd sess., Serial 1117, vol. 1: 650–51; John Ross to Opothleyahola, Oct. 8, 1861, Annual Report of the Commission of Indian Affairs for 1865, 338; E. H. Carruth to William G. Coffin, Sept. 19, 1862, Annual Report of the Commissioner of Indian Affairs for 1862, vol. 2: 309–10.
5. Swanton, "Religious Beliefs," 366, 481–82, 547; Hudson, *Southeastern Indians*, 121, 128, 155–56, 194, 232; Gregory and Strickland, *Creek Seminole Spirit Tales*, n.p.
6. Green, *The Politics of Indian Removal*, 4–7; Hudson, *Southeastern Indians*, 234–37; Swanton, "Religious Beliefs," 111–14.
7. Swanton, "Religious Beliefs," 339–45; Hudson, *Southeastern Indians*, 230–31.
8. Carruth to Hopoeithleyahola and Oktahahassee, in U.S. War Department, *War of the Rebellion*, vol. 8: 25; Stephen R. Lewis interview; Monaghan, *Civil War on the Western Border*, 223–24.
9. Gill, "Thesis," 25–29.

CHAPTER TEN. THE PROMISE

1. Little is known of E. H. Carruth except that he was a teacher or missionary. Virtually all teachers at Indian schools were missionaries. Their function was to teach the word of God. Abel, *The American Indian As Slaveholder*, 242–45; Trickett, "The Civil War in the Indian Territory," 18: 151–52; Abel, *The American Indian As Participant in the Civil War*, 59–64, 133, 246–47.
2. Abel, *The American Indian As Slaveholder*, 242–45; Trickett, "The Civil War in the Indian Territory," 18: 151–52; Abel, *The American In-*

dian As Participant in the Civil War, 59–64, 133, 246–47; Debo, *The Road to Disappearance,* 143–44, 148–49.

3. Abel, *The American Indian As Slaveholder,* 242–45; Trickett, "The Civil War in the Indian Territory," 18: 151–52; Abel, *The American Indian As Participant in the Civil War,* 59–64, 133, 246–47.

4. Wendall Holmes Stephenson, *The Political Career of James H. Lane,* 16–161; Trickett, "The Civil War in the Indian Territory," 18: 56–58, 151–52; Abel, *The American Indian As Participant in the Civil War,* 37–70; idem, *The American Indian As Slaveholder,* 229–31, 248–49; Debo, *The Road to Disappearance,* 148–49.

5. Evan Jones to William P. Dole, Oct. 31, 1861, Report of the Commissioner of Indian Affairs for 1861, 658–59; Evan Jones to William P. Dole, Dec. 14, 1861, in Abel, *The American Indian As Participant in the Civil War,* 63–64, 88; Trickett, "The Civil War in the Indian Territory," 18: 152, 403.

6. Tom Holman, "William G. Coffin, Lincoln's Superintendent of Indian Affairs for the Southern Superintendency," 491–514; Gill, "Thesis," 27–32.

7. Tom Holman, "William G. Coffin, Lincoln's Superintendent of Indian Affairs for the Southern Superintendency," 491–514; Gill, "Thesis," 27–32; Jones to Dole, Oct. 31, 1861, Report of the Commissioner of Indian Affairs for 1861, 658–59; Trickett, "The Civil War in the Indian Territory," 18: 152–53.

8. Coffin to Dole, Oct. 2, 1861, Annual Report of the Commissioner of Indian Affairs for 1861, 654–55; Jones to Dole, Oct. 31, 1861, Annual Report of the Commissioner of Indian Affairs for 1861, 658–59; E. H. Carruth to Hopoeithleyahola and Oktahahassee, Sept. 10, 1861, in U.S. War Department, *War of the Rebellion,* vol. 8: 25; E. H. Carruth to Chickasaws and Choctaws, Sept. 11, 1861, in ibid., vol. 8: 26; E. H. Carruth to Tusaquach, Sept. 11, 1861, in ibid.

9. As with several figures in our story, material on White King, or Micco Hutke, is contradictory. Sometimes he is depicted as remaining with Opothleyahola and helping lead the Muskogees in battle against the Confederates. Yet most sources clearly state that he was with both the first and the second Indian delegations that rode to Kansas. Abel, *The American Indian As Slaveholder,* 249–50, 266–70; Porter, "Billy Bowlegs," 394; Trickett, "The Civil War in the Indian Territory," 18: 153.

10. George A. Cutler to William P. Dole, Nov. 4, 1861, in Abel, *The American Indian As Participant in the Civil War,* 65–69; George A. Cutler to William P. Dole, Sept. 30, 1862, Annual Report of the Commissioner of Indian Affairs for 1862, 282–84; Trickett, "The Civil War in the Indian Territory," 18: 56–59; Castel, *A Frontier State at War,* 19–24, 34, 49–55.

11. Jones to Dole, Dec. 14, 1861, Annual Report of the Commissioner of Indian Affairs for 1861, 658–59; Cutler to Dole, Sept. 30, 1862, Annual Report of the Commissioner of Indian Affairs for 1862, 282–84; Debo, *The Road to Disappearance,* 149; Gill, "Thesis," 31–32.

12. David Hunter to Adjutant-General Thomas, Jan. 15, 1862, in Abel, *The American Indian As Participant in the Civil War,* 70–72, 74–

75; Abel, *The American Indian As Slaveholder,* 228–43; Trickett, "The Civil War in the Indian Territory," 18: 58–61; Gill, "Thesis," 31.

CHAPTER ELEVEN.
THE PREDATOR BEAST

1. Cutler to Dole, Nov. 4, 1861 in Abel, *The American Indian As Participant in the Civil War,* 65–69; Cutler to Dole, Sept. 30, 1862, Annual Report of the Commissioner of Indian Affairs for 1862, 282, 284.

2. Andrew Sinclair, *Corsair: The Life of J. Pierpont Morgan,* 18–20.

3. Since at least the mid-twentieth century, chaos theory has undermined Newtonian philosophy as a foundation of contemporary thought. Yet most still approach the topic of science and the scientific method from the perspective of Sir Isaac Newton. This is particularly true of those in the social sciences. See John Briggs and F. David Peat, *The Turbulent Mirror: An Illustrated Guide to Chaos Theory;* James Gleick, *Chaos: Making a New Science.*

4. Carl Sandburg, *Abraham Lincoln: The War Years,* vol. 2: 186–89, 208–209, 272–73, 619.

5. Ibid., vol. 1: 9–10; vol. 2: 186–89, 208–209, 272–73.

6. Expense account of journey in Abel, *The American Indian As Participant in the Civil War,* 73; idem, *The American Indian As Slaveholder,* 208; Herman J. Viola, *Diplomats in Buckskins: A History of Indian Delegations in Washington City,* 26–27, 54, 92, 113–17.

7. Abel, *The American Indian As Participant in the Civil War,* 73; idem, *The American Indian As Slaveholder,* 208; Viola, *Diplomats in Buckskins,* 26–27, 54, 92, 113–17; Sandburg, *Abraham Lincoln,* vol. 2: 186–89, 272–73.

8. Sandburg, *Abraham Lincoln,* vol. 2: 186–89, 208–209, 619; vol. 3: 15–16; Sinclair, *Corsair,* 18–25.

9. However much the topic may be ignored—or denied—the promotion of war by third parties who stand to benefit is an old story. It was practiced against Indians on the American frontier for three hundred years. But such activity was by no means limited to Indians. During the Civil War, millions of dollars in gold, credits, supplies, and munitions were lent or sold to the Confederacy by third parties in the North who had much to gain. Some European banking firms were also linked to a labyrinth of business connections with ties to both North and South, strategically placing themselves to benefit from war. That such a topic is rarely discussed, much less researched, is a comment on scholarship in the modern era. It was common throughout the Civil War to hear or read of financial profiteering mixed with charges of treason. The most vocal critics of the financiers were labor leaders, newspaper editors, high-ranking government officials, and the president. But their complaints were largely drowned out in a chorus of public hosannas for the lords of money. Sandburg, *Abraham Lincoln,* vol. 2: 186–89, 208–09; vol. 3: 123–25; Sinclair, *Corsair,* 18–25.

❖ NOTES

CHAPTER TWELVE. A VISION

1. Cooper to Benjamin, in U.S. War Department, *War of the Rebellion,* vol. 8: 7–8; Sebron Miller interview, Indian-Pioneer History, WPA Project, Oklahoma Historical Society, vol. 60: 370; Stephen R. Lewis interview; Swanton, "Religious Beliefs," 409, 478–82, 616–17; Hudson, *The Southeastern Indians,* 128, 319.

CHAPTER THIRTEEN. THE TRICKSTER

1. Cooper to Benjamin, in U.S. War Department, *War of the Rebellion,* vol. 8: 7–8; McIntosh, "Exodus Statement," 5.

2. Colonel John Drew wrote days after the fact that Daniel McIntosh concurred in the decision to meet with Opothleyahola. Our research into the life and personality of Daniel McIntosh suggests the opposite would have occurred. We think John Drew was concerned with being singled out as a scapegoat for what had happened to his regiment. Thus, he hoped to shield himself from blame by implicating others. Cooper to Benjamin, in U.S. War Department, *War of the Rebellion,* vol. 8: 7–8; John Drew to Colonel Cooper, Dec. 18, 1861, in ibid., vol. 8: 16–18; Gaines, *The Confederate Cherokees,* 43–46.

3. Cooper to Benjamin, in U.S. War Department, *War of the Rebellion,* vol. 8: 7–8; McIntosh, "Exodus Statement," 5; Gaines, *The Confederate Cherokees,* 21–46.

4. Drew to Cooper, in U.S. War Department, *War of the Rebellion,* vol. 8: 16–18; Gaines, *The Confederate Cherokees,* 46–47.

5. Drew to Cooper, in U.S. War Department, *War of the Rebellion,* vol. 8: 17; Gaines, *The Confederate Cherokees,* 21–24, 46–49.

6. Cooper to Benjamin, in U.S. War Department, *War of the Rebellion,* vol. 8: 7–8; Gaines, *The Confederate Cherokees,* 48.

7. Cooper to Benjamin, in U.S. War Department, *War of the Rebellion,* vol. 8: 7–8; Gaines, *The Confederate Cherokees,* 49–50.

CHAPTER FOURTEEN. VENGEANCE

1. Stephen R. Lewis interview; Swanton, "Religious Beliefs," 406–36; Cooper to Benjamin, in U.S. War Department, *War of the Rebellion,* vol. 8: 7–8; D. N. McIntosh to Colonel Cooper, Dec. 16, 1861, in ibid., vol. 8: 16; LeRoy H. Fischer and Kenny A. Franks, "Confederate Victory at Chusto-Talasah," 452–76.

2. Some historians have described the ravine as void of trees. Our inspection of the site has led us to a different conclusion. Also, Gaines's *The Confederate Cherokees* places the cabin and corn crib at the center of the horseshoe and on the opposite bank. His description of Indian positions and fortifications are in keeping with traditional Muskogee battle placements, yet so are ours. Source materials have led us to position the

cabin and crib at a different location. Stephen R. Lewis interview; Cooper to Benjamin, in U.S. War Department, *War of the Rebellion*, vol. 8: 7–8; McIntosh to Cooper, in ibid., vol. 8, 16; Gaines, *The Confederate Cherokees*, 49–52; Swanton, "Religious Beliefs," 406–36; Fischer and Franks, "Confederate Victory at Chusto-Talasah," 452–76.

3. Cooper to Benjamin, in U.S. War Department, *War of the Rebellion*, vol. 8: 7–8; McIntosh to Cooper, in ibid., vol. 8: 16; Gaines, *The Confederate Cherokees*, 49–52.

4. The Treaty of Washington, 1826, was signed by Opothleyahola. It ceded nearly all Muskogee lands in Georgia to the federal government, resulting in the removal of the Lower Creeks, including the McIntosh, to Indian Territory.

5. As with the Battle of Round Mountain, primary source materials on the engagement at Bird Creek are often contradictory. Cross referencing of primary materials has convinced us, in fact, that portions of the official record are incorrect. Thus, we have been forced to reconstruct events to the best of our ability from a variety of often conflicting sources. McIntosh to Cooper, in U.S. War Department, *War of the Rebellion*, vol. 8: 16; Jackson McCurtain to Colonel Cooper, Jan. 18, 1862, in ibid., vol. 8: 20–21; Joseph R. Hall to Colonel D. H. Cooper, n.d., in ibid., vol. 8: 19–20; Captain William B. Pitchlynn to Colonel D. H. Cooper, Jan. 18, 1862, in ibid., vol. 8: 21–22; Cooper to Benjamin, in ibid., vol. 8: 7–9.

6. Colonel William B. Sims to Colonel D. H. Cooper, Dec. 15, 1861, in U.S. War Department, *War of the Rebellion*, vol. 8: 18; Hall to Cooper, in ibid., vol. 8: 19–20; Wright, "Colonel Cooper's Civil War Report," 18; Swanton, "Religious Beliefs," 406–36.

7. Sims to Cooper, in U.S. War Department, *War of the Rebellion*, vol. 8: 18; Hall to Cooper, in ibid., vol. 8: 19–20; Cooper to Benjamin, in ibid., vol. 8: 7–9; McIntosh to Cooper, in ibid., vol. 8: 16; McCurtain to Çooper, in ibid., vol. 8: 20–21; Hall to Cooper, in ibid., vol. 8: 19–20; R. A. Young to D. H. Cooper, n.d., in U.S. War Department, *War of the Rebellion*, vol. 8: 15; Pitchlynn to Cooper, in ibid., vol. 8: 21; Sparks, *The War between the States*, 41–45; Wiley Britton, *The Civil War on the Border*, vol. 1: 168–71; Fischer and Franks, "Confederate Victory at Chusto-Talasah," 452–78; Sims to Cooper, in U.S. War Department, *War of the Rebellion*, vol. 8: 18–19; Douglas Cooper to James McIntosh, Dec. 11, 1861, in ibid., vol. 8: 709.

8. McIntosh to Cooper, in U.S. War Department, *War of the Rebellion*, vol. 8: 16; Cooper to Benjamin, in ibid., vol. 8: 6–11.

CHAPTER FIFTEEN. THE SPIRITS

1. Cooper to Benjamin, in U.S. War Department, *War of the Rebellion*, vol. 8: 11–12; Sparks, *The War between the States*, 44–45; McIntosh, "Exodus Statement," 6–7; Griscom, *Fighting with Ross' Texas Cavalry Brigade*, 10; Victor M. Rose, *Ross' Texas Brigade*, 42; Britton, *The Civil War on the Border*, 168–71; Abel, *The American Indian As Slaveholder*, 256; Trickett, "The Civil War in the Indian Territory," 18:

275–76; Edwin C. Bearess, "The Civil War Comes to Indian Territory, 1861: The Flight of Opothleyahola," 17–18; Bearess, "The Civil War Comes to Indian Territory," 17–18.

2. Cooper to Benjamin, in U.S. War Department, *War of the Rebellion,* vol. 8: 11–12; Sparks, *The War between the States,* 44–45; McIntosh, "Exodus Statement," 6–7; Griscom, *Fighting with Ross' Texas Cavalry Brigade,* 10; Rose, *Ross' Texas Brigade,* 42; Britton, *The Civil War on the Border,* 168–71; Abel, *The American Indian As Slaveholder,* 256; Trickett, "The Civil War in the Indian Territory," 18: 275–76; Edwin C. Bearess, "The Civil War Comes to Indian Territory, 1861: The Flight of Opothleyahola," 17–18; Angie Debo refers to this person as James Larney, although it was in fact James Scott. This is in no way a criticism of Angie Debo, for we stand in awe of her life's work. See Debo, *The Road to Disappearance,* 151–52.

3. Cooper to Benjamin, in U.S. War Department, *War of the Rebellion,* vol. 8: 11–12; Report of Colonel James McIntosh, Jan. 1, 1861, in ibid., vol. 8: 22; Rose, *Ross' Texas Brigade,* 18–47; Abel, *The American Indian As Slaveholder,* 258; Britton, *The Civil War on the Border,* 171–72; Trickett, "The Civil War in the Indian Territory," 18: 276–77.

4. Report of Colonel James McIntosh, Jan. 1, 1861, in U.S. War Department, *War of the Rebellion,* vol. 8: 22; Cooper to Benjamin, in ibid., vol. 8: 11–12; Trickett, "The Civil War in the Indian Territory," 18: 277–78.

5. Report of Colonel James McIntosh, Jan. 1, 1861, in U.S. War Department, *War of the Rebellion,* vol. 8: 22; Trickett, "The Civil War in the Indian Territory," 18: 277; Britton, *The Civil War on the Border,* 172.

6. Report of Colonel James McIntosh, Jan. 1, 1861, in U.S. War Department, *War of the Rebellion,* vol. 8: 22; Stephen R. Lewis interview; Britton, *The Civil War on the Border,* 173; Trickett, "The Civil War in the Indian Territory," 18: 278.

CHAPTER SIXTEEN. TO DIE WELL

1. As with the other battles, the conflict at Chustenahlah is clouded by contradictory accounts of what happened. This is not uncommon for troops, who experience the trauma of combat and try later to put their recollections on paper. In addition, many of those who wrote of Chustenahlah did so months or even years after the fact. The shock of battle coupled with the lapse of time served, no doubt, to dim memories and confuse facts. Once again, we have picked through all materials to reconstruct what happened. Report of Colonel James McIntosh, Jan. 1, 1861, in U.S. War Department, *War of the Rebellion,* vol. 8: 23; Stephen R. Lewis interview; W. P. Lane to James McIntosh, Dec. 26, 1861, in U.S. War Department, *War of the Rebellion,* vol. 8: 29; Rose, *Ross' Texas Brigade,* 42–47; Arthur Shoemaker, "The Battle of Chustenahlah," 180–84; Bearess, "The Civil War Comes to Indian Territory," 34–42.

2. Rose, *Ross' Texas Brigade,* 43; Swanton, "Religious Beliefs," 406–36; Report of Colonel James McIntosh, Jan. 1, 1861, in U.S. War Depart-

ment, *War of the Rebellion,* vol. 8: 22–25; Shoemaker, "The Battle of Chustenahlah," 34–42.

3. Report of Colonel James McIntosh, Jan. 1, 1861, in U.S. War Department, *War of the Rebellion,* vol. 8: 22–25; Report of Colonel W. C. Young, n.d., in ibid., vol. 8: 26–27; Report of Lieutenant Colonel John S. Griffith, Dec. 27, 1861, in ibid., vol. 8: 27–28; Lane to McIntosh, in ibid., vol. 8: 28–29; Report of Captain William Gipson, Dec. 28, 1861, in ibid., vol. 8: 29–30; Report of Captain H. S. Bennett, n.d., in ibid., vol. 8: 30–31; Rose, *Ross' Texas Brigade,* 44; McReynolds, *The Seminoles,* 300–302; Porter, "Billy Bowlegs," 395–96; Trickett, "The Civil War in the Indian Territory," 18: 278–79.

4. The documents are unclear as to whether Stephen R. Lewis (interviewed July 9, 1937 and cited earlier) and S. R. Lewis (interviewed Feb. 20, 1937) are the same person. We are citing the S. R. Lewis interview of Feb. 20, 1937, as a separate source. S. R. Lewis interview, Indian-Pioneer History, WPA Project, Oklahoma Historical Society, vol. 6: 257 (hereafter S. R. Lewis interview); James Scott interview; Stephen R. Lewis interview; Rose, *Ross' Texas Brigade,* 43–44.

5. S. R. Lewis interview; James Scott interview; Stephen R. Lewis interview; Rose, *Ross' Texas Brigade,* 43–44; untitled statement, Opothleyahola File, Oklahoma Historical Society; Report of Colonel James McIntosh, Jan. 1, 1861, in U.S. War Department, *War of the Rebellion,* vol. 8: 22–25.

6. Two thousand to three thousand combatants fought the Battle of Chustenahlah. Confederate records report hundreds of Indians slain, yet no wounded. That such a battle would be fought, with so many lives lost and no wounded is beyond credibility. That leaves only one inescapable and chilling conclusion about what happened to the Indian wounded. Report of Colonel James McIntosh, Jan. 1, 1861, in U.S. War Department, *War of the Rebellion,* vol. 8: 22–25; Report of Colonel W. C. Young, in ibid., vol. 8: 26–27; Bearess, "The Civil War Comes to Indian Territory," 34–38.

7. Kenny Franks, *Stand Watie and the Agony of the Cherokee Nation,* 121–23.

8. This letter was found in Opothleyahola's camp after the Battle of Chustenahlah. James McIntosh to General S. Cooper, Jan. 4, 1862, in U.S. War Department, *War of the Rebellion,* vol. 8: 25; Rose, *Ross' Texas Brigade,* 42–43; Gill, "Thesis," 65; Grant Foreman, *A History of Oklahoma,* 107.

CHAPTER SEVENTEEN.
A WORLD OF WHITE

1. S. R. Lewis interview; James Scott interview; Lindy Scott interview, Indian-Pioneer History, WPA Project, Oklahoma Historical Society, vol. 44: 29 (hereafter Lindy Scott interview); Stephen R. Lewis interview; William G. Coffin to William P. Dole, Oct. 15, 1862, Annual Report of

the Commissioner of Indian Affairs for 1862, 279; George A. Cutler to William Coffin, Sept. 30, 1862, in ibid., 283; Bearess, "The Civil War Comes to Indian Territory," 38–41; Foreman, *A History of Oklahoma,* 107; Fischer and Franks, "Confederate Victory at Chusto-Talasah," 473–76; Debo, *The Road to Disappearance,* 151; Rose, *Ross' Texas Brigade,* 44, 51; Report of Colonel James McIntosh, Jan. 1, 1861, in U.S. War Department, *War of the Rebellion,* vol. 8: 24–25.

2. S. R. Lewis interview; James Scott interview; Lindy Scott interview; Stephen R. Lewis interview; Coffin to Dole, Oct. 15, 1862, Annual Report of the Commissioner of Indian Affairs for 1862, 279; Cutler to Coffin, Sept. 30, 1862, in ibid., 283; Bearess, "The Civil War Comes to Indian Territory," 38–41; Foreman, *A History of Oklahoma,* 107; Fischer and Franks, "Confederate Victory at Chusto-Talasah," 473–76; Debo, *The Road to Disappearance,* 151; Abel, *The American Indian As Slaveholder,* 259–61.

3. Stand Watie to Colonel McIntosh, Dec. 28, 1861, in U.S. War Department, *War of the Rebellion,* vol. 8: 32; E. C. Boudinot to Colonel Stand Watie, Dec. 28, 1861, in ibid., vol. 8: 32–33; Report of Colonel James McIntosh, Jan. 1, 1861, in ibid., vol. 8: 24; Report of Colonel James McIntosh, Jan. 10, 1861, in ibid., vol. 8: 31; Porter, "Billy Bowlegs," 396; McReynolds, *The Seminoles,* 220, 226–27; Britton, *The Civil War on the Border,* 165, 174; Franks, *Stand Watie,* 121–23; Trickett, "The Civil War in the Indian Territory," 18: 279.

4. McIntosh, "Exodus Statement," 8–10; Cooper to Benjamin, in U.S. War Department, *War of the Rebellion,* vol. 8: 12–14.

CHAPTER EIGHTEEN. THE HUNTED

1. Colonel Daniel McIntosh indicates in his "Statement Relative to the Exodus of Opothleyahola" that the land was not encased in ice and snow as his men pursued fleeing Indians. This refutes all other primary sources—Indian as well as white. The Exodus Statement was written more than seven years after the fact. We suspect Daniel McIntosh was confusing weather conditions with other and earlier circumstances in the campaign. In addition, his comment that all Indian survivors of Chustenahlah were treated humanely and quickly sent home casts suspicion on the entire document. Many survivors of Chustenahlah were enslaved, some were executed, and others were retained as prisoners. McIntosh, "Exodus Statement," 8–10; Jackman Pigeon interview, Indian-Pioneer History, WPA Project, Oklahoma Historical Society, vol. 107: 361–62; Lindy Scott interview; Stephen R. Lewis interview; Cooper to Benjamin, in U.S. War Department, *War of the Rebellion,* vol. 8: 12–14; Rose, *Ross' Texas Brigade,* 44, 51; Cutler to Coffin, Sept. 30, 1862, Annual Report of the Commissioner of Indian Affairs for 1862, 283; Bearess, "The Civil War Comes to Indian Territory," 38–41; Foreman, *A History of Oklahoma,* 107; Abel, *The American Indian As Slaveholder,* 259–61; Debo, *The Road to Disappearance,* 151; McReynolds, *The Seminoles,* 220–27, 302–304.

CHAPTER NINETEEN. THE GODS

1. Rose, *Ross' Texas Brigade*, 48; Cooper to Benjamin, in U.S. War Department, *War of the Rebellion*, vol. 8: 12–13; McIntosh, "Exodus Statement," 8–10; Coffin to Dole, Oct. 15, 1862, Annual Report of the Commissioner of Indian Affairs for 1862, 280; Bearess, "The Civil War Comes to Indian Territory," 40–41; Trickett, "The Civil War in the Indian Territory," 18: 280; McReynolds, *The Seminoles,* 302–304.

2. Cooper to Benjamin, in U.S. War Department, *War of the Rebellion,* vol. 8: 12–13; "Cooper's Report," Opothleyahola File, 18.

3. One blizzard followed by several days of fair weather and then another storm is in keeping with weather patterns in the American Southwest. It is also, of course, a depiction of events from several primary sources. Cooper to Benjamin, in U.S. War Department, *War of the Rebellion,* vol. 8: 12–14; "Cooper's Report," Opothleyahola File, 18.

4. Cooper to Benjamin, in U.S. War Department, *War of the Rebellion,* vol. 8: 12–14; "Cooper's Report," Opothleyahola File, 18.

5. S. R. Lewis interview, vol. 6: 257; James Scott interview; Lindy Scott interview; Stephen R. Lewis interview; Swanton, "Religious Beliefs," 409, 478–80, 486–87, 616–17.

CHAPTER TWENTY. THE GREAT FATHER

1. Sandburg, *Abraham Lincoln*, vol. 1: 56–58; vol. 2: 207–10, 232–45; vol. 3: 77; Viola, *Diplomats in Buckskins,* 113–16; Abel, *The American Indian As Slaveholder,* 244–49; Abel, *The American Indian As Participant in the Civil War,* 64–75; Debo, *The Road to Disappearance,* 148–49.

2. Sandburg, *Abraham Lincoln,* vol. 2: 207–10, 232–45; Viola, *Diplomats in Buckskins,* 54–67, 113–28, 146–47.

3. Sandburg, *Abraham Lincoln,* vol. 1: 120–21; Viola, *Diplomats in Buckskins,* 137–45.

4. Photographs in Sandburg, *Abraham Lincoln,* vol. 2, after pp. 212 and 628; Viola, *Diplomats in Buckskins,* 137–45.

5. Photographs in Sandburg, *Abraham Lincoln,* vol. 2, after pp. 212 and 628; Viola, *Diplomats in Buckskins,* 137–45. Not a shred of evidence exists to suggest that Abraham Lincoln met with any Indians during the period the miccos were in Washington. Neither official documents nor personal papers even hint at a meeting. There is no evidence to suggest that Lincoln even knew the miccos were in town. Yet the Indians were clearly under the impression that while in Washington they had met the president.

6. Thaddeus Hyatt is one example of a railroad crony parading as an abolitionist in Kansas. After the Civil War, he was manager of the Missouri, Kansas & Texas Railroad, the first line to build across Indian Territory. Foreman, *A History of Oklahoma,* 134–39, 172–80, 206–207, 210; Debo, *The Road to Disappearance,* 197–99.

CHAPTER TWENTY-ONE. THE CYCLE

1. Henry Jackson interview, Indian-Pioneer History, WPA Project, Oklahoma Historical Society, vol. 5: 459–62 (hereafter Henry Jackson interview); Stephen R. Lewis interview; Coffin to Dole, Oct. 15, 1862, Annual Report of the Commissioner of Indian Affairs for 1862, 280; Cutler to Coffin, Sept. 30, 1862, in ibid., 282–83; Dr. A. B. Campbell to Dr. James K. Barnes, Feb. 8, 1862, in ibid., 294–95; John Connor, Head Chief et al., Jan. 3, 1862 in Abel, *The American Indian As Slaveholder*, 268–269; Bearess, "The Civil War Comes to Indian Territory," 40–41.

2. Dr. Campbell to Dr. Barnes, Annual Report of the Commissioner of Indian Affairs for 1862, 294–95; George W. Collamore to William P. Dole, April 21, 1862, in ibid., 299–301.

EPILOGUE

1. Henry Jackson interview; Collamore to Dole, Annual Report of the Commissioner of Indian Affairs for 1862, 299–302; Captain Jno. W. Turner to William P. Dole, Feb. 11, 1862, in ibid., 296–98; McReynolds, *The Seminoles*, 294; Debo, *The Road to Disappearance*, 152–53; Helga Harriman, "Economic Conditions in the Creek Nation, 1865–1871," 325; M. Thomas Bailey, *Reconstruction in Indian Territory*, 34–35; Edmund Danziger, Jr., "The Office of Indian Affairs and the Problem of Civil War Refugees in Kansas," 261–63.

2. Coffin to Dole, Oct. 15, 1862, Annual Report of the Commissioner of Indian Affairs for 1862, 280–81; Cutler to Coffin, Sept. 30, 1862, in ibid., 282–84; G. C. Snow to William Coffin, Sept. 29, 1862, in ibid., 286–87; Peter P. Elder to William G. Coffin, Sept. 12, 1862, in ibid., 287–88; William Dole to C. B. Smith, Feb. 13, 1982, in ibid., 291–93; Dr. Campbell to Dr. Barnes, in ibid., 295–96; Turner to Dole, in ibid., 296–98; Danziger, "The Office of Indian Affairs," 263–65.

3. Collamore to Dole, Annual Report of the Commissioner of Indian Affairs for 1862, 264–65; Danziger, "The Office of Indian Affairs," 264–65; Abel, *The American Indian As Participant in the Civil War*, 82–83.

4. Elijah Sells to D. N. Cooley, Oct. 16, 1865, Annual Report of the Commissioner of Indian Affairs for 1865, 436–37; George A. Reynolds to Elijah Sells, June 28, 1865, in ibid., 447; Helga H. Harriman, "Economic Conditions in the Creek Nation, 1865–1871," 326, 333; Danziger, "The Office of Indian Affairs," 272–73; Annie Heloise Abel, *The American Indian under Reconstruction*, 59–65.

5. Collamore to Coffin, Annual Report of the Commissioner of Indian Affairs for 1862, 301; Report of the Commissioner, Annual Report of the Commissioner for Indian Affairs for 1865, 206–07; Abel, *The American Indian under Reconstruction*, 59–72.

6. Dr. Campbell to Dr. Barnes, Annual Report of the Commissioner of Indian Affairs for 1862, 296–96; Collamore to Coffin, in ibid., 299–302.

7. W. G. Coffin to Charles E. Mix, Sept. 1, 1862, in ibid., 311–13; Holman, "William G. Coffin," 491–514; Castel, *A Frontier State at War,*

220–21; Abel, *The American Indian under Reconstruction*, 57; Leverett Wilson Spring, *Kansas: The Prelude to the War for the Union*, 300–305; Stephenson, *The Political Career of James H. Lane*, 150–52.

8. Castel, *A Frontier State at War*, 220–21; Abel, *The American Indian under Reconstruction*, 230–55; H. Craig Miner, *The Corporation and the Indian: Tribal Sovereignty and Industrial Civilization in Indian Territory, 1865–1907*, xii, 4–6, 14–18, 22–23, 30, 77–78; Sinclair, *Corsair*, 19–24; Abel, *The American Indian under Reconstruction*, 320–27; Danziger, "The Office of Indian Affairs," 259; Bailey, *Reconstruction in Indian Territory*, 66–67, 114.

9. Abel, *The American Indian under Reconstruction*, 67–68, 320–27; Bailey, *Reconstruction in Indian Territory*, 76–77; Miner, *The Corporation and the Indian*, 9–11, 77–95, 116–17.

10. The MKT was a subsidiary of the Union Pacific Railroad Company at this time. Controlling interest in the Union Pacific, as well as its construction company, Crédit Mobilier, was in the hands of individuals tied by career, finance, and lifelong personal friendships to the House of Rothschild and J. P. Morgan. Bailey, *Reconstruction in Indian Territory*, 105, 138–39; Miner, *The Corporation and the Indian*, 91, 104, 117; Charles Edgar Ames, *Pioneering the Union Pacific: A Reappraisal of the Builders of the Railroad*, 425; Gustavus Myers, *History of the Great American Fortunes*, 437–45; Robert Edgar Riegel, *The Story of the Western Railroads: From 1852 through the Reign of the Giants*, 104–39.

11. James Scott interview; Lindy Scott interview.

12. Abel, *The American Indian under Reconstruction*, 57; Joel D. Boyd, "Creek Indian Agents, 1834–1874," 51–52; Holman, "William G. Coffin," 504–14.

13. Miner, *The Corporation and the Indian*, 55; Abel, *The American Indian As Participant in the Civil War*, 181, 198.

14. Oral interviews with members of the Muskogee Nation; Meserve, "The MacIntoshes," 310–25.

15. Franks, *Stand Watie*, 123–211.

16. Dr. Campbell to Dr. Barnes, Annual Report of the Commissioner of Indian Affairs for 1862, 295–96; Cutler to Coffin, Sept. 30, 1862, in ibid., 282–84; Meserve, "Chief Opothleyahola", 439–53.

17. Muriel Wright Letters, June 25–July 1, 1938, Opothleyahola File; Morrison, *A Forgotten Hero*, 10–12.

BIBILIOGRAPHY

INTERVIEWS

Oral interviews with members of the Muskogee Nation, Muskogee, Okmulgee, Tulsa, Oklahoma, 1985–86.

ARCHIVES

Alabama Department of Archives and History, Montgomery
    Executive Letterbook
    Journal of the Senate
    Journal of the House of Representatives
Georgia Department of Archives and History, Atlanta
    Executive Letterbook
National Archives, Washington, D.C.
    Record Group 75. Records of the Bureau of Indian Affairs
    Correspondence of the Office of Indian Affairs
        Letters Received (M234), 1824–81
        Letters Sent (M21), 1824–81
    Documents Relating to the Negotiations of Ratified and Unratified
        Treaties with Various Indian Tribes (T494), 1801–69
    Records of the Secretary of War Relating to Indian Affairs
        Letters Received (M271), 1800–23
        Letters Sent (M271), 1800–24
    Record Group 107. Records of the War Department
        Letters of the Secretary of War Relating to Military Affairs (M6),
            1800–89
        Letters Sent to the President by the Secretary of War (M127), 1800–63

Reports of the Commissioners of Indian Affairs, 1837–74
Superintendent for the Five Civilized Tribes. Creek Files
Oklahoma Historical Society, Oklahoma City
    Checote Manuscript
    Creek Nation, Tribal Records
    Indian-Pioneer History, WPA Project
    Opothleyahola File
Thomas Gilcrease Institute of American History and Art Library, Tulsa
    Confederate Papers
    Creek Papers, 1783–1892
    Grant Foreman Papers
    Thomas Gilcrease Institute Collection
    Benjamin Hawkins Papers
    Ethan Allen Hitchcock Papers
    Andrew Jackson Papers
    Jesup Papers
    William McIntosh Papers
    Samuel Bell Maxey Papers
    Albert Pick Papers
    John Ross Papers
University of Oklahoma Library, Norman
    Battle of Round Mountain Files
    Cherokee Advocate, 1844–53, 1876–77
    Cherokee Phoenix, 1828–34
    Grayson Family Papers, 1834–1919
    Historic Oklahoma Collection, 1854–1959
    Issac McCoy Papers, 1808–74
    Chilly McIntosh Manuscripts. Division of Manuscripts, 1774–1956
    Roley McIntosh Papers, 1871–1907
    Phillips Collection
    John Ross Papers, 1815–66
University of Tulsa Library, Tulsa
    Robertson and Worcester Family Papers, 1815–1932

GOVERNMENT DOCUMENTS

U.S. Congress
    House of Representatives
        Executive Document 1. 37th Cong., 3rd sess. Serial 1157
        Executive Document 1. 39th Cong., 1st sess. Serial 1248
        Executive Document 15. 33rd. Cong., 2nd sess.
        Executive Document 59. 19th Cong., 2nd sess. Serial 151
        Executive Document 79. 19th Cong., 2nd sess. Serial 152
        Report 98. 19th Cong., 2nd sess. Serial 161
        Executive Document 102. 22nd Cong., 1st sess. Serial 288
        Executive Document 149. 23rd Cong., 1st sess. Serial 256

Executive Document 219. 27th Cong., 3rd sess., Hitchcock
    Report
Executive Document 248. 20th Cong., 1st sess. Serial 174
Executive Document 276. 24th Cong., 1st sess. Serial 292
Senate
Executive Document 1. 37th Cong., 2nd sess. Serial 1117
Executive Document 3. 25th Cong., 2nd sess. Serial 314
Executive Document 53. 21st Cong., 1st sess. Serial 193
Executive Document 198. 50th Cong., 1st sess.
Executive Document 319. 58th Cong., 2nd sess. Indian Affairs,
    Laws and Treaties
Executive Document 425. 24th Cong., 1st sess. Serial 284
Executive Document 512. 23rd Cong., 1st sess. Serials 245,
    246, 247
Executive Document 616. 26th Cong., 1st sess. Serial 361
Report 1278. 49th Cong., 1st sess.
Report 5013. 59th Cong., 2nd sess.

NEWSPAPERS/MAGAZINES

Arkansas Gazette, 1839
Arkansas Intelligencer, 1845–46
Cherokee Advocate, 1883
Fort Smith Herald, 1852–53
The Indian Advocate, 1850–53
Indian Record, 1887
Louisville Weekly Journal, 1848
Mobile Commercial Register, 1820–35
Montgomery Advertiser, 1836
Montgomery Republican, 1822
National Intelligencer, 1825–30
Niles Weekly Register, 1818–29
St. Louis Republican, 1853
Tulsa Tribune, 1939
United States Magazine and Democratic Review, 1844

PUBLISHED SOURCES

Abel, Annie Heloise. *The American Indian As Participant in the Civil War.*
    Cleveland: Arthur H. Clarke Co., 1919.
———. *The American Indian As Slaveholder and Secessionist.* Cleveland:
    Arthur H. Clarke Co., 1915.
———. *The American Indian under Reconstruction.* Cleveland: Arthur
    H. Clarke Co., 1925.
———. "The History of Events Resulting in Indian Consolidation West of
    the Mississippi." *American Historical Association Annual Report for
    1906.* Washington, D.C.: Government Printing Office, 1908; 233–450.

————. "Indian Reservations in Kansas and the Extinguishment of Their Title." *Transactions of the Kansas State Historical Society* 8 (1903–04): 72–109.

————. "The Indians in the Civil War." *American Historical Review* 15 (March, 1910): 281–96.

Abernathy, Thomas P. *The Formative Years in Alabama, 1815–1828.* 2nd ed. Tuscaloosa: University of Alabama Press, 1965.

Aldon, John R. *John Stuart and the Southern Colonial Frontier.* Ann Arbor, Mich.: N.p., 1944.

Ames, Charles Edgar. *Pioneering the Union Pacific: A Reappraisal of the Builders of the Railroad.* New York: Meredith Corp., 1969.

Bailey, M. Thomas. *Reconstruction in Indian Territory: A Story of Avarice, Discrimination, and Opportunism.* Port Washington, N.Y.: Kenniket Press, 1972.

Banks, Dean. "Civil War Refugees from the Indian Territory in the North, 1861–1864." *Chronicles of Oklahoma,* 41 (Fall, 1963): 286–98.

Barron, S. B. *The Lone Star Defenders: A Chronicle of the Third Texas Calvary, Ross' Brigade.* New York: Neal Publishing, n.d.

Bearess, Edwin C. "The Civil War Comes to Indian Territory, 1861: The Flight of Opothleyahola." *Journal of the West* 11 (Spring, 1972): 9–42.

Berkhofer, Robert F., Jr. "The Political Context of a New Indian History." *Pacific Historical Review* 40 (August, 1971): 357–82.

Bernard, Jesse. "Political Leadership among North American Indians." *American Journal of Sociology* 34 (September, 1928): 296–315.

Blunt, James G. "General Blunt's Account of His Civil War Experiences." *Kansas Historical Quarterly* 1 (May, 1932): 222–63.

Bonner, James C. "Tustunugee Hutkee and Creek Factionalism on the Georgia-Florida Frontier." *Alabama Review* 10 (April, 1957): 111–25.

————. "William McIntosh." In *Georgians in Profile: Historical Essays in Honor of Ellis Merton Coulter,* ed. Horace Montgomery. Athens: University of Georgia Press, 1958; 119–28.

Botkin, B. A., ed. *Lay My Burden Down: A Folk History of Slavery.* 2nd ed. Chicago: University of Chicago Press, 1946.

Boyd, Joel D. "Creek Indian Agents, 1834–1874." *Chronicles of Oklahoma* 51 (Spring, 1973): 37–58.

Brannon, Peter A. "Aboriginal Towns in Alabama." In *Handbook of the Alabama Anthropological Society.* Montgomery: Brown Printing Co., 1920; 42–58.

————. "Creek Indian War, 1836–1837." *Alabama Historical Quarterly* 13 (Summer, 1951): 156–58.

————. "Tuckabatchee Chiefs." *Arrow Points* 14 (May, 1929): 33–34.

————, ed. "Distribution of Troops at Fort Mitchell." *Alabama Historical Quarterly* 21 (Spring, 1959): 14.

Briggs, John, and F. David Peat. *The Turbulent Mirror: An Illustrated Guide to Chaos Theory and the Science of Wholeness.* New York: Harper & Row, 1989.

Britton, Wiley. *The Civil War on the Border.* New York: Knickerbocker Press, 1899.

Bryant, Keith L., Jr. *History of the Atchison, Topeka, and Santa Fe Railroad.* New York: Macmillan, 1974.

Bunge, Robert. *An American Urphilosophe: An American Philosophy (Before Pragmatism).* New York: University Press of America, 1984.

Caldwell, Taylor. *Captains and the Kings.* Garden City, N.Y.: Doubleday, 1972.

Campbell, John A. "The Creek War of 1836." *Transactions of the Alabama Historical Society* 3. N.p.: The Society, 1899; 162–66.

Carter, Blue Clark. "Opothleyahola and the Creeks during the Civil War." In *Indian Leaders: Oklahoma's First Statesmen,* eds. H. Glenn Jordon and Thomas M. Holm. Oklahoma City: Oklahoma Historical Society, 1979; 48–61.

Castel, Albert. *A Frontier State At War: Kansas, 1861–1865.* Ithaca, N.Y.: Cornell University Press, 1958.

Caughey, John Walton. *McGillivray of the Creeks.* Norman: University of Oklahoma Press, 1938.

Clay, Mrs. Clement C. "Recollections of Opothleyahola." *Arrow Points* 4 (February, 1922): 35–36.

Cleveland, Frederick A., and Powell, Fred Wilbur. *Railroad Promotion and Capitalism in the United States.* New York: Longman's, Green & Co., 1909.

Cochran, Thomas C., and Thomas B. Brewer, eds. *Views of American Economic Growth in the Industrial Era.* New York: McGraw-Hill, 1966.

Corkran, David H. *The Creek Frontier 1540–1783.* Norman: University of Oklahoma Press, 1967.

Cumming, William P. *The Southeast in Early Maps.* Chapel Hill: University of North Carolina Press, 1962.

Danziger, Edmund, Jr. "The Office of Indian Affairs and the Problem of Civil War Indian Refugees in Kansas." *Kansas Historical Quarterly* 35 (Autumn, 1969): 257–75.

Debo, Angie. "The Location of the Battle of Round Mountain." *Chronicles of Oklahoma* 41 (Summer, 1963): 70–104.

———. *The Road to Disappearance.* Norman: University of Oklahoma Press, 1941.

———. "The Site of the Battle of Round Mountain, 1861." *Chronicles of Oklahoma* 27 (Summer, 1949): 187–206.

Deloria, Vine, Jr., ed. *Of Utmost Good Faith.* New York: Bantam Books, 1972.

Du Chateau, Andre Paul, "The Creek Nation on the Eve of the Civil War." *Chronicles of Oklahoma* 52 (Fall, 1974): 290–315.

Edmunds, R. David. *The Shawnee Prophet.* Lincoln: University of Nebraska Press, 1983.

Fairbanks, Charles H. "Creek and Pre-Creek." In *Archeology of the Eastern United States,* ed. James B. Griffin. Chicago: University of Chicago Press, 1952; 285–91.

Fehrenbach, T. R. *Lone Star: A History of Texas and the Texans.* New York: Collier Books, 1980.

Fenton, William N. "Factionalism in American Indian Society." In *Actes du Ne Congrès International des Sciences Anthropologiques et Ethnologiques* 2. Vienna: N.p., 1952; 330–40.

Fischer, LeRoy. "The Civil War Era in Indian Territory." *Journal of the West* 12 (July, 1973): 345–55.

Fischer, LeRoy, and Kenny A. Franks. "Confederate Victory at Chusto-Talasah." *Chronicles of Oklahoma* 49 (Winter, 1971–72): 452–76.

Foreman, Carolyn Thomas. "The Light-Horse in the Indian Territory." *Chronicles of Oklahoma* 34 (Spring, 1956): 17–43.

Foreman, Grant. *Advancing the Frontier.* Norman: University of Oklahoma Press, 1933.

———. *The Five Civilized Tribes.* Norman: University of Oklahoma Press, 1934.

———. *Fort Gibson.* Norman: University of Oklahoma Press, 1936.

———. *A History of Oklahoma.* 2nd ed. Norman: University of Oklahoma Press, 1945.

———. *Indian Removal.* Norman: University of Oklahoma Press, 1932.

———. *Indians and Pioneers: The Story of the American Southwest before 1830.* Norman: University of Oklahoma Press, 1936.

———, ed. *A Traveler in Indian Territory: The Journal of Ethan Allen Hitchcock, Late Major-General in the United States Army.* Cedar Rapids, Ia.: Torch Press, 1930.

Franks, Kenny A. "An Analysis of the Confederate Treaties with the Five Civilized Tribes." *Chronicles of Oklahoma* 50 (Winter, 1972–73): 458–73.

———. "Operations against Opothleyahola, 1861." *Military History of Texas and the Southwest* 10 (Summer, 1972): 187–96.

———. *Stand Watie and the Agony of the Cherokee Nation.* Memphis, Tenn.: Memphis State University Press, 1979.

Fundaburk, Emma Lila, and Mary Douglas Fundaburk Foreman, eds. *Sun Circles and Human Hands: The Southeastern Indians, Art and Industries.* Luverne, Ala.: The editors, 1957.

Gaines, W. Craig. *The Confederate Cherokees: John Drew's Regiment of Mounted Rifles.* Baton Rouge: Louisiana State University Press, 1989.

Gardner, James H. "One Hundred Years Ago in the Region of Tulsa." *Chronicles of Oklahoma* 11 (Winter, 1933): 764–85.

Gates, Paul Wallace. *Fifty Million Acres: Conflicts over Kansas Land Policy, 1854–1890.* Ithaca, N.Y.: Cornell University Press, 1954.

Gatschet, Albert S. *A Migration Legend of the Creek Indians.* Philadelphia: Daniel G. Brinton, 1884.

———. "Towns and Villages of the Creek Confederacy in the XVIII and XIX Centuries." *Alabama Historical Society Miscellaneous Collections* 1 (N.p.: The Society, 1901): 398.

Glaab, Charles N. *Kansas City and the Railroads.* Madison: State Historical Society of Wisconsin, 1962.

Gleick, James. *Chaos: Making a New Science.* New York: Penguin Books, 1987.

Green, Donald E. *The Creek People.* Phoenix, Ariz.: Indian Tribal Series, 1973.

Green, Michael D. "Federal-State Conflict in the Administration of Indian

Policy: Georgia, Alabama, and the Creeks, 1824–1834." Ph.D. diss., University of Iowa, 1973.

———. *The Politics of Indian Removal: Creek Government and Society in Crisis*. Lincoln: University of Nebraska Press, 1982.

Greer, E. S., Jr. "A Tuckabatchee Plate from the Coosa River." *Journal of Alabama Archaeology* 12 (Summer, 1966):156–58.

Gregory, Jack, and Renard Strickland. *Creek Seminole Spirit Tales*. Pensacola, Fla.: Indian Heritage Association, 1971.

Griffith, Benjamin W., Jr. *McIntosh and Weatherford, Creek Indian Leaders*. Tuscaloosa: University of Alabama Press, 1988.

Griscom, George L. *Fighting with Ross' Texas Calvary Brigade, C.S.A.: Diary of Lieutenant George L. Griscom, Adjutant, 9th TX Calvary*. Homer L. Kerr, ed. Hillsboro, Tex.: Hill Junior College Press, 1976.

Haas, M. R. "Creek InterTown Relations." *American Anthropologist* 42 (September, 1940): 479–89.

Hacker, Louis *The Triumph of American Capitalism: The Development of Forces in American History to the End of the Nineteenth Century*. New York: Columbia University Press, 1940.

Halbert, Henry S., and T. H. Ball. *The Creek War of 1813 and 1814*. 1895. Reprint. Birmingham: University of Alabama Press, 1969.

Hall, Arthur H. "The Red Stick War: Creek Indian Affairs during the War of 1812." *Chronicles of Oklahoma* 12 (Fall, 1934): 264–93.

Hamilton, J. P., Sr. "Indian Refugees in Coffey County." *LeRoy Reporter* (August 14, 21, 1931).

Harriman, Helga H. "Economic Conditions in the Creek Nation, 1865–1871." *Chronicles of Oklahoma* 51 (Winter, 1973): 325–35.

Hawkins, Benjamin. *Letters of Benjamin Hawkins, 1796–1806*. Georgia Historical Society Collections, no. 9. Savannah: Published for the Society, 1916.

———. *A Sketch of the Creek Country in the Years 1788 and 1789*. Georgia Historical Society Collections, no. 3. Savannah: Printed for the Society, 1848.

Hill, Edward E. *The Office of Indian Affairs, 1824–1880: Historical Sketches*. New York: Clearwater Publishing Co., 1974.

Holland, James W. "Andrew Jackson and the Creek War: Victory at the Horseshoe." *Alabama Review* 21 (July, 1968): 243–75.

Holman, Tom. "William G. Coffin, Lincoln's Superintendent of Indian Affairs for the Southern Superintedency." *Kansas Historical Quarterly* 39 (Winter, 1973): 491–514.

Hryniewicki, Richard J. "The Creek Treaty of Washington, 1826." *Georgia Historical Quarterly* 48 (December, 1964): 425–41.

Hudson, Charles M. *Four Centuries of Southern Indians*. Athens: University of Georgia Press, 1975.

———. *The Southeastern Indians*. Knoxville: University of Tennessee Press, 1976.

———, ed. *Black Drink: A Native American Tea*. Athens: University of Georgia Press, 1979.

Hultkantz, Ake, et al. *Seeing with a Native Eye: Essays on Native American Religion*. New York: Harper & Row, 1976.

Jack, Theodore H. "Alabama and the Federal Government: The Creek Indian Controversy." *Journal of American History* 3 (December, 1916): 301–17.

Jahoda, Gloria. *The Trail of Tears.* New York: Holt, Rinehart and Winston, 1975.

Johnson, Robert V., and Clarence C. Buel, eds. *Battles and Leaders of the Civil War.* New York: Thomas Yoseloff, 1956.

King, Jerlena. "Jackson Lewis of the Confederate Creek Regiment." *Chronicles of Oklahoma* 41 (Spring, 1963): 66–69.

Kinnaird, Lawrence. "International Rivalry in the Creek Country." *Florida Historical Society Quarterly* 10 (January, 1930): 59–85.

Lankford, George E. *Native American Legends.* Little Rock, Ark.: August House, 1987.

Lasswell, Harold D. "Faction." In *Encyclopedia of Social Sciences,* ed. Edwin R. A. Seligman. New York: Macmillan, 1931; 49–51.

Lincoln, Abraham. *Abraham Lincoln: His Speeches and Writings.* Roy P. Basler, ed. New York: Grosset & Dunlap, 1946.

Linton, Ralph. ed. *Acculturation in Seven American Indian Tribes.* New York: D. Appleton–Century Co., 1940.

———. *The Study of Man: An Introduction.* New York: D. Appleton–Century Co., 1936.

Lowie, Robert H. "Some Aspects of Political Organization among the American Aborigines." *Journal of the Royal Anthropological Institute* 78 (January, 1948): 11–24.

McElroy, Robert. *Levi Parsons Morton: Banker, Diplomat and Statesman.* New York: Arno Press, 1975.

McNeil, Kenneth. "Confederate Treaties with the Tribes of Indian Territory." *Chronicles of Oklahoma* 42 (Winter, 1964–65): 408–21.

McReynolds, Edwin C. *The Seminoles.* Norman: University of Oklahoma Press, 1957.

———. *Oklahoma! A History of the Sooner State.* Norman: University of Oklahoma Press, 1954.

Martin, Joel W. *Sacred Revolt: The Muskogee's Struggle for a New World.* Boston: Beacon Press, 1991.

Mason, Carol I. "Eighteenth Century Culture Change among the Lower Creeks." *Florida Anthropologist* 16 (September, 1963): 65–80.

Meserve, John Bartlett. "Chief Opothleyahola." *Chronicles of Oklahoma* 9 (Winter, 1931): 439–53.

———. "The MacIntoshes." *Chronicles of Oklahoma* 10 (Winter, 1932): 310–25.

Metcalf, P. Richard. "Who Should Rule at Home? Native American Politics and Indian-White Relations." *Journal of American History* 61 (December, 1974): 651–65.

Miner, H. Craig. *The Corporation and the Indian: Tribal Sovereignty and Industrial Civilization in Indian Territory 1865–1907.* Columbia: University of Missouri Press, 1976.

Monaghan, Jay. *Civil War on the Western Border, 1854–1865.* Boston: Little, Brown and Co., 1955.

Moore, Frank, ed. *The Rebellion Record: A Diary of American Events.* Vol. 4. New York: D. Van Nostrand, n.d.

Morrison, T. F. *A Forgotten Hero: A True Story of a Creek Indian Chief of Civil War Times.* Chanute, Kan.: Printed by the author, n.d.

Morton, Ohland. "Confederate Government Relations with the Five Civilized Tribes." *Chronicles of Oklahoma* 31 (Summer and Autumn, 1953): 189–204, 299–322.

————. "Reconstruction in the Creek Nation." *Chronicles of Oklahoma* 8 (Spring and Summer, 1931): 42–64, 189–225.

Myers, Gustavus. *History of the Great American Fortunes.* New York: Modern Library, 1937.

Nunez, Theron A., Jr. "Stiggins Narrative, Creek Nativism and the Creek War of 1813–1814." *Ethnohistory,* 5 (Spring, 1958): 1–47, 131–75, 292–301.

O'Beirne, H. F., and E. S. O'Beirne. *The Indian Territory: Its Chiefs, Legislators and Leading Men.* St. Louis: N.p., 1892.

Opler, Morris E. "The Creek "Town" and the Problem of Creek Indian Political Reorganization." In *Human Problems in Technological Change,* ed., Edward H. Spicer. New York: Russell Sage Foundation, 1952; 165–80.

————. "The Government of the Creek Indians." *Chronicles of Oklahoma* 8 (Spring, 1930): 44.

————. *Report on the History and Contemporary State of Aspects of Creek Social Organization and Government.* Washington: Bureau of Indian Affairs, 1937.

Otterbein, Keith F. "Internal War: A Cross-Cultural Study." *American Anthropologist* 70 (July, 1968): 277–89.

Paredes, J. Anthony, and Kenneth J. Plante. *Economics, Politics, and the Subjugation of the Creek Indians: Final Report for the National Park Service.* Tallahassee, Fla.: U.S. National Park Service, 1975.

Payne, John Howard. "The Green Corn Dance." *Chronicles of Oklahoma* 10 (Summer, 1932): 170–95.

Pennington, Edgar LeGare, ed. "Some Ancient Georgia Indian Lore." *Georgia Historical Quarterly* 15 (September, 1931): 192–98.

Pickett, Albert James. *History of Alabama and Incidentally of Georgia and Mississippi, from the Earliest Period.* 2 vols. The First American Frontier Series. New York: Arno Press, 1971.

Pickett, Andrew J. "The Death of McIntosh, 1825." *Arrow Points* 10 (February, 1925): 31–32.

Porter, Kenneth W. "Billy Bowlegs (Holata Micco) in the Civil War." *Florida Historical Quarterly* 45 (April, 1967): 390–401.

Remini, Robert V. *Andrew Jackson and the Course of American Empire, 1767–1821.* New York: Harper & Row, 1977.

Riegel, Robert Edgar. *The Story of the Western Railroads: From 1852 through the Reign of the Giants.* New York: Macmillan, 1926.

Robertson, Alice M. "The Creek Indian Council in Session." *Chronicles of Oklahoma* 11 (Winter, 1933): 895–98.

Rose, Victor M. *Ross' Texas Brigade.* 2nd ed. Kennesaw, Ga.: Continental Book Co., 1960.

Russell, Orpha. "Ehvn-hv lwue: Site of Oklahoma's First Civil War Battle." *Chronicles of Oklahoma* 29 (Winter, 1951–52): 401–07.

Sandburg, Carl. *Abraham Lincoln.* 6 vols. New York: Harcourt, Brace & World, 1936–39.

Savage, William W., Jr. "Creek Colonization in Oklahoma." *Chronicles of Oklahoma* 54 (Spring, 1976): 34–43.

Sears, William H. "Creek and Cherokee Culture in the Eighteenth Century." *American Antiquity* 21 (December, 1955–56): 143–49.

Shirk, George. "The Place of Indian Territory in the Command Structure of the Civil War." *Chronicles of Oklahoma* 45 (Winter, 1967–68): 464–71.

Shoemaker, Arthur. "The Battle of Chustenahlah." *Chronicles of Oklahoma* 38 (Summer, 1960): 180–84.

Sinclair, Andrew. *Corsair: The Life of J. Pierpont Morgan.* Boston: Little Brown & Co., 1981.

Spalding, Phinizy. *Oglethorpe in America.* Chicago: University of Chicago Press, 1977.

Sparks, A. W. *The War between the States As I Saw It.* Tyler, Tex.: Lee & Burnett Printers, 1901.

Spoehr, Alexander. "Creek Inter-Town Relations." *American Anthropologist* 43 (March, 1941): 132–33.

Spring, Leverett W. "The Career of a Kansas Politician." *American Review* 4 (1899): 80–104.

———. *Kansas: The Prelude to the War for the Union.* Boston: Houghton Mifflin, 1896.

Starkloff, Carl F. *The People of the Center: American Indian Religion and Christianity.* New York: Seabury Press, 1974.

Stephenson, Wendall Holmes. *The Political Career of James H. Lane.* Topeka: Kansas State Printing Plant, 1930.

Swanton, John R. "Early History of the Creek Indians and Their Neighbors." *Bureau of American Ethnology Bulletin 103.* Washington, D.C.: Government Printing Office, n.d.

———. "Religious Beliefs and Medical Practices of the Creek Indians." and *Bureau of American Ethnology Forty-Second Annual Report.* Washington, D.C.: Government Printing Office, 1928.

———. "Social Organizations and Social Usages of the Indians of the Creek Confederacy." *Bureau of American Ethnology Forty-Second Annual Report.* Washington, D.C.: Government Printing Office, 1928.

———. "The Social Significance of the Creek Confederacy." *Proceedings of the International Congress of Americanists.* Washington, D.C.: The Congress, 1917.

Thorton, J. Mills, III. *Politics and Power in a Slave Society: Alabama, 1800–1860.* Baton Rouge: Louisiana State University Press, 1978.

Trickett, Dean. "Ad Interim Report on the Site of the Battle of Round Mountain." *Chronicles of Oklahoma* 28 (Winter, 1950–51): 492–94.

———. "The Civil War in the Indian Territory." *Chronicles of Oklahoma* 17 and 18 (Winter and Spring, 1940–41): 315–27, 401–12; 55–69, 142–53, 266–80.

U.S. *Statutes at Large. Treaties between the U.S. and Indian Tribes.* Boston: N.p., 1948.

U.S. War Department. *War of the Rebellion: A Compilation of the Official Records of the Union and Confederate Armies.* 70 vols. Washington, D.C.: Government Printing Office, 1800–1904. Serial 1.

Viola, Herman J. *Diplomats in Buckskins: A History of Indian Delegations in Washington City.* Washington D.C.: Smithsonian Institution Press, 1981.

Walker, William. "Tukabahchi Sons-in-Law." *Arrow Points* 14 (May, 1929): 43.

Wallace, Anthony F. C. "Revitalization Movements: Some Theoretical Considerations for Their Comparative Study." *American Anthropologist* 58 (September, 1956): 264–81.

Waring, Antonio J., Jr. "The Southern Cult and Muskhogean Ceremonial." In *The Waring Papers: The Collected Works of Antonio J. Waring, Jr.,* ed. Stephen Williams. Athens: University of Georgia Press, 1965; 30–67.

White, Christine S. "Opothleyahola, Factionalism, and Creek Politics." Ph.D. diss., Texas Christian University, 1986.

Wilkins, Thurman. *Cherokee Tragedy: The Story of the Ridge Family and of the Decimation of a People.* New York: Macmillan, 1970.

Williams, Walter L., ed. *Southeastern Indians since the Removal Era.* Athens: University of Georgia Press, 1979.

Wood, Dion Carlos. "The Creek Indians and International Relations in the Southeast, 1775–1805." Master's thesis, University of Oklahoma, 1935.

Woods, Clee. "Oklahoma's Great Opothele Yahola." *North South Trader* 4, no. 2 (January–February, 1979): 22–36.

Woodward, Thomas S. *Woodward's Reminiscences of the Creek, or the Muscogee Indians, Contained in Letters to Friends in Georgia and Alabama.* Montgomery, Ala.: Barrett and Wimbish, 1859.

Wright, Muriel. "Colonel Cooper's Civil War Report on the Battle of Round Mountain." *Chronicles of Oklahoma* 39 (Winter, 1961): 352–97.

———. "General Douglas H. Cooper, C.S.A." *Chronicles of Oklahoma* 32 (Summer, 1954): 142–84.

———. *A Guide to the Indian Tribes of Oklahoma.* Norman: University of Oklahoma Press, 1951.

———. "Lieutenant Averiall's Ride at the Outbreak of the Civil War." *Chronicles of Oklahoma* 39 (Spring, 1961): 2–14.

———. "Oklahoma Civil War Sites in Oklahoma." *Oklahoma Historical Society* (May, 1965): 16–57.

Young, Mary E. "The Creek Frauds: A Study in Conscience and Corruption." *Mississippi Valley Historical Review* 42 (December, 1955): 411–37.

———. *Redskins, Ruffleshirts, and Rednecks: Indian Allotments in Alabama and Mississippi.* Norman: University of Oklahoma Press, 1961.

BIBLIOGRAPHY ❖

INDEX

98, 103, 117, 137, 143, 159, 160
Muskogees, 12, 16, 23, 24, 34, 37, 92, 103, 110, 114, 120, 121, 137, 148, 151, 154, 155, 156, 157, 159, 160, 161, 171. *See also* People

Nebraska Territory, 133
New York City, 78, 82–85, 138, 153, 154, 155
North, 50, 68, 82, 139, 153, 154, 156, 169
Northern troops, 26. *See also* Union troops

Oklahoma, 160
old country, 4, 11, 33, 66, 114, 115. *See also* Alabama; Georgia
omens, 5, 32–33
Opothleyahola, 9, 11, 20, 31; battle strategies of, 44, 57, 63, 95–99, 103–107, 113–16, 118, 120–21; death of, 156–57; dreams and visions of, 5, 92–93, 98, 131, 149, 154; family of, 14, 115, 148, 157; health of, 36, 44, 109, 114–16, 125, 148, 156–67; as leader, 7–8, 12, 28, 109, 124, 131, 134–35, 137, 142, 143, 148–49, 150, 154, 157, 160; and McIntosh, 16–18, 101–102, 115, 171; physical description of, 10, 64, 91; removal of, 7–8; as Speaker of the Nation, 16, 42; of Tucka-batchee, 16, 48, 124, 161; wealth of, 149

Osage, 38, 65
Osage War Trail, 38

Pacific Railroad, 155–56
Pea Ridge, Battle of, 156
Peeksville, N.Y., 81
People, 5, 12, 19, 24, 26, 37, 44, 66, 93, 101, 108–10, 114, 116, 119, 122, 123, 125–27, 130–32, 136–37, 148, 154, 155, 156, 157, 160. *See also* Creeks; Muskogees
Philadelphia, Pa., 78, 138
Piankasaws, 37
plantation pills or Drake's Bitters, 81
Potomac River, 138–39, 140
Poughkeepsie, N.Y., 81
predator beast, xvi, 77, 154. *See also* wolves

Quapaws, 37

railroad men, 78, 79, 143, 153–55
railroads, 142–43
Rappahannock River, 85
Rector, Elias, 60
Red Fork of the Arkansas, 44, 53
Red Stick War, 161. *See also* Creek War of 1813–14
removal, 7–8, 160
Richmond, Va., 139
Rockefeller, John D., 154
Ross, John, 25–26, 37, 65, 66, 95–96, 109
Rothschild, 154, 180
Rounded Mountain, 41, 94
Rounded Mountain, Battle of, 55–58, 65, 136, 165–66

Sac and Fox Reservation, 157
sacred fire, 7, 160
Sands, 23, 68, 73, 109, 143
Santa Fe, New Mexico Territory, 60